HUNTING SERIAL PREDATORS

*A Multivariate
Classification Approach
to Profiling
Violent Behavior*

HUNTING SERIAL PREDATORS

A Multivariate Classification Approach to Profiling Violent Behavior

Grover Maurice Godwin, Ph.D.

CRC Press

Boca Raton   London   New York   Washington, D.C.

Library of Congress Cataloging-in-Publication Data

Godwin, Grover Maurice
    Hunting Serial Predators: a multivariate classification appoach to profiling violent behavior/Grover Maurice Godwin
        p. cm.
    Includes bibliographical references and index.
    ISBN 0-8493-1398-8 (alk. paper)
    1 Serial murderers—United States—Psychology 2 Criminals—United States—Classification 3.
Criminal behavior—United States. 4. Criminal behavior, Prediction of—United States. I. Title.
    HV6529.G58 1999
    364.15 '.23—dc21   99-31298
                                                             CIP

Visit the CRC Press Web site at www.crcpress.com

© 2000 by CRC Press LLC

No claim to original U.S. Government works
International Standard Book Number 0-8493-1398-8
Library of Congress Card Number 99-31298
Printed in the United States of America   2 3 4 5 6 7 8 9 0
Printed on acid-free paper

Prologue

Since the *Hunting Serial Predators* manuscript was completed, there has been a relatively large debate as to the definition of deductive and inductive reasoning as the terms relate to offender profiling. As a result of the vexing opinions concerning exactly what deductive and inductive profiling entails, I felt that it was necessary to address some important issues surrounding the use of these terms.

Deductive reasoning was first developed by Thales, Pyuthagoras, Aristotle, and other Greeks of the Classical Period (600–300 B.C.). However, anyone who has read the Sherlock Holmes stories by Sir Arthur Conan Doyle is aware that Sherlock Holmes used a form of deductive reasoning. Holmes, for example, would observe that Watson's clothes were dry in spite of the fact that it had been raining all day. From this Holmes would guess or deduce that Watson had spent the day at his club — of course, Watson could have spent the day at some other location.

Profiles constructed by the FBI profilers, clinical psychologists, criminologists, and the police routinely drawn inferences about, for example, serial murderers and their behaviors based solely on work experience, gut feelings, and the motivation of the offender. This form of deductive profiling is where the profiler assumes one or more facts as self-evident about a crime or offender and then, following work experience and hunches, arrives at other facts commonly called conclusions. Hence, the FBI profiles are deductive rather than inductive. However, some argue that the FBI profiling method is inductive.

Broadly, the argument put forth for the FBI method being inductive is, since the FBI relies on data collected from interviews with serial murderers, as a foundation for developing their profiles, then their reasoning must be inductive. The basis for this argument is flawed, because the data collected by the FBI has never been empirically analyzed, or it has been properly organized in a systematic manner so that profilers could refer to it in future. Rather, the information has been passed down over the years based on memories of past experiences and inferences gleaned from the interviews in order to arrive at conclusions about a particular case. To be sure, deductive reasoning is from the general (passed down information) to the specific (case).

The "truth" of the conclusions reached by deductive profiling is a contingent truth; that is, it depends upon the truth, or the basis for the truth, for theories formed when the investigator first arrives on scene or during interviews. These statements or beliefs are taken as starting points for the argument. Deductive profiling processes available information by application of personal experiences as opposed to theoretically driven inductive profiling based on all available instances of a crime. The guarantee of the deductive profiling method is that IF the premises are true and IF the hypotheses are valid, then the conclusions are also true. However, this could hardly be the case, since rarely is a profiler's deductive opinions about what may have occurred at a crime empirically or theoretically driven by research and hypothesis testing. Drawing deductive inferences about crime scene behavior produces truths and conclusions out of thin air. Consequently, for deductive profiling to be robust there must be truths that are known a priori, which can only be achieved through empirical research.

It is further argued that there are a number of factors that interfere with adequate empirical evaluation into the variables that contribute to the success or failure of a profile, and what is needed is more of a systematic and empirical approach to offender profiling than currently exists. Contrary to deductive profiling where generalizations guide the profiles, inductive profiling is an empirically based approach where conclusions are derived from scientific analysis. Inductive reasoning is from the specific to the general. For example, inductive profiling derives general principles about the behavior of serial murderers by empirically examining and testing particular facts or instances of a large number of solved cases. Briefly, not including information on unsolved cases in the inductive analysis would not be helpful, because no background information on the offender is available. In contrast to the deductive process, which starts with assumptions about behavior, inductive profiling relies on data gathered from the crime scenes, police reports, psychological evaluations, method examiners' reports and victimology reports in order to be empirically analyzed and subsequently to support a theory. In all instances the internal validity of the data is confirmed.

An important step in the inductive profiling method is to formalize operational definitions (hypotheses) for testing. Once this step has been completed, the next step involves coding the data for statistical analysis in which the results are supported with theories. The important item that makes inductive profiling more robust than deductive profiling is, through research, observable patterns in the data can be found that lead to new theories. Rather than being stagnated with held views of behavior, inductive profiling is like a revolving door — researchers are always striving to look for emerging patterns in crime data, which leads to new ways to assist investigators.

If, for example, a profiler or an investigator in a serial murder investigation deduced from specific knowledge that serial murderers were preferential about selecting particular victims, they may decide only to include cases for consideration where the victim targeting is similar. However, profilers and investigators should not make such an assumption and cases should only be excluded where there is inductive reasoning for exclusion or there is alternative information which can exclude the cases. As previously mentioned, current profiling decisions are made deductively on the basis of experience of the individual decision makers. However, this book argues that such expertise must be validated through the development of theories and statistical models of criminal behaviors, which are based on empirical data relationships. That is, decision-making in criminal investigations should move from deductive to inductive. Adopting this approach would help to minimize the biasing effect of individual experience upon decisions which are based on all the circumstances of any particular case available to the individual making the decision.

Preface

Serial murder. This topic has received attention from both the academic community and the entertainment world since the FBI first published accounts of its profiling principles. The topic was made popular by the novel and Oscar-winning film *Silence of the Lambs*, with recent follow-ups such as *Seven*, *Copycat*, and *The X-Files* making the headlines. However, beyond the victims' pin pictures that help create the sensationalism in these movies and books, until now there have been few, if any, reliable empirical studies about serial murderers.

The idea of psychologically classifying serial murderers is premised on the assumption that to understand crimes of this nature, we need to consider the range of psychological issues relevant to behavior in general; for example, the offender's perception and interpretation of his actions and their likely consequences, and the emotional framework within which the person operates. Crime scene behavior, like any other behavior, is assumed to be a function of the whole personality of the individual. Equally important, it is assumed that human behavior does not take place in a vacuum but always occurs in a concrete social situation. Hence, the specific circumstances of a set of actions need to be understood in order to give a useful account of any related serial murderer's behavior.

The extrapolation of behavioral characteristics of serial murderers from information about their crimes as an aid to police investigations has been the thrust of most psychological profiling. However, in order for the classification of serial murderers to be more than educated guesswork, conclusions must be based on empirical research of consistencies in criminal behavior, and the relationship those actions have to aspects of an offender available to the police in an investigation. The present book represents a subsample of American serial killers who traveled throughout the U.S. to abduct and murder three or more victims, on different dates, and in different geographical locations. The data sample does not represent a subsample of sexually sadistic serial murderers nor a subsample of offenders found exclusively in any one particular database. On the contrary, offenders in this book were drawn from 40 states and displayed a broad range of crime scene actions and background characteristics.

To that end, in the present book the crime scene actions of 107 U.S. serial murderers, who killed a total of 728 victims, were examined in relation to their first, middle, and last offenses, in order to test three hypotheses: that serial murderers will have some structure in their actions within a series that are common to those offenses; that there will be certain thematic behavior underlying any murder committed by a sample of serial murderers that is more typical than any other committing serial murders; and there will be consistency across the three offense series for the offender samples. A two-faceted behavioral organization and attachment model was hypothesized, with four thematic classifications. Multivariate statistical analysis using Smallest Space Analysis (SSA) supports the faceted, four thematic classification model.

The empirically derived Facet Model of Serial Murder found that serial murderers' crime scene actions were similarly structured across their first, middle, and last offenses. Important information that is currently not found in the literature on serial murder was revealed by the analysis. For example, the SSA found a distinct subgroup of affective-type serial murderers who viewed their victims as vehicles that targeted, attacked, and murdered victims in their residences. Also, cognitive serial murderers, who viewed their victims as objects, tended to show organization at their crime scenes and hid the victims' bodies. Broadly, the results found that serial murderers who were sadistic were highly organized in their behavior. The analysis also found that serial murderers' behavior became refined and consistent over time.

Using Partial Order Scalogram Analysis (POSA), several relationships between offenders' crime scene behavior, criminal, sexual, and personal histories were revealed. For example, serial murderers with affective crime scenes and who viewed their victims as vehicles were more likely to have a violent criminal history for murder, rape, and kidnaping. However, cognitive serial murderers who viewed their victims as objects were more likely to have a history of fondling and sexual crimes, such as cunnilingus and fellatio. Generally, there was little difference in whether the offenders' behavior was affective or cognitive, with no bearing on their educational and employment histories. However, there was some indication that affective serial murderers were more likely to be employed than cognitive type murderers, and that cognitive serial murderers with sadistic crime scenes were likely to be better educated.

The three primary goals of this book, therefore, were: 1) to develop an empirical model of serial murderers' crime scene behaviors; 2) to find out if offenders remained consistent in their behavior over a number of offenses; and 3) to link crime scene behavior to the background character-istics of the offender.

These considerations give rise to four questions: 1) Do serial murderers who commit a series of homicides display behavioral actions within the series that are common to their offenses? 2) Are there unique signature behaviors committed by a sample of serial murderers that are more typical of them than any others committing serial murders; 3) Will these relate to background characteristics? Finally, 4) is there consistency across behavioral actions and offenders over time?

The book is divided into seven parts: An introductory section; a data acquisition and methodology section; a descriptive section; an empirical research section; an applicability section; and a concluding section. A summary of each chapter of these six sections is outlined below.

The introduction presents a review of the literature relevant to the three research questions outlined above.

Chapter 1 is a general overview of the different ways in which motives for murder have been classified. Topics of discussion include various ways in which offenders' aggression have been classified.

Chapter 2 presents a discussion of the extant typologies used to classify serial murderers, including a review of the FBI's organized and disorganized serial murder typology. It is concluded that most classifications of serial murderers are inherently flawed due to weak operational definitions, and unsubstantiated assumptions made about offender actions and characteris-tics. As an alternative to the rigid classification models, it is suggested that a Facet Theory approach to modeling the crime scene actions of serial mur-derers may be more robust and valid.

Chapter 3 describes a possible Facet Model of Serial Murder. Two facets, behavioral organization and attachment, are proposed as describing the type of aggression exhibited by the killers and the cognitive significance that the offenders placed on their victims. The behavioral facet consists of two elements — affective and cognitive — while the attachment facet also has two elements: victim as vehicle and victim as object.

Chapter 4 outlines the book's research objectives.

Chapter 5 describes the data acquisition and content analysis of the crime information data used in the book.

Chapter 6 discusses the book's research design and methodology, including a rationale for the use of non-metric multidimensional scaling procedures.

Chapter 7 describes the characteristics of 728 serial murder victims. This chapter outlines descriptive statistics with the background characteristics of the murdered victims. For example, the victims' ages, races, and genders are covered.

Chapter 8 provides an examination of 107 American serial murderers, of whom 11 are a part of a team. Examined are the possible characteristics that make up the serial murder sample with reference to characteristics such as the offenders' ages, races, and genders, and background history relating to criminality, sexuality, employment, and education.

Chapter 9 provides a descriptive overview of the murderers' crime scene behaviors.

Chapter 10 describes the first analysis of the book. Using 65 crime scene actions in the analysis, the SSA supports the two proposed facet elements, affective and cognitive; and the attachment elements, victim as vehicle and object. The four facet elements were thus used to classify the crime scene actions of serial murderers into four thematic regions: 1) Affective — Vehicle (AV); 2) Affective — Object (AO); 3) Cognitive — Vehicle (CV); and 4) Cognitive — Object (CO), describing modes of offender-victim interaction. Subsequent SSA tests found that the structure of the SSA appears to remain consistent across the killers' first, middle, and last offenses.

Chapter 11 analyzes 38 mid-frequency crime scene actions from the SSA analysis, using POSA analysis in order to better understand the possible interplay between the facets, behavioral and attachment, and the four thematic classifications highlighted in Chapter 10.

Chapter 12 describes a final analysis carried out on a more limited sample of 38 crime scene actions, using SSA to model serial murderers' crime scene behaviors. The chapter also describes how more conventional statistics, such as Kendall's coefficient of concordance *(W)*, Cochran's *Q* analysis, and Spearman's *rho*, were used to test the hypothesis that serial murderers were consistent in their crime scene behaviors across their first, middle, and last offenses.

Chapter 13 describes the use of POSA and conventional statistics to model elements of crime scene behavior and background characteristics. Each of the four thematic classifications were compared with background characteristics describing the killers' criminal, sexual, personal history, and age data.

Chapter 14 describes the application of the Facet Model of serial murder to real-life solved serial murder cases.

Chapter 15 describes how the methodology used in the book was applied in developing a psychological profile of the serial murderer John Williams, Jr., in addition to the summary and conclusions.

The present book is the result of intensive research carried out by this author over a period of four years. The implications of the research propounded in this book have a number of practical consequences for police investigations and, if the results are replicated with other data sets, could form the basis of a powerful investigative decision support tool.

Grover Maurice Godwin, Ph.D.
Raleigh, North Carolina — 1998

Acknowledgements

First, I would like to take this opportunity to express my sincere thanks to my Ph.D. supervisor Dr. Graham Wagstaff, for his consistently excellent supervision throughout my doctorate studies at The University of Liverpool. Secondly, I would like to thank the many other people without whom I would never have been able to complete this book. These include my mother and father; Priscilla McKinnie and Halford Godwin; and Dr. Robert Keppel and the entire staff at the Homicide Investigation Tracking System Unit (HITS) in Seattle, Washington for giving me the unique opportunity to visit their office and collect my research data. I would also like to thank Thomas J. Long of Vance-Granville Community College, Henderson, N. C. for his continued support over the past 12 years. My appreciation also goes to Mr. Timothy McKinnie. Finally, I would like to express my gratitude to all those at CRC Press who helped make this book possible, and especially to my editor, Becky McEldowney.

About the Author

Dr. Maurice Godwin is an adjunct professor at Vermont College of Norwich University in their distance learning MA Degree program, with a concentration in criminal investigative psychology. He is a former police officer in the State of North Carolina. Dr. Godwin was one of the first project coordinators for a National Institute of Justice grant for implementing community policing in a rural area. Dr. Godwin is also the author of journal articles on psychological and geographical profiling. He has worked as a consultant to police and others in developing psychological and geographical profiles. He has lectured in the U.S. and Europe on serial murder, cyber stalking, and criminal investigative analysis. Dr. Godwin received his undergraduate degree from Trevecca Nazarene University; his Master's Degree from Indiana State University, and his doctorate from The University of Liverpool, England.

Web Site: http://www.investigativepsych.com

Introduction

Classifications of serial murderers that are empirically formulated are necessary in order to make logical decisions about how to detect, apprehend, and eventually access their dangerousness. Similarly, without meaningful classifications, predications about aspects of crime scene behavior and how those actions relate to background characteristics can only be, at best, vague and limited to general factors. Until there is a classification model of serial murderers' crime scene actions that is built from the ground up, based on empirical and repeatable studies, then it will not be possible to make significant advances in any of these three areas: police investigations, aetiology, and treatment. The difficulty, of course, is in finding the distinct behaviors and characteristics which will classify serial murderers into meaningful groups.

A reliable and robust classification scheme should meet three broad criteria. First, classifications must be reliable. When different people use it, they must come up with the same results. Schemes that seem intuitively obvious to those devising the classification often fall apart when others use them. For instance, one offender's necessary aggression may be another person's sadism. Secondly, the classification must be practical and straightforward to interpret and use. If it requires years of dynamic psychological study before it produces results, chances are that it will not be very widely applied. Thirdly, the classification model must be valid for the task it is developed to fulfill. It must either lead to meaningful predictions or create facets of behavior to further our understanding of serial murderers.

How well do existing attempts at classifying serial murderers meet these criteria? Most fail, and outside of criminologist Eric Hickey's attempt, researchers do not even try. Many classification models of serial murderers tend to hone in on psychological motivation as if it is a given. These classifications provide explanatory models that are never tested to see whether they can be applied to actual serial murder cases. On the whole, current attempts to classify the behavior of serial murderers have been failures. The models are embedded with demographic statistics, offender self-reports, and offense descriptions mixed in an intuitive manner to create groups that conform to the researcher's preconceptions. For instance, the FBI's classification model of serial murderers is a good example of this.

The FBI profilers divide serial murderers into two types, according to the interplay of aggression and sex. The first serial murderer type is one who struggles against his impulses. His crimes are posited to be disorganized, and he often leaves his crime scenes in disarray. His driving motive is sexual gratification. The disorganized serial murderer has an aggressive aim and is called a displaced anger murderer. Such men seek to hurt, humiliate, and defile their victims, and sex is in the service of an aggressive impulse. In other words, sexual and aggressive impulses are not well differentiated, but do feed off each other. The second serial murderer type is labeled a sociopath. He is driven by sadistic urges, seeking to humiliate his victims. However, his crimes are organized, have a degree of planning involved, and he rarely leaves any forensic clues. The organized serial murder is one where violence is only instrumental in achieving a sexual end. This type of offender is often referred to as a serial sex murderer. Other research also points out that sex is an integral part of the serial murderer's attack.

In light of the FBI's classifications of serial murderers, other researchers argue that it is not aggression and sex that drives the serial murderer, but power and control. For example, some researchers suggest that sex in the crime of serial murder is pseudo-sexual, not a sexual act. In this theory, the serial murderer has inherent doubts about his general adequacy, including sexual inadequacy, and seeks to control his victims through intimidation. To alleviate these feelings of sexual inadequacy, the individual seeks revenge on women for wrongs believed to have been done to himself in past experiences. The serial murderer then uses violence in a sadistic way to take back control over women.

All these classifications have a certain logic to them. However, they tend to mix the sexual serial murderer in with killers who act on emotional impulses by suggesting that sex is behind *all* serial murders. In reality, though, there is no real reason why one should be preferred to another; nor is it clear how to decide which type befits a particular serial murderer. For example, is the serial murderer who commits a blitz-style attack, leaves the victim fully clothed, shows no forensic awareness, and steals the victim's car a sadistic serial murderer? None of the literature on serial murder classification schemes have tested those for reliability or validity; when others have done so to some degree, it has been found that they do not produce reproducible results when different researchers test the same population. The need, then, is for a classification system of serial murderers based on clear rules and verifiable data. However, important questions must be asked before any attempt is made to classify serial murderers.

The development of a classification model of serial murder requires that questions need to be answered by research, rather than relying solely on the work experiences and hunches of a few selected investigators. Given that any classification system of serial murderers must draw upon knowledge of the relationships between offense behavior and offender characteristics, the development of a classification model of serial murder requires establishing increasingly precise relationships between these two sets of variables. This then raises the question of whether those variables *do* relate to each other. With regard to behaviors of the offender, this is the question of whether the variation among offenders is so great that no systematic model can be developed.

Classifications can take on many different forms from clusters, regions, or sequential causal path analysis. However, some of these approaches to offense interpretation make strong assumptions about the type of framework that will emerge — others, less strong. It is argued in this book that a general but empirical framework, which makes minimum assumptions and can incorporate stronger models when appropriate, is the Facet Theory. Facet Theory works well with qualitative categories and builds up models of the underlying structure of the data from those categories, such as information contained in police files.

The ultimate purpose of any offender classification system is to aid police in identifying potential suspects and select between them. But which behaviors and characteristics can be specified with any consistency; and of those, which are the most useful in helping police identify the perpetrator? The impetus of this book is to provide empirical support for answering these questions.

The book introduces an "inductive" rather than a "deductive" approach to classifying the crime scene behavior of serial killers. The main difference between the present book and other literature on serial murder: *Hunting Serial Predators* is empirically and theoretically supported by solid research, data, and analysis. The other books involve no analysis and are mainly semi-autobiographical accounts of serial murder cases that draw unsubstantiated conclusions. Also, the other books rely solely on anecdotal accounts of serial murder cases, and do not provide any useful investigative decision-making strategies.

To that end, the majority of the available published accounts of serial murderers are not in scholarly or technical publications. Indeed, even such few academic reviews as do exist typically commence with reference to fictional accounts, such as *The X Files* or *Millennium*. It is therefore not surprising that a robust profile of the serial murderer, as described in current serial murder books, is far from clear or precise. Therefore, what makes this book unique is the fact that it does not cloud the topic with fictional and semi-autobiographical accounts based on particular experiences or hunches of the writer. Each chapter is clearly written, explaining in detail how to *psychologically* research and interpret the crime scene actions of serial killers. The book provides the reader with an Empirical Facet Model of the crime scene actions of serial murderers, based on information available to a police inquiry.

Serial murder is a controversial subject, full of potent myth. The object of this book is to provide an empirical overview of the related scientific knowledge, introduce a new method to classify the serial predator, and present accounts of the process and difficulties of profiling the serial murderer. It will be useful and interesting to most scientists and professionals in the fields of criminology, psychology, criminal justice, and police studies. It is the applied side of the book which will make it a standard reference for detectives and police officers, now and in many years to come.

Dedication

This book is dedicated to my wife, Helen, who has graciously endured
my long working hours during the project, and whose encouragement,
help and support has sustained me throughout.

For the known and unknown victims.

All the scientists in the world could not bring a criminal investigation to
a successful conclusion without the involvement of artists, the detectives who
link the components of a case into a complete package.

Larry Ragle
Blood will tell: Crime scene investigations (1995)

Detection is, or ought to be, an exact science and should be treated in
the same cold and unemotional manner.

Sir Arthur Conan Doyle
The Sign of Four

Contents

12 Consistency in Serial Murderers and Their Crime Scene Behaviors   183

13 Modeling Crime Scene Behavior and Background Characteristics   193

Motives For Murder: What Differentiates Killers?

1

Motives for serial murder have typically been classified within one of four broad explanatory frameworks. First, there is the sociogenic approach, which assumes criminal behavior develops out of societal processes. This explanation would lead to a classification of offenders on the basis of variations in their social backgrounds. Examples can be found in sociological theories such as social structural theory and social process theory.

1.1 Sociogenic Motives for Murder

Social structure theory suggests that individuals commit murder because they are stifled in their low socioeconomic standing. Similarly, social process theories contend that criminal behavior is a function of a socialization process, whereby the offender interacts with institutions and social organizations. Individuals may turn to crime as a result of family difficulties, failures in school, or peer group pressure. For example, Storr suggests that human cruelty, such as sadistic acts often committed by serial murderers, is a phenomenon which can only be understood if we take into account the fact that many people suffer from persistent feelings of powerlessness and helplessness which date back to early childhood experiences.[1] It is further suggested by Egger that as a result of this powerlessness, often formed as a result of some traumatic childhood event, individuals develop rage and intense hatred which is eventually taken out on targeted victims.[2] For example, in a separate study that looked at the case histories of murderers, Ellis and Gullo found that whenever sufficient material is given on a murderer's background, it is consistently found that: 1) his upbringing, particularly in relation to being treated kindly by his parents and his being emotionally close to them and to

1

his other family members, was often negative; and 2) from an early age, he acted peculiarly, especially in his interpersonal relationships with others — and began to get into trouble both in social relationships and at school.[3] However, the sociogenic approach is just one emphasis for murder; it does not directly examine the behavioral differences in serial murderers. Moreover, as Hickey points out, sociogenic theories offer compelling explanations for many types of crimes; however, they are inappropriate for serial murder.[4]

1.2   Culture Motives for Murder

Culture motives for serial murder are a relatively recent addition to the serial murder literature. For example, Leyton views serial murder as a consequence of social class conflict and frustration. From this culture conflict perspective, the offender perceives the outcomes of his or her social interaction to be below desired levels.[5] Consequently, the offender seeks out alternatives. The individual may choose to isolate himself from the disturbing environment in order to resolve the conflict, or to rebel against the perceived source(s) of conflict. However, the suggestion that violent criminal behavior is caused by a culture that alienates individuals, by making them feel entrapped and not allowing them to succeed in life, fails to explain why some individuals are exposed to these social forces and do not become violent criminals.

Another culture motive propounded by feminists is that serial murderers are basically misogynistic males who are acting out society's gender attitudes in an extreme form.[6] However, Leyton takes a position against the feminists' claims and points out that this motive fails to consider that it is males who are the majority of homicidal victims in every civilization in the world, not women.[7]

1.3   Biogenic Motives for Murder

According to the biogenic motive perspective, the explanation for serial murder develops from biological predispositions.[8–9] For example, Bailey has theorized that human action is heavily linked to the functioning of the limbic system.[8] Bailey argues that behavioral impulses of serial killers come from the more primitive structures of the brain which are more urgent than those of the cerebral cortex, and that most individuals engage in phylogenetic regression and progression.[10] Bailey posits that the killer's brutal aggression is an atavistic expression that is reptilian, automatic, and instinctual in nature. For example, impulsive behavior of serial murderers is said to evolve out of the cortical arousal which induces stimulation for sensation-seeking and narcissistic games with the police. However, Restak disagrees with Bailey, arguing that serial murderers have not been found to have episodic dyscontrol, but that serial murderers often plan and stalk their victims prior to killing them.[11-12] Restak also points out that the current state about knowledge of the brain of serial murderers is at a very elementary level.

1.4 Psychogenic Motives for Murder

Finally, there is the interpretation based on clinical and psychiatric analysis that murder is a product of the person's psychological characteristics.[13] For example, some see serial murder developing from unresolved psychological conflicts, or inappropriately learned behavior.[14-15] Such classifications of criminals can also be seen in the work of Cleckley's concept of psychopaths, and the FBI's motivational classification model of serial murder proposed by Ressler et al. and Burgess et al.[16-18] For example, Cleckley identifies several attributes of those he terms psychopaths that are not understood in terms of mental deficiency or psychosis. In a later study, Cleckley outlines 16 characteristics describing the makeup of a psychopath.[19] These attributes include pathological lying, poor judgment, egocentricity, and impulsiveness, along with charismatic, intelligent, hedonistic, narcissistic and antisocial behavior. Since serial murderers are generally viewed as possessing all these types of behaviors, researchers and the public alike often refer to all serial murderers as psychopaths.

1.5 Murder Typologies

There exist several problems in classifying serial murderers as psychopaths. First, not all psychopaths can be considered violent. Another problem with the term is that researchers and clinicians alike have yet to arrive at a consensus as to the accepted definition of the term psychopath.[20] However, beyond these issues, researchers who apply psychopathological concepts to profile serial murderers have yet to develop a set of empirically related behaviors common to serial murderers.

One of the earliest researchers to construct a psychological typology of different motives for murder was Jesse.[21] She provides six individual motives for murder:

1. Gain
2. Revenge
3. Elimination
4. Jealousy
5. Lust for killing (no sexual connection with victim)
6. Conviction (sexual gratification with victim)

The first four of these motives are self-explanatory. The fifth and sixth motive types, however, describe the lust murderer. Jesse divided five and six into lust-murders, where the satisfaction is the actual killing, without any sexual connection with the victim; and lust-murders committed at the same time or directly after the sexual act as part of the sexual gratification. Jesse's typology is one of the first-ever homicide models that actually draws a distinction between expressive and instrumental aggression. In this one respect, Jesse's motive typology for murder is useful; however, the typology does not provide any information on the different emphases between offenders within each motive category.

Later, Willie proposed these ten motives for murder:[22]

1. Depressive
2. Psychotic
3. Affiliated with organic brain disorder
4. Psychopathic
5. Passive aggressive
6. Alcoholic
7. Hysterical
8. Juvenile
9. Mentally retarded
10. Sex murderers

Willie argues that the depressive murderer is seldom involved in legal proceedings and does not display antisocial behavior. He often feels that suicide is a way out of his hopeless life. The paranoid type is often labelled as psychotic or schizophrenic. This type of murderer often hears voices that threaten to murder him or her and responds in a defensive manner. The next category is the murderer with organic brain damage who kills due to trauma received to his or her head in earlier life. The psychopathic personality has a history of social maladjustment which may result in him leaving clues at the crime scene. The fifth type, passive aggressive personality, has life experiences that cause him to turn violent when an individual, for example a lover, threatens to cut him off or rejects his dependency needs. Similar characteristics have been used in describing exploitative and displaced anger rapists.[23] The alcoholic character has an intrinsically aggressive nature, which when combined with alcohol, is unleashed. The hysterical personality-type murderer is more likely to be a female and only engages in threats of murder rather than actually going through with the act. The juvenile is classed as a child killer. The mental retarded type allegedly murders because of brain diseases. The final type of murderer is the sex killer. This type of murderer is most likely to display acts, such as cannibalism, postmortem sexual activity, and mutilation. However, Willie provides no motive for these type of crimes.

Willie's murder typology describes a broad range of explanations for murder ranging from sociogenic, biogenic, and psychogenic drives. However, similar shortcomings that are evident in Jesse's typology can also be found in Willie's ten motive categories. First, all offenders are lumped into rigid types, none of which focus on the fact that there may be offenders within each type who have different reasons for murder. Secondly, it is possible that hybrids exist within each motive type; therefore, offenders' behaviors are most likely to overlap; hence, the categories may not be mutually exclusive.

Also, while sociogenic, biogenic, and psychogenic explanations divide murderers into various subclasses based on different aetiological emphases, this is little help to those who hunt serial murderers. So, for example, just by looking at these three types of explanations we cannot tell exactly how we might expect behavior to be manifested. To fill this obvious gap in the literature, researchers began merging sociogenic, biogenic, and psychogenic explanations of crime with theories of aggression to distinguish between an offender's level of aggression.[24–28]

1.6 Theories on Instrumental and Reactive Aggression

One influential theory on aggression is propounded by Wolfgang and Ferracuti.[25] Based on an empirical study, Wolfgang and Ferracuti concluded that there are three basic types of criminals: 1) violent subculture; 2) psychopathological; and 3) dominant culture members. The first type, violent subculture, have internalized violent norms and values. Violent values prescribe the use of violent action and proscribe the use of nonviolent action when one has been provoked in some way. Violent values operate hand in hand with the norms. The second type, the psychopathological criminal, is posited to suffer from a severe mental disorder which makes him or her aggressive. The individual has internalized non-violent norms and values, and these are unleashed when the person is provoked. The violent action is a result of some perceived threat. The final criminal type describes members of the dominant culture; they have internalized nonviolent norms and values. They are similar to the psychopathological criminal, except they neither suffer from severe mental disorder nor engage in violent actions under any circumstances not authorized by their governments. The members of the dominant culture are presumably spread across all the classes.

However, the Wolfgang and Ferracuti theory has several inherent weaknesses. Monahan argues that the classifications are constructed upon concepts pertaining almost exclusively to the psychological composition of the offenders, leaving the offender and victim interaction relatively silent.[29] Furthermore, the study did not examine offenders who repeatedly murdered.

Thus, Wolfgang and Ferracuit suggest that members of the subculture of violence neither continuously engage in violence nor seek out violent situations, and they mention nothing about repeated violence beyond making these obvious points.[30]

Another theory used to classify aggression is Megargee's under- and over-controlled personality.[31–32] Megargee constructed his theory primarily from the results of psychological tests given by him and others to violent offenders. According to Megargee, there are two basic types of violent criminals: the under-controlled and the overcontrolled. The under-controlled individual is outwardly aggressive and has a very low threshold for frustration. The under-controlled person suffers from a lack of inhibitions against the expression of aggression, so that when he or she experiences frustration, there is nothing to prevent his or her subsequent drive to aggression from expressing itself in violent action. The overcontrolled person is outwardly nonaggressive and usually has a very high threshold for frustration.[32] However, overcontrolled individuals often suffer from excessive inhibitions against the expression of aggression, so that when they become frustrated, their subsequent drive to aggression is usually prevented from immediately expressing itself in violent action or even in some less severe form of overt aggression. Consequently, the drive to aggression in the overcontrolled person is not discharged, but is stored up until it finally reaches the point where it overcomes the excessively high degree of self-control. Once the individual reaches this extreme point, any event can trigger the rage. Therefore, overcontrolled individuals have a high probability of engaging in extremely violent behavior when they finally do become aggressive. The under-controlled persons can also engage in extremely violent behavior if they too become extremely frustrated.

In a later study, Megargee classified aggressive acts into those characterized by instrumental or extrinsic motivation, in which extrinsic aggression is goal oriented, and intrinsic aggression is the injury to the victim as an end in itself.[33] However, the major difference between Megargee's violent types is their level of control during the crime and not the degree of the violent behavior which they display. The distinction between Megargee's under-controlled and overcontrolled violent types become obfuscated when it is used to interpret crime scene behavior of serial murderers. Indeed, the major shortcoming of the Megargee violent type is that he mentions nothing at all about violent situations. Megargee suggests that all that is necessary for an under- or overcontrolled person to engage in violence is a frustrating stimulus of sufficient strength.[34] But as Bartol points out, the Megargee typology ultimately does not explain the various types of violence displayed.[35]

Another theory on aggression was proposed by Toch, who describes two main types of violent men.[28] The first is the self-image defender. This is a person who is extremely sensitive to the implications of other people's actions to his integrity, manliness, or worth. He uses violence as a means of getting revenge for perceived slights to his self-conception. The second violent type is the catharter. This is a person for whom violence is associated with relief and peace of mind. When the individual's emotions become all pent up, he explodes into a rage. Since violence is merely a means of emotional release, virtually any victim will do. The catharter in Toch's classification is similar to the aggression in Felson's theory; he proposes that aggression is a means of impression management, which restores one's threatened identity.[36] However, Toch seems to treat violent situations as only the settings for the expression of a particular dysfunctional ego. As a consequence, he does not provide any analysis of the nature of the immediate situations in which people become violent. Additionally, he seems to exclude the victim's role in the crime completely.

1.7 The Distinction Between Instrumental and Expressive Behavior in Murder

Other researchers have attempted to look more specifically at the offenders' ability to regulate their aggression in a crime. For example, Berkowitz reviewed evidence in support of a distinction between reactive (emotional), unregulated aggression, elicited in response to frustration; and instrumental aggression, which is more purposeful and goal directed.[37] Berkowitz concluded that reactive aggression conforms to the classic frustration-aggression model, whereas instrumental aggression can be understood from a social learning perspective. However, Berkowitz cautioned that individuals can exhibit both reactive and instrumental aggression, which raises the possibility of relatively more specific types of instrumental and reactive violent offenders. Some studies have examined the instrumental-reactive distinction in youthful offenders. For example, Hartup distinguished instrumentally aggressive children who pushed and shoved to obtain some object, such as a toy, apart from hostile aggressors whose intent was to harm their peer.[38] The idea of dividing offenders into different types based on the instrumental reactive destination has a long history.[39–42]

In one of the first studies to develop a dichotomous typology of murder, Feshbach divided homicides into either instrumental, where the murder served some goal, such as profit in a robbery; or expressive, where the murder is the result of the offender's emotional state — for example, killings that occur during the course of an argument.[41] However, in a more recent study on the differences in instrumental and expressive murder, Cornell and colleagues looked at criminal defendants charged with murder, attempted murder, and malicious wounding.[43] They found that offenders classified as reactive, who carefully planned and carried out the murder of an estranged

spouse, often reported no immediate provocation by the victim and denied
a state of angry arousal at the time of the offense. In contrast, though, they
found instrumental offenders often claimed they acted impulsively in a state
of anger. Overall, the findings concluded that instrumental and reactive
aggression are not mutually exclusive.

When the instrumental and expressive dichotomy is applied to lust or
sadistic murders, the distinction becomes blurred.[44] For example, De River
defines lust-murder as when death has occurred through torture brought
about to relieve sexual tension.[45] De River points out that lust-murderers only
gain sexual gratification through physical injury or torture of the victim
where the offender enjoys acts of perversion such as vampirism, cannibalism,
and necrophilia. Research by Nettler concurs with De River, and refers to
killers who perform perversions as intentional lust or sadistic murderers.[46]
Nettler goes on to point out that sadistic murderers commit butcher murders
without being legally insane. However, Revitch and Schlesinger define lust-
murders more generally as compulsive homicides that are stimulated through
a combination of social pressures, resulting in weakening of authority and
controls.[47] Within such definitions, the distinction between murder as a
means to an end, and as a reaction to a stimulus situation, is not at all obvious.

Additional problems can occur when looking at instrumental and expressive aggression. One is that many offenders may have a history of both types
of aggression. For example, an offender committing an otherwise instrumental offense, robbery for instance may become angry at the victim and engage
in reactive aggression, such as shooting the victim. To try and avoid the
obvious conflict in this approach to classifying aggression, several researchers
have attempted to distinguish between offenders in terms of psychopathy.[43–48]
However, within such models, the emphasis is mainly on pathology rather
than actual behavior. Classifying offenders based on elements of pathology
also has built-in selective legal biases — plea bargaining, arrest, and referral
for psychiatric examination, among others — thus incarcerated criminal
populations may not be representative of criminals at large or groups of
criminals selected by type of offense. Banay notes that the reasons given for
the act of murder by killers can be misleading since the true cause is masked
by other logically understandable explanations.[49] In seems, therefore, that the
traditional classification of instrumental and expressive aggression lacks
strong empirical support.[30]

1.8 Classifying Aggression in Serial Murderers

One of the major weaknesses of traditional classifications of aggressive
behavior, particularly as they apply to murder, is that they are based on the

assumption that there are only two types of people: the violent and nonviolent. This is due in part to the fact that, historically, traditional studies on aggression in murder have used single homicides as case studies, without any exploration of murderers.

Nevertheless, a number of studies have classified the actions of serial murderers for a variety of etiological reasons. Most published accounts of variations in serial murderers have tended to classify levels of aggression in an offense with some form of motivational drive and inferred offender characteristics.[4,13,17,50–52] These published studies traditionally classify serial murderers by how the offender's aggression is channelled and controlled during the crime, and how it is accommodated and regulated by internal mechanisms. Those who research serial murder typically borrow from traditional studies on aggression, such as those mentioned above, to classify serial murderers or their crime scene behaviors.

Two distinctions are usually made about the serial murderer's crime scene actions: 1) the actions are emotional or reactive; and 2) actions involve some sort of planning. For example, the FBI's organized and disorganized dichotomy essentially derives from the instrumental and expressive aggression theories. In the early FBI interviews with convicted serial murderers, the offenders claimed that their crimes were reactive, with no planning involved.[17] However, the FBI later questioned whether such a thing as a spontaneous murder really exists, suggesting that due to extensive fantasizing, serial murderers must, to some degree, be planning their murders.[17] As a result of this thinking, the FBI profilers insist that among serial murderers who have little or no conscious plans of murder, there is still a great deal of evidence in their belief structures for fantasy and planning.[17] The planning is thought to be reflected in the crime scene actions of the killer, which tends to be methodical, and signifies ritualized behavior and careful planning with dominance, power and control as the most frequent motivational themes.[53] Regardless of the similar or dissimilar attributes serial murderers share, many researchers insist on dividing them into subgroups or types based on whether the offender's aggression is consistent or not.[4,17,50] Broadly, the literature discussed above is considered the stepping stone for what is the most widely accepted method of psychological profiling in use today, that of the Federal Bureau of Investigation (FBI) in the U.S. Currently, researchers and investigators around the world use the FBI's motivational model of organized and disorganized scheme to profile serial murderers.[54] The FBI's motivational classification model was developed to assist in the investigation of serial murders rather than contribute to the literature, but because of the attention that has been paid to the model as a basis for classifying serial murderers it is useful to examine this work in some detail.

Reliability, Validity, and Utility of Extant Serial Murderer Classifications

2

The FBI's initial project on serial murder began in 1978.[17,55] The impetus for the project was to conduct personal interviews with serial murderers about their crimes in order to find out how they were successful at avoiding capture.[55] The FBI serial murder project was given added attention in Washington, D.C. in the early 1980s due to public outcry of the murder of a six-year-old boy in Florida by a serial murderer.[17] Therefore, due to public pressure, the FBI serial murder project was brought to the forefront and given the necessary U.S. government funding, which eventually lead to a unit being established in Quantico, Virginia called the Behavioral Science Unit (BSU). In 1995, a restructuring phase combined the Behavioral Science Unit, Violent Criminal Apprehension Program (VICAP) , and the National Center for the Analysis of Violent Crime into one unit, calling it the Critical Incident Response Group (CIRG).[56]

2.1 The Origins of the FBI Serial Murder Project

The primary purpose of the serial murder project was to use interviews with convicted killers as a basis for constructing future classifications, which then could be used to aid police investigations. A series of interviews with 36 incarcerated offenders, of whom 25 were defined as serial murderers (i.e., the killing of three or more individuals over time), took place between 1979 and 1983 in the U.S. The interviews were guided by an unstructured checklist of questions. Prior to the interviews, data sources on each offender and their crimes were obtained by reviewing crime scene photos, physical evidence, court transcripts, victim reports, autopsy reports, prison records, and psychiatric reports. However, no detailed analysis of this material has ever been presented. Instead, a simple dichotomy was claimed to emerge from the project, by which offenders were classified either as organized or disorganized. The assignment of the offenders to either the organized or disorganized category was based on the appearance of the victim's attire or nudity, the exposure of victim's sexual parts, the insertion of foreign objects in body cavities, or evidence of sexual intercourse.

The FBI posits in the literature that the organized and disorganized scheme was developed to classify a subgroup of serial murderers; that is, sex-related murderers, where motive was often lacking.[17] This also can be interpreted like so: where the murderer is emotional and no organization can be deciphered from his actions at the crime scene, there is no motive. Because of the apparent lack of motive, FBI profilers decided to look for evidence of planning, irrationality, or some form of discord at the crime scene in order to determine whether the offender was organized or disorganized. The organized and disorganized typology is then used to classify the murderer's personality, depending on which category the crime scene falls into.

There are weaknesses in the organized and disorganized dichotomy. For example, there is no one single explanation in the literature of the differences between the organized and disorganized serial murderer. Rather, what the organized and disorganized dichotomy actually seems to describe is the different levels of aggression in serial murderers, although no literature source acknowledges this. The differences in the organized and disorganized crime scenes are usually explained in the form of a psycho-dynamic drive. The dynamic drives are: 1) revenge; and 2) sadism.[17,52] The focus of these drives is seen in terms of lasting urges, formed through early life experiences. These experiences are organized especially around conflict, such as defenses, conscience, and reality at times arrayed against the drives.

The differences between the two types therefore appear to originate from several traditional theories of aggression and personality disorders. For example, it is alleged that the organized offender has the ability to maintain some control over his aggressive behavior, while the disorganized offender is unable to maintain control. There is, however, a third type: the mixed offender, which is rarely discussed in the literature. The mixed type was added to accommodate offenders who did not fit into either the organized or disorganized category.[57]

2.1.1 The Organized Serial Murderer

According to the FBI classification, the organized (nonsocial) serial murderers are generally assumed to be cunning and spend vast amounts of time planning their murders, whether consciously or not, and this behavior is reflected at their crime scenes.[17] Another assumption is that the serial murderer's planning is expressed in his preoccupation with and constant need for control.[58] For example, the FBI profilers claim that crime scenes tend to echo this aspect through the condition of the body, the body's state of dress, selection of restraints and weapons, body disposal sites, and method of approach.[4,59]

The organized serial murderer is described as one who is positively anti-social but often more gregarious, quite normal on the outside, maintaining normal relationships. He will be more forensically aware, mobile, creative, and adaptive; he often has a preferential victim, a certain type. Although victims' bodies are normally concealed, he will tease the police by leaving some bodies open to view. The FBI profilers suggest that the organized type serial murderer is out to shock and offend the community and taunt the police because he feels so much more powerful than them.[59] The offender will likely be a police buff and usually collects items relating to law enforcement.[17,59]

In the FBI study, imprisoned serial murderers classified as organized were assumed to have had an angry frame of mind at the time of the murder, but their behavior was calm and relaxed during the commission of the crime. For example, the organized crime scene is described as having a "semblance of order existing prior to, during, and after the murder."[17] It is suggested that the murder is planned, and the offender is likely to use a con or ploy to lure his victims to their deaths. For example, the individual may strike up a conversation or pseudo-relationship with his victims. For organized killers who consciously plan their murders, selection of the victim is believed to be a first step in acting out their fantasy; victims are thought to be chosen because of their symbolic similarity to someone in the killer's life or because of meanings the offender assigned to particular actions, such as hitching. However, the FBI provides no empirical research supporting the theory that serial murderers target specific victims for psychological reasons.

The organized offender is seen as one who usually remembers his thoughts prior to each murder and improves on his planning with each subsequent killing. The offenders' planning and control over their victims is noted by the use of restraints: ropes, chains, handcuffs, belts, clothing, etc. The offender is most likely to bring a weapon to the crime scene and take it with him when he leaves. The organized serial murderer is also forensically aware and rarely leaves incriminating evidence behind. The FBI suggests that the organized serial murderer is more likely to rape and torture victims prior to death, while the disorganized types are more likely to mutilate and to perform post-mortem sexual acts. However, these assumptions have been challenged by several researchers.[20,60]

The organized typology has several shortcomings. The FBI suggests that organized serial murderers kill to act out their "control and dominance," while at the same time they maintain that prior to the murder, the offender is feeling frustration, hostility, anger, agitation, and excitement, all of which indicate the crime is emotional and revenge seems to be the primary drive.[17,61]

In other words, the FBI claims that serial murderers who kill in an emotional rage have control of their behavior at the crime scene.

The revenge (nonsocial) drive explanation for repetitive murder is supposedly that it is the offender's unconscious effort to discharge aggressive drives toward another person who represents a significant other from past life experiences. The act supposedly originates from the Oedipal trauma — trauma by a seductive or rejecting mother and a punitive or absent father. The ego's defenses cannot prevent the action, but direct it towards an alternative object — the victim. The rationale of the revenge formulation is that the relationship between a child's parents sets the patterns not only for the sexual and aggressive behavior, but also for general standards of expressing and prohibiting all sorts of behavior.

The drawback to the aggressive revenge drive theory is that it assumes conflicts invariably express themselves in Oedipal language. This may well have an emphasis for some serial murderers; for example, David Berkowitz "Son of Sam," who shot couples in their cars, apparently as stand-ins for the biological parents who had abandoned him. The revenge focus for serial murder may have some validity; however, the Oedipal theory neither explains why some serial murderers would need to seek revenge repeatedly nor why convicted killers do not necessarily demonstrate weakened defenses in other aspects of their lives. It seems reasonable to conclude that an individual who is so tortured by Oedipal thoughts that he acts them out is going to reveal similar behavior in other realms of his life. Clearly, the revenge focus seems too broad an explanation for describing individual differences in serial murderers.

2.1.2   The Disorganized Serial Murderer

In Freud's Theory of Sexuality, he concluded that in such perversions as sexual murder and necrophilia, "It is impossible to deny that in their case a piece of mental work has been performed which, in spite of its horrifying result, is the equivalent of an idealization of the instinct." [62] Freud's statement seems to set the direction for the classification of the serial murderer's aggression as a sexual perversion; many researchers have argued that the disorganized murderer kills primarily for sexual gratification. [17]

The asocial (disorganized) serial murderer is described as a loner, withdrawn, and more cowardly in his crimes. [50] His crimes are often committed without a plan, and the victims are usually attacked in a blitz style. Some researchers suggest that the disorganized crime scene indicates a serial murderer whose motivation consists of uncontrolled sexual drives, reflected by his inability to control impulsive behavior or change his action in consideration of others. [52] Other researchers suggest that the psychological gain for the disorganized serial murder is sexual exploitation of the victim in the form of sadistic acts. [17] For example, it is advocated in the literature that a sadistic sexual drive is the impetus for the disorganized serial murderer.[4,17] However, what is derived from this perspective are biases gleaned from offenders' self-reports. Consequently, no exploration of the various emphases murder has for different offenders is considered.

The sadistic aggressive explanation for disorganization suggests that the offender derives sexual gratification by the infliction of pain and degradation on his victims. For example, it is argued by some that the aetiology for serial murder is sexual gratification.[63] The sexual attack is a way to degrade, subjugate, and ultimately destroy the victim. In the sadistic drive formulation, it is postulated that the offender kills out of sexual frustration because of a specific need for an object he can humiliate and torture. Some researchers also claim that sadism reassures the individual of his power by easing his worries about, for example, castration.[47] However, Storr discounts the sadistic sexual gratification theory.[1] Rather, he suggests that the murder has less to do with "sex" and more to do with pseudo-sexual activity, power relations, and control. Fox and Levin concur with Storr's view and point out that domination is a crucial element in serial crimes with a sexual theme.[64]

The disorganized offender is also described as one who shows no forensic awareness, often leaving fingerprints, bloody footprints, semen, and evidence of little or no preparation for the murder by selecting weapons of opportunity. For example, the FBI profilers point out that the disorganized serial murderer is not likely to use restraints because the victim is killed immediately.[17] In the disorganized-type murder, the victim is depersonalized by cuts and stab wounds to specific areas of the body. Other examples of depersonalization and sadistic acts on victims occur in the form of inserted objects, which the FBI suggests is a form of regressive necrophilia and sexual substitution rather than an act of mutilation or control.[17,59] Additional sexual exploits may include sadistic features such as mutilation, disembowelment, amputation, and vampirism.

The literature suggests that victims of the disorganized killer typically show signs of overkill and excessive blunt trauma to the facial area, which is thought to indicate that the victim knew the attacker.[17] Also, the lack of organization in the disorganized serial murderer is often noted by the offender making no attempts to conceal the victim's body and leaving him/her in the same location in which he/she was killed.[59]

2.2 Discrepancies in the Organized and Disorganized Dichotomy

If we look closely at the FBI's description of organized and disorganized types, there appear to be some discrepancies in their text descriptions when compared to the respective crime scene check-list. For example, the text version of the disorganized type actually seems to contain a number of organized types of behaviors that require extensive planning and forethought. For instance, behavior such as postmortem sexual activity, revisiting the crime scene, and the use of gloves would appear to indicate cognitive planning and an instrumental focus. However, the checklist — the list of actions assigned to each crime scene type — seems to reflect more a mixture of revenge and expressive aggression.[17] For example, the actions of blunt trauma to the face and blitz attack are embedded with a primary focus, that being a sexual gratification. The combination of these modes of behavior is commonly cited as indicative of the organized serial murderer; actually, they appear to represent disorganization rather than organization. It seems, therefore, the hypothesis that serial murderers who perform mutilations, postmortem sex, and cannibalism are also disorganized is certainly open to question.

In addition to these discrepancies, there are two further shortcomings in the organized and disorganized offender typology. First, the behavior that describes each type is not mutually exclusive; a variety of combinations could occur in any given murder scene. This is, of course, a weakness in all the murder classification schemes discussed in this chapter. Next, there is no discussion as to why serial murderers have the need to repeatedly kill. Both the revenge and sadistic drives seem too vague. It can also be noted that the organized and disorganized scheme also provides no reason why serial murders select some victims and pass up others. The organized and disorganized labels appear to be clinical assessments, similar to those found in the DSM-III-R. Hare argues that the antisocial personality disorder criteria in DSM-III-R are primarily a measurement of antisocial and criminal behavior and do not consider the affective and interpersonal characteristics of the personality disorder commonly associated with individuals displaying psychopathological behavior.[48]

2.2.1 Reliability of the FBI Serial Murderer Sample

In the FBI project, 36 killers were interviewed, 25 of whom were classified as serial murderers and 11 single or double killers[17,52,61] A subsample of the 36 offenders was classified as disorganized and organized.[17] Thirty-three of the offenders who participated in the interviews were white. The offenders who agreed to participate in the final project were reportedly motivated by various reasons, such as making restitution to victims, to obtain attention, or to gain some legal advantage. For example, some of the offenders interviewed "had not completely exhausted their legal appeals prior to the interviews." [55] Furthermore, the offenders who refused to be interviewed were predominately white, intellectual, and motivated not to participate on advice from their attorneys and were most likely to have organized behavior, which could account for the higher ratio of disorganized to organized murderers. Rather than interviewing a representative sample of killers, the FBI examined a small selected set of incarcerated offenders who were interested in volunteering. Thus, the FBI sample must be thought of as biased, although exactly how much is difficult to tell without a description of the population they were drawn from with which to compare the sample.

2.2.2 Inferring Behavior from Fantasy in the FBI Model

One theme that dominates serial murder classifications is the role that fantasy has in facilitating the murders. Ressler and his colleagues concluded that "sexual murder is based on fantasy." [17] Several methodological constraints become relevant when inferring motivation through fantasy, such as the distortion most likely found in self-report studies. The FBI's serial murder classification relies on self-reports of personal history background and elements of how the crime was committed. However, research by Lewis and his colleagues, in a study that required independent confirmation of reports of trauma (e.g., those found in hospital or police reports at the time of the incidents) found that convicted killers tend to underreport histories of trauma and deny symptoms of psychiatric disorders.[65] For example, during the interviews with serial murderers, the FBI researchers ultimately found the disorganized murderers' unanimous assertion of heterosexuality to be unreliable, but their suspicions were not aroused about whether retrospective accounts of the offenders' fantasy states prior to the murders were accurate.

In a later study, Prentky and his colleagues examined the role of fantasy in serial sexual murder by comparing 25 serial sexual murderers taken from the FBI sample with 17 single-victim sexual killers.[23] The results of the study found that the serial group differed significantly from the single homicide group on measures of intrusive fantasy. However, the Prentky study has several weaknesses. First, part of the data sample was borrowed from the FBI serial murder project, which, as discussed earlier, has inherent biases. Similar to the FBI's studies, the Prentky report is so embedded with a mixture of clinical and motivational assumptions that no clear differences are made between fantasy and planning. Shapiro cautioned that historical explanations of pathology are simply too narrow a base from which to derive the complicated forms of sadism.[66] Second, the Prentky study used a control group — single sexual murderers — but did not match its study methods to those used with the serial murderer group. This is rather vexing, because there were no interviews of the offenders in the single-victim group. Instead, data were taken from police archives. DeHart and Mahoney point out that researchers who choose to distinguish between one-victim murderers and serial murderers run into ambiguities in scientific and legal classification of serial murderers, which may diminish the validity of the data.[10] Third, the Prentky study compared a distinct subgroup of serial sex murderers with single-victim murderers who, over time, may not be likely to have the opportunity to exhibit bizarre sexual behaviors as the serialists. Finally, the study used fantasy to distinguish between the offenders, which is highly susceptible to subjective interpretation.

Further complications come to light when using inferred motives and fantasies to develop a classification model of serial murder. Serial murderers often alter or exaggerate claims for egocentric or status reasons. For example, the FBI classification model of serial murder is constructed under the assumption that normal people do not have sadistic fantasies, or if they do, they are different from those experienced by serial murderers. One assumption is that childhood fantasy is usually positive, and thus serial murderers' childhood fantasies are oddly violent. Another assumption is that serial murderers show an unusually early onset of fetishistic behavior, when in fact the literature suggests that fetishism begins to develop somewhere around the age of five.[67]

Fantasy is described in the FBI motivational model as a linear relationship between a dominant mother, abusive personality, and arousal levels.[18] However, research by Terr found that abused children could become either aggressive or withdrawn, and children with non-abusive backgrounds demonstrated a range of responses from psychosis through neurosis.[68] This suggests that subtle yet crucial distinctions may be overlooked when an interviewer inquires only whether or not the offender's mother was dominant in his childhood. Research by Lion further suggests that inferring fantasy from violence crimes such as rape and serial murder is problematic.[69]

2.3   Validity of the FBI Serial Murder Model

Using a five-stage development criteria, Busch and Cavanaugh examined two classification models of serial murder proposed by the Ressler et al.[70,71] In the author's opinion, Busch and Cavanaugh determined that the FBI classification model fits two stages: 1) unfounded statements not supported by data collection; and 2) unevaluated case reports without rigorous evaluation of other contributory factors.[72] The remaining three stages of the criteria were: 3) scientific case reports of individuals or small groups; 4) select population studies of particular subgroups under study; and 5) epidemiological studies of larger random samples or a significant proportion of a small population.

Busch and Cavanaugh also concluded that the FBI serial murder classifications were weak because they were descriptive and were not generalizable to the full population of serial murderers at large. They also found that the two studies depended on *ad hoc* data, which, combined with a small sample

size, introduce biases that tend to confirm the assumptions of the researchers.[72] Busch and Cavanaugh further argued that the motivational model for
serial murder proposed by the FBI lacked statistical support and warn that
the conclusions they draw from the crime scene variables inevitably produce
a bias favoring confirmation of the assumptions. A study by Canter also
questions the motivational-based murder classifications by pointing out that
it is the offender's actions that are known to police, not his motivation.[73]

2.3.1 Lack of Empirical Operational Definitions

A continual source of conflict in the FBI's serial murder model is the lack of
defined concepts in the organized and disorganized dichotomy. An example
of lack of defined concept is, in the FBI project, fantasy which was positively
coded if the daydreaming content included intentional infliction of harm in
a sadistic or sexually violent way.[74] The problems with this form of *post hoc*
reasoning are demonstrated in one serial murder case where, on the one
hand, the FBI profilers interpreted the bizarre positioning of a victim's body
that represented a Hebrew letter as evidence of planning rather than fantasy;
and on the other hand, they interpreted the refinement in techniques used
to immobilize victims as evidence of fantasy rather than planning.[17] A study
by Katz also points out that any model of serial murder which accepts blanket
statements on motivation and that does not clearly examine victim/offender
interaction and the interaction of behavioral sequences in the actual murder
may be misleading.[75]

2.3.2 False Dichotomization of Variables

A typical example of false dichotomization of variables and the lack of mutually exclusive concepts in the FBI serial murder typology is demonstrated in
the following scenario: how would a police investigator classify an organized
serial murderer with good intelligence, sexual competence, and who is geo-
graphically mobile (i.e, has a car) who commits a spontaneous, depersonal-
izing murder in which the victim's body is left at the crime scene — all of
which are characteristics of a disorganized killer? In this example, the profilers
assume that the motivational factor that caused the violent criminal behavior
will be indicated by the study of the patterns in the external characteristics
of violent offenders. Their assumption is that the antecedent factor for a
series of murders is due to both an emotional outburst and some intrinsically
abnormal personality in the offender, and that the offender's personality will
be reflected in the way he carries out his crimes. This perspective sees motivation and personality as the same process and neglects different emphases
that each explanation may have for different individuals.

2.4   Utility of the FBI Serial Murder Model

The theories on which the profiles of serial murderers are built are rather perplexing. There is the clinical classification which sees the differences in offenders, not so much in the crimes, as in the internal emotional dynamics of the killer. These type classification models seem to paint a picture of the offenders' mental illnesses, rather than trying to distinguish between their crimes. Here, motive is thought to be some form of anger or rage towards society or a targeted group of individuals, and the offender harbors his emotional reactions to the point where they explode. These trends may be explained in terms of displacement of anger from other targets, or the feeling of lack of power. However, Stephenson has reviewed such displacement theories as general explanations of criminal behavior and found little evidence for them.[76] Secondly, there is the motivational classification to suggest the internal forces or predispositions that drive a sadistic killer to murder repeatedly are mental representations of vicarious gratifications.[13,17] In other words, the murderer, who has no conscious emotion, is driven by thoughts and fantasies. This perspective is usually derived by relying on self-reports of serial murderers to classify the offender's mental state, and in turn to classify crime scenes. However, the FBI profilers suggest that the sadistic personality is influenced by a continual fantasy. Moreover, the problem with this form of deductive reasoning is that motives are inferred and are assumed to be related to intrinsic thoughts and mental illness, and that the exploration of behavior is totally neglected. Not surprisingly, in a recent study on different profiling approaches, researchers examined the validity and utility of diagnostic evaluations and profiles developed from crime scene analysis.[77] The study concluded that the "majority of profiles are mildly to severely flawed." [77] Other approaches to the profiling of serial murderers appear not to be much better. Given this, it might be more productive to adopt an approach that focuses more on behavior.

2.5   The Personality to Behavior Confusion

From a behavioral approach, the actions of serial murderers are examined through those behaviors that can be observed, rather than the individual's internal workings. As John B. Watson argued many years ago, only individuals can observe their perceptions and feelings, but someone else can observe your actions.[78] Consequently, it seems more reasonable to consider crime scene actions as experiences of behavior rather than particular manifestations of intrinsic psychopathology.

The behavioral approach to classifying serial murderers' actions suggests that an individual's actions are the result of interaction between personality characteristics, social habits, and the physical conditions of the situation. An inductive behavioral approach to modeling serial murderers sees behavior as mostly being consistent across a number of situations rather than specific to a particular environmental context. By employing the inductive behavioral approach, trends in how serial murderers behave, from one crime to the next, can be explored. Researchers often assume that personality traits are consistent, so that an offender can be characterized according to enduring personality characteristics. However, individuals are not uniformly rewarded across different crimes. The offender may learn to discriminate those contexts in which certain behavior is appropriate and those in which it is not. Rather, it is aggressive actions that are differentially rewarded, and learned discriminations determine the situations in which the individual will display a particular behavior. This suggests that diverse behaviors do not necessarily reflect variations on the same underlying motive; they often are discrete responses to different situations. Therefore, a behavioral classification model of serial murder may be likely to be more representative of serial murderers at large rather than one developed from personality traits.

2.6 Other Perspectives on Classifying Serial Murderers

2.6.1 Sewell's Approach

Using Megargee's aggression theories, research by Sewell analyzed the serial murderer Ted Bundy from literature dealing with Bundy and Sewell's own involvement as an investigator on the Chi Omega sorority house murders at Florida State University. Sewell applied Megargee's algebra of aggression to Bundy's crime scene behavior for this one crime event. Briefly, Megargee's theory of criminal behavior argues that "an individual automatically weighs alternatives and chooses a response to a situation which maximizes his or her benefit and minimizes potential pain distress." [79] Sewell's analysis found that Ted Bundy's behavioral characteristics provide a clear application of Megargee's algebra aggression by stating that:

> Bundy's overall violent response exemplified an instigation to aggression which was grounded in his rage against women and magnified by his need for excitement, attention, and ego gratification. His habit strength drew on his repeated successful acts of violence...to obtain control of the victims and the unsuccessful attempts by a number of states to charge him with these crimes. A number of situational factors added to his predisposition towards violence as an acceptable response.

Sewell's study concluded that Ted Bundy's motive for murder was that he chose a violent response as an acceptable reaction to many situations. However, a review of Sewell's study found that he omitted some critical behavioral information concerning Ted Bundy's killing career. Although it could be argued that the Chi Omega murders were opportunistic and relatively unplanned, Bundy's other murders were very much thought out with deliberation and intent. To use Bundy's behavior in murders towards the end of his killing career is misleading, because in those murders Bundy was more emotional due to the pressure of trying to elude the police. Therefore, his instrumental need for postmortem sexual activity had dissipated. Sewell failed to acknowledge this difference in his study. In other words, Sewell's study used one murder incident in which Bundy was clearly frustrated, and extrapolated it to Bundy's entire criminal career.

2.6.2 The Holmes Approach

Serial murderers have been classified by other researchers[20,50,80,81] For example, Holmes and DeBurger classified serial murderers into four types: 1) visionary serial murderers, whose impetus to kill is propelled by voices they hear or visions they see; 2) mission serial murderers, whose impetus to kill is a need on a conscious level to eradicate a certain group of people; 3) hedonistic serial murderers, who are labeled lust- or thrill-murderers and whose crimes have sexual overtones; and 4) power/control serial murderers, whose motivation to kill is driven by a need for sexual gratification and the complete domination of their victims.

The Holmes and DeBurger classification scheme appears to be a type of "story line," offering up reasons why serial murderers kill, rather than an empirical model distinguishing between offenders or offenses. A study by Gresswell and Hollin points out three weaknesses in the Holmes serial murder typology: 1) the classifications are not mutually exclusive; 2) the classifications are not exhaustive; and 3) the classifications fail to pick up interactions between the murderer, the victims, and the environment, and do not appear to be flexible enough to accommodate a serial murderer who may have different motives for different victims or changing motives over time.[82] Also, another weakness in the Holmes classification model is that the data on which the conclusions are based are not provided.[52]

2.6.3 Hickey's Approach

Hickey's study on serial murderers and their victims is based on data collected on 203 serial murderers, of whom 34 were females and 169 males.[20] The dates of their crimes range from 1795 to 1988. Hickey's research mainly focused on victims of serial murderers rather than the offenders' crime scene behaviors.

Hickey's study on serial murder is considered to be one of the most thorough in the literature. Hickey developed a taxonomy of motives from his data, and he states that serial murderers' motives appear to focus on "financial security, revenge, enjoyment and sexual stimulation." [20] However, there are several problems with Hickey's motive types. For one, it is most likely that most researchers would exclude many of the female serial murderers who Hickey included in his study. For instance, he included females who could be labeled as "black widows," meaning that they usually killed for profit. Of the 34 female murderers in his study, 53% killed for profit sometimes, while for 41% the motive for murder was entirely financial profit.

The data on male serial murders was less than forthcoming in Hickey's study. For example, he did not discuss many behavioral characteristics, and when they were highlighted, they were used descriptively. Consequently, no attempt was made to empirically explore the relationship between serial murderers who acted out of revenge and the distances they traveled to commit their crimes; although he did discuss differences in spatial behavior, it was not in relation to crime scene actions.

Despite the shortcomings in Hickey's study, he does provide a useful descriptive model on predispositional factors and facilitators that could influence the serial murderer. He refers to his model as the "trauma-control model for serial murder." [20] Hickey suggests that the triggering mechanism in the serial murderer may well be some form of trauma in which the individual is unable to cope with the stress of traumatic events. For example, he proposes that the most common childhood traumatization, in his population of killers, was rejection by relatives and parents.[20] Hickey further points out that individuals deal with traumatic events differently; for example, some deal with past trauma in a more destructive framework.

One interesting finding in Hickey's study was, although no exact percentage figure is given, he found that the serial murderers who were serial rapists were also abused. In a similar vein, Hazelwood and Warren reported in their study on 41 serial rapists that 76% had been sexually abused as children.[83] This finding is interesting because it gives an indication that a common feature in serial murderers' backgrounds could be some form of a traumatic experience.

2.6.4 The Dietz Approach

Dietz and his colleagues made a descriptive study of 30 sexually sadistic serial murderers.[80] The purpose of their study was to gather information on personal characteristics and crime scene details common among such murderers. Seventeen of the subjects were classified as serial murderers, five of whom were originally in the FBI's sample population. The remaining subjects were drawn from a pool of cases maintained in the FBI's National Center for the

Analysis of Violent Crime. The data used were archival documents (i.e., self-reports and police records) describing the offenders' crimes. The study found that 93% of the sexual sadists were organized and suggested that fantasy was the motivational factor behind the murders.

The ratio of organized to disorganized offenders in the Dietz study was considerably higher than in the FBI's project. The high proportion of organized offenders was probably due to biases in the sample; that is, a distinct subgroup of offenders, sexual sadistic murderers who were most likely to have organized behavior. Another form of bias in the Dietz study was the combination of a small sample size with *a priori* diagnosis suppositions made about the offenders, which appear to confirm the assumptions of the researchers.

2.7   Investigative Process Management (IPM)

Given the problems with these approaches, how should we proceed? One way might be through what could be termed the Investigative Process Management (IPM) approach.

2.7.1   Induction as Systematization

The view adopted here is that induction is not a method of inference to the best explanation, but to the best "systematization." Induction, in this way, is used as an instrument of inquiry; it affords a mechanism for arriving at our best available estimate of the correct answer to our factual questions. For example, during a criminal investigation, questions arise most pressingly where the information- in- hand does not suffice, when they are not answerable in terms of what has already been established. Here arises what C. S. Peirce calls the *ampliative* methodology of inquiry — the sense of going beyond the evidence in hand.[84] Investigators need to do their very best to resolve questions that transcend accreted experience and outrun the reach of the information already at their disposal. In this regard, it becomes necessary to have a device for obtaining the best-available, "rationally" optimal answers to the information- in- hand. Arriving at answers inductively is not to be a matter of mere guesswork, but of responsible estimation in a serious sense of the term. It is not just an estimate of the true answer that we want, but an estimate that is sensible and defensible; tenable, in short.

Here induction represents a cognitively serious effort at closing all information- gaps in such a way that, everything considered, we can regard it as epistemically well-advised to accept the indicated results. In this sense, the inductively derived answers are arrived at by systematization with "real world" experience.

2.8   Deriving Inductive Profiles from Deductive Experiences

Providing answers to a criminal inquiry requires systematization of information in hand. Using this information, we want to arrive at rational conclusions or answers rather than depend on "leap in the dark" suppositions. But why should IPM be a matter of the systematization of question-resolving conjecture with *experience*? The answer lies in the consideration that system-building is not an end in itself; it is a process subject to objectives and the systematization of data in its original form.

The starting point in any police inquiry is set by factual questions — questions about the world or the case to which we want to and need to have the best available answers. Now at this juncture, a "this-or-nothing" argument comes into operation. Only the investigator's access to information about cases is through interaction with past criminal cases. The same applies to those individuals who have studied criminal behavior in a clinical environment — and such interaction is what experience is all about. Here, of course, experience must be broadly construed to encompass the whole gamut of interaction, with nature-generated cues and clues that serve as grist to the mill of inquiry. The investigator, researcher, or clinician must have inputs to provide knowledge of nature, and experience is the only source of inputs that is available. The empiricist insight holds well; we have no alternative but to fall back on experience as the factual information about the world.

To be sure, experience itself cannot do the whole job. For one thing, it only relates to particular cases. Questions about the world usually involve some element of generality, and empiricists have always had to confront the vexing problem of rationalizing the cognitively crucial step from particular experiences. There is simply no alternative to relying on experience for the reference points of the theoretical triangulation through which our knowledge of the world is generated. If information about criminal matters of objective fact is to be obtainable at all, then this must be so on the basis of experience, supplemented by whatever principles and rules of inductive systematization are needed to make its rational exploitation possible. Past observations are our only avenue of contact with what happens in the world. If anything can validate claims to generalized factual knowledge, then experience, while limited and no doubt imperfect, can validate such claims.

As John Henry Newman wrote: "We are in a world of facts, and we use them, for there is nothing else to use." [85] If we do not call on experience to validate our cognitive claims in the factual sphere, then nothing can do so: if anything can, then experience can. In this sense, the inductive approach used within IPM, the view adopted in this research, is thus a matter of not only systematization with experience but the systematization of experience as well.

On the whole, extant classifications reviewed in this chapter are inherently flawed due to weak operational definitions and inferred deductive assumptions made about offender actions and characteristics. This leads to the profiling of serial murderers in its present form being empirically unsound and misleading for police investigations. For example, as mentioned earlier, Prentky and Ressler suggests that fantasy is the motive for serial murder; however, they provide no supporting literature to support their theory. Their claims appear to be deductive conclusions, based on offenders' self-reports, which are highly susceptible to misleading and false information.

The serial murder models reviewed in this chapter, outside of Hickey's study, seem rather vexing. For example, no explanations are given regarding exactly how the offender's criminal personality is formed. On the one hand, some researchers will argue that the offender is affected by some manifestation of mental illness, while on the other hand, others will conclude fantasy is the motive for murder. The problem is that neither mental illnesses nor fantasies are motives; therefore, it is not possible to specify what exactly is responsible for the serial murderer's actions. For example, an offender who is mentally ill may have different reasons for murder than those offenders who appear normal, yet may be driven by fantasies.

The IPM approach is genuinely ampliative rather than merely inferential; it does not lie in unravelling the inner ramifications of the preexisting state of informational affairs, but in bringing about new information at our disposal. Accordingly, inductive profiling in this vein is the operative method of a goal-oriented method to classifying serial murders; it is at bottom a matter of *praxis*, a process of ultimately practical rather than strictly theoretical character. This fact is critically important from the standpoint of justification or validation research. Experience plays a substantial role in filling in the gaps. Thus, while recognizing that humans sometimes see illusory associations between variables when actually there is none, it is likewise important to recognize that associations between variables may go unnoticed due to lack of experience. Such an approach requires an appropriate methodology; perhaps the most appropriate is Facet Theory.

2.9 A Move Towards a Facet Classification of Serial Murderers

An alternative to classifying serial murderers into rigid types, such as organized and disorganized, is the inductive thematic Facet Model that sees the criminal's behavior as being shaped by daily life experiences and interpersonal relationships with others. In other words, the way the individual treats others when he is not offending may affect the way he carries out his crimes.

Facet Theory offers a new approach to classifying serial murderers that may be sufficiently and empirically robust and practical for police investigations.[86] There are two immediate advantages. To begin with, serial murder investigations are faced with a great deal of information of investigative value that may be derived from simple overt aspects of an offense. Facet Theory can be helpful in that often serial murders involve subtle behavioral information which has value, but the detailed analysis of the overt actions of the murder usually overshadowed these actions. One example of how the inductive faceted profiling process could assist police in a serial murder investigation is a study carried out on the spatial behavior of 54 U.S. serial murderers. The study found that the locations at which victims were abducted were centrally located close to the offenders' home bases rather than at any number of the body dump locations.[87] Next, Facet Theory can use offense and offender variables that have been inductively related and empirically replicated for linking crimes to a common offender.

A Thematic Facet Model of Serial Murder

3

The use of Facet Theory enables explanatory models to be derived from data not readily amenable to conventional statistical analyses. Briefly, a facet is defined as "a set of playing the role of a component set of a Cartesian set." [88] A less formal definition was offered by Brown, saying that a facet is a "conceptual categorization underlying a group of observations.[89]

3.1 The Facet Approach

Facet Theory (FT) offers a different solution to the problem of classifying the actions of serial murderers. According to Canter, the facet approach combines the following:[90]

1. Complementary interplay between hypothesis generation and hypothesis testing. The generation of hypotheses is facilitated by representation of complex relationships in geometric forms. The testing of hypotheses and their replicability draws upon a formal framework, with minimal assumptions.
2. A formal system for representing sets of interrelated, multivariate hypotheses that is combined with empirical procedures for examining their validity.
3. A set of nonmetric multivariate statistical procedures for revealing the structures inherent in complex data, together with principles for the interpretation of the products of those analyses.

3.1.1   Facet Structures

There are three basic facet structures: 1) background facets; 2) domain facets; and 3) range facets (i.e., content facets).[92] Background facets describe what may be considered the context of the research or its sample population parameters. Domain facets describe what may be considered as the "body" of the area of interest. Background and domain facets represent different foci for the research study. Generally, the domain facets are concerned with the internal structure of a domain (i.e., what it consists of), while background facets are considered to discover individual differences in relation to that domain. Range facets are described as the possible responses to the stimuli provided by the domain facets. In other words, it is the response of the sample population described by the background facets to the domain as described by the domain facets. For example, the range facet may consist of simple responses, such as "yes" or "no," or the range may be ordinal. When the range facet of each item is ordered, indicating that it has the same underlying meaning, it is considered a common range.[92] The general mapping sentence for the study in this book is shown in Chapter 6.

3.1.2   Constituents of Facets

All facets consist of a number of elements. These are defined as the different values or points that logically and completely describe all the variations of the facet. An element is a discrete component of a facet.[95] For example, the variables White, Spanish, or African-American would be elements of the facet race.

In a robust model of serial murder, facets and facet elements should ideally be mutually exclusive in relation to the other facets and their elements. Variables not being mutually exclusive is a continual criticism of the FBI organized and disorganized serial murder model. For example, the classification of a crime scene behavior should belong to one facet and should be independent of it belonging to another facet. However, to determine whether facets and facet elements are mutually exclusive or not will be tested in the analysis section of this book.

3.2   Narrative Themes

In contrast to the FBI's motivational model of serial murder, it is proposed that such behavior develops out of the context of relations with others through interpersonal relations. Thus, as Sullivan points out, that personality is made manifest in interpersonal situations, and not otherwise.[93] Likewise, Klein posited that aggression is an informed personal, purposive hatred, bound up with specific relations with specific others.[94]

A recent approach used to explain the inference process that links action and interpersonal behavior is that of Narrative Theory.[95] McAdams views personality as multilayered, with a three-level approach for understanding the whole person. This understanding includes dispositional traits, motives, and the narrative identities. The first level of understanding the person is through individual traits. These are broad, decontextualized, and relatively nonconditional constructs, which provide a signature for personality description. These are the implicitly comparative dimensions of personality that go by such labels as extroversion, dominance, and neuroticism. The second level of understanding consists of strategies. These personality descriptions invoke personal strivings; for example, life tasks, coping strategies, or domain-specific skills and values. Also at this level, other descriptions can be included, such as motivational development or strategic constructs that are contextualized in time, place, or role. McAdams defines these as the general description of personal concerns.[95] They speak to what people want, often during particular periods in their lives or within particular domains of action. This level also includes methods which people use in order to get what they want or avoid getting what they do not want over time. The third level, McAdams argues, involves an exploration of the identity of the individual's narrative or life story; without this, psychology can never understand how and to what extent the person living in modern society is able to find unity, purpose, and meaning in life. While McAdams' work has mainly focused on the life stories of noncriminals, Canter applied narrative theory to the study of criminals.[96]

3.2.1   Criminal Narratives

Central to Canter's narrative approach is that people live their lives as a form of a "story," with themselves as the central characters. These stories, or identity narratives, can be analyzed to discern the *themes* and *roles* that guide an individual's behavior. The specific themes and patterns in a person's past behavior can provide important insight into the person's "self-story." Once reconstructed, this self-story can be used both to predict future behavior as well as other characteristics. For example, in a study by Bartol and Bartol, they point out that these life stories are intimately connected to behavior such as crime that is outside of socially approved boundaries.[97] Canter states that "narratives are expressed in the actions and traces left in the aftermath of crimes, they are like shadow puppets telling us a life story in a stilted, alien language." [96] It is suggested that by drawing attention to the subjective aspects of how serial murderers view their victims, a theoretical framework for classifying the behavior of serial murderers can be proposed. For example, in a study by Meloy of serial murderers' projective test results, he found evidence of needs for self-mirroring and symbiotic relations due to traumatic relations with significant others.[98] Meloy found that the inherent conflict between the wish to join but also to be perfectly reflected by the same significant other leads to the offender's mixture of pseudo-autonomy and indifference toward others, punctuated by violent forays into society. Another study found that in homicides involving the victim and offender in semi-relationships, the amount of aggression in the murder was "dependent upon the psychological state of the offender and the meaning the victim had for him." [99]

The thematic classification considers underlying patterns or thematic trends that are characteristic of both offense behavior and other aspects of the offender's lifestyle, whereas such characteristics are unspecified in many typological models, including the FBI's model of serial murder. In a thematic classification framework, the links are made explicit and are grounded within theoretical concepts. Also, in the thematic approach it is expected that offenders will have some overlapping sets of repertoires; however, they will also have behavior most common to them. Briefly, a thematic variable is a general description or title assigned to cover many possible variations of observed behavior or phenomena. Thus, Holsti points out that a *theme* is a single assertion about some subject, the most useful unit of content analysis: for example, using a knife to control the victim.[100] One methodological approach that seems appropriate to inductively reveal and classify the destructive actions of serial murderers is Facet Theory.[101]

Facet Theory requires the researcher to match a conceptual framework to a body of empirical data as demonstrated in the Facet Model of serial murder in Figure 3.1. One advantage of Facet Theory is that it allows a strong test of the model's utility, which has more value in decision making compared to models where the procedures rely entirely on assumptions. In other words, once facets have been derived with some consistency, it is possible to produce replicates of the facets using different data samples. As Canter points out, it is this interplay between substantive theory and empirical results that makes the facet approach so attractive for classifications and decision-orientated research.[90] Figure 3.1 shows a hypothesized facet classification model of serial murder; that is, a conceptual framework that can be matched to the behavior of serial murderers.

3.3   Rationale for the Facet Model of Serial Murder

3.3.1   The Behavioral Organizational Facet

To develop a Facet Model of serial murder requires defining each thematic element, and how each contributes to the Facet Model. The model in Figure 3.1, the behavioral organizational facet, defines the type and level of the offender's aggression during the crime. Briefly, it is imperative to point out that the term organized and disorganized as used in the Facet

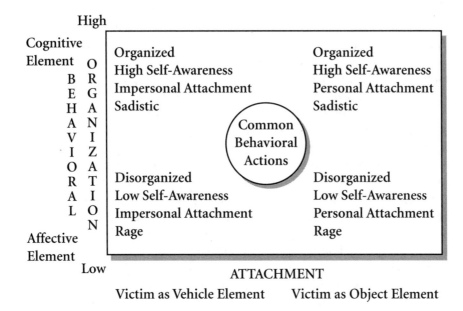

Figure 3.1 Thematic Facet Behavioral Classification Model of Serial Murder

Model does not have the same meaning as defined by the FBI. Rather, the two words were chosen simply because they best describe controlled aggression versus uncontrolled aggression. The two terms as used here do not imply certain personality characteristics. The behavioral facet is one dimension that is divided into two elements: affective and cognitive. These two components were termed some years earlier by Rosenberg.[102] He defined "affect" as feelings and emotions and "cognition" as beliefs. The affective and cognitive components were further elaborated by Levy, where he defines cognitive component as the thoughts about the attitude object, implying a rationality in the attitude, and the affective component as concerning feelings or emotions towards the attitude object.[103]

3.3.2 Affective Element

Affective behaviors are hostile aggressive actions that allegedly result from the offender's emotional state.[37,104] The goal-oriented behavior is simply to injure someone. Behavior is motivated by a desire for a noxious outcome in an expressive way; it is an expression of rage. The affective action is a search for direct gratification. One example of affective behavior might be where the serial murderer shows no preplanning in his crimes; the victims are blitz attacked; and he leaves forensic clues at the crime scene, which demonstrates low self-awareness.

It is argued that affective behavior can involve various processes by which the offender invests the victim with affective significance. For example, the victim may superficially represent someone from the past who the offender might want to injure. According to Levy and Guttman, affective actions involve an interpersonal focus that represent the elicitation of a response aimed towards the self; that is, behavior is directed towards self-gratification.[105]

It is worth noting that in a study by Moyer, he divided aggression into seven types: predatory, inter-male, fear-induced, irritable, territorial, maternal, and instrumental.[106] In a later study however, Meloy collapsed Moyer's seven types of aggression in two categories, describing difference emphases of aggression in serial murderers: they were affective and predatory aggression.[98] Affective aggression is seen as the result of external or internal threatening stimuli that evoke an intense and patterned activation of the autonomic nervous system, accompanied by threatening vocalization and attacking or defending postures.[98] Predatory aggression, on the other hand, is a concept that was borrowed from animal behavior; it may involve activities such as stalking for food or protecting one's territory. In humans, though, Meloy contends that predatory aggression is the hallmark of psychopathic behavior.[107] He argues that predatory aggression requires intent, planning, and emotional detachment. For example, Meloy points out that any one predatory act in a pattern of violent behavior significantly increases the likelihood that psychopathic character disturbance exists in the individual.[98] Meloy thus defines crimes that involve random and impulsive violent acts, where there is no apparent pattern to the killer's victim selection, as affective aggression.

As we have noted, a similar distinction is made by the FBI's organized and disorganized classification of serial murderer types.[17] Meloy hypothesizes several causes for affective aggression. First, the individual's internalized object representations of others may be so diffused and primitive on both a conceptual and perceptual level that others are defined only by their physical presence. The individual's reality testing is thus distorted. Liebert argues that this view of the victim is similar to that manifested in revenge aggression as where the explanation for the drive to injure is an effort to discharge aggression towards another person who represents, for example, a parent or abandoning girlfriend.[13] Also, Revitch and Schlesinger expressed a similar opinion, and noted that often the serial murderer's crimes have a sexual component, and, in many cases, suggests displaced matricide.[47] Meloy contends that the cause of the rage and revenge in such cases is attributed to being abandoned by others.[60] As a result, the violence that occurs may have no pattern.

On the basis of these considerations, one would expect the affective element category to include crime scenes that suggest the main focus is the actual murder of the victim, rather than for some other instrumental reason. The crime scene would suggest a killer who vents his anger and rage on the victim by a frenzied attack; also, one might expect the victim to show signs of overkill. Affective violence is not to destroy the victim, but to restore a tenuous sense of integrity and stability to the individual's crumbling self-experience; an opportunity to solidify a more cohesive sense of self. Meloy also contends that affective violence is an immediate response to a perceived threat and results in a lowering of the sense of agency.[60] Research by Terr suggests that this sense of lowering of agency appears to be the main reason for disorganized behavior.[68]

Affective serial murderers commit a sudden killing, which is impulsive and rarely well thought-out; their actions have no obvious purpose or hope for personal advantage.[108] For example, Ruotolo clinically examined five affective type of murderers.[109] He found that two psychologically significant events had taken place. First, a blow was dealt to the individual's pride system, triggering off enormously intense self-hate. This anger was projected onto the victim, which allowed for a temporary shoring up of the unstable pride. Second, he found that there was prolonged tension and disorganization in the murderer long before actual contact with the victim. This finding suggests that it may be likely that serial murderers who fit the affective category could have unstable background histories. For example, they may have a criminal history and are not likely to be educated. David Carpenter, a contemporary American serial murderer, could be considered to provide a classic example of the affective serial murderer. Carpenter was convicted of killing seven individuals. He surprised and attacked his victims as they walked along trails in national parks in the U.S. His method of death was to immediately shoot his victims. Hence, there was no pattern to his victim targeting.

Therefore, the three main characteristics hypothesized to define the affective element are disorganization, low self-awareness, and rage.

3.3.2.1 *Consistency in the Affective Element*

Arguably, the regulation of aggressive drive in affective violence should remain consistent. One reason for this is that once a particular and characteristic form of behavior is achieved from early experiences by the offender, the maintenance of the behavior (slowly evolving) itself may become an independent force in the functioning of the offender, both during the crime and when being non-offensive. For example, forms of reactive aggressive behavior may develop in response to physical restraint in early relations and other interferences with directed activity, such as repeatedly taking toys away, or preventing goal-oriented activity.[68]

3.4   The Cognitive Element

It is hypothesized that cognitive violence appears to be aggressive behavior that is directed toward attaining non-injurious goals.[110] In this regard, behavior is seen as instrumental rather than expressive. Instrumental behavior, as focusing towards some goal, has received attention from a number of researchers, for example, Berkowitz and Buss.[37,111] These traditional theories of instrumental aggression argue that the goal of aggression is to harm, and the action is performed automatically; that is, with little cognitive meditation.[37] However, this description of instrumental aggression is overly simplistic. It could be argued that all harm-doing behavior is cognitively mediated, but may have different emphases and meaning for different offenders. For example, serial murderers who kill to achieve a goal may likely have a sense of agency.[112] This sense of awareness results in more evidence of organization and control at the crime scene. It may also suggest that these types of offenders could have more stability in their backgrounds; for example, one hypothesis may be that they will likely be married and educated.

As previously mentioned, in some respects Meloy's predatory classification resembles the FBI's organized serial murderer type, where crimes are planned and the offender is in control of his behavior at the crime scene. However, differences between the two become apparent on further examination. For example, the predatory serial murderer is presumed to be in control of his crime scene behavior, leaving very little forensic evidence behind, while also committing sadistic sexual acts.[60,98] In contrast, though, the FBI profilers argue that serial murderers who mutilate and perform cannibalistic acts are most likely to display sloppiness at their crime scenes by leaving an abundance of forensic clues behind.[17] Arguably, however, Meloy's analysis could be considered more viable, as sadistic acts could be construed as more thought-out and cognized rather than as opportunistic expressions of rage. A further distinction can be made between the FBI's and Meloy's classification models in that Meloy's approach was to study serial murder from a victim-targeting perspective rather than focusing solely on the offender's personality and motivation as in research by Liebert.[13]

In Meloy's study of serial murderers, he found that the level of aggression of the predatory killer's behavior is at such intensity before the abduction that there appears to be an objectless state at the time of violence.[98,107] The victim is perceived as fitting in with the internalized object percept, a visual image in the offender's mind that is both a desperately pursued and hatefully unwanted fantasied person. For example, Meloy argues that the victim for the predatory serial murderer may be, at first, ragefully devalued or initially idealized, despite the offender's lack of any actual emotional attachment to him or her.

Cognitive behavior is methodical, and the offender is likely to be able to maintain control during his crimes. For example, in a study by Williams, he compared the criminal histories of 45 psychopaths with 46 nonpsychopaths, and found that psychopathic criminals committed more violent and sadistic crimes than the nonpsychopaths.[113] For example, the psychopaths' actions were significantly more instrumentally motivated, whereas the non-psychopaths' acts were significantly more often expressive, due to strong emotional arousal. A later study found that 93% of sexually sadistic murderers carefully planned their crimes.[114] Meloy suggests that the reason that the predatory killer is able to maintain control is his ability to adequately test reality while maintaining the capacity to distinguish between his internalized object world, regardless how bizarre it is, and his actual relations with people. Due to his ability to remain focused, the predatory serial murderer has no confusion about the boundaries of the self, which often occurs in crimes with affective aspects. For example, Theodore (Ted) Bundy, a contemporary American serial murderer, provides a possible classic example of a predatory serial murderer. Bundy was convicted of 13 murders of young college girls. Bundy carefully targeted his victims; often, he used cons and ploys to lure the victims to their deaths. The instrumental drive behind Bundy's murders was to have postmortem sex with his victims.[115]

It should be emphasized that according to this analysis, both the affective and cognitive types of serial murderers can imbue their victims with symbolic significance. However, the distinction is that the affective serial murderer selects targets randomly and imbues them with symbolic significance, whereas the cognitive serial murderer specifically targets victims who show a fit with their symbolic person. Other researchers have argued that serial murderers often target specific victims.[2,116]

Consequently, the culminating phase of a sequence of preparatory activities — in other words, a plan of action — sets serial murderers found in the cognitive element apart from those in the affective element. The cognitive murderer might also leave crime scenes that suggest the main focus of the attack was less to do with the actual murder and more to do with the need to possess the victim's body. For example, cognitive serial murderers may relive their crimes by revisiting their victims' grave sites.

In summary, therefore, one might expect the following characteristics to define the cognitive element: organization, high self-awareness, and elements of sadistic behavior.

3.4.1 Consistency in the Cognitive Element

It could be hypothesized that the offender's aggressive drive, in relation to the cognitive element, requires *ongoingness*: it has a lasting quality.

Constancy in the cognitive theme is seen as proactive behavior as opposed to reactive. The constructive aggressive behavior develops from mastery and exploration.[117,118] This link to aggression, as some researchers argue, originates from our animal forebears, as in food-getting, mate-getting and cub-protection instincts, as well as territorial protection. In humans, though, it has been linked to high mastery of traumatic experiences.[120] These experiences of aggressivity are allegedly tied to pleasure, though embedded in early traumatic relations, and assumed to ensure a lasting place within the individual's behavior. For this reason, behavior in the cognitive element will remain stable over time.

3.5   The Attachment Facet

Attachment Theory describes a behavioral system which is regarded as an integral part of human nature. Attachment has been variously operational-ized in terms of coherent patterns of behavior which indicate the quality of the attachment bond within a relationship.[120] In Bowlby's opinion, the goal of the attachment system is to maintain proximity to the primary caretaker (not necessarily the mother) to ensure protection from dangers such as predators. Due to this danger, the individual is therefore especially prone to activation under conditions of anxiety, fear, and fatigue.

Present attachments in people are supposedly based on past attachment relationships. Thus in Bowlby's conceptualization of attachment, he views it as functioning continuously to provide the person with a secure base from which to engage in exploration.[121] Thus, the goal of the attachment system is the maintenance of *felt security.* For example, a study that required children to construct working models or internal representations of themselves and others found that the internal representations of how they viewed others provided the foundation for later personal relationships.[122] Bowlby also points out that attachment underlies the capacity to make affectional bonds, and may relate to a whole range of adult dysfunctions including marital problems and personality disorders.[121] He states that the stability of interac-tion patterns in specific attachment relationships mediates continuities in attachments with others. A similar picture emerges from child trauma studies carried out by Suttie.[123] Klein also argues that an individual's experience of his behavior is not influenced only by *reality* of traumatic relationships, but also by the imagined meaning the person assigns to them.[124] This is similar to the narrative concept where a person's life story could be reflected in his criminal behavior.

A study by Swann discusses a *self-verification* process through which people induce others to verify their self-images.[125] This process has been demonstrated in the maintenance of both positive and negative relationships, thus people tend to adopt interaction strategies that elicit self-confirmatory feedback from others. It might be expected then that individual differences in interpersonal styles of serial murderers in the affective and cognitive elements would be highlighted in their interactions with their victims.

Using a psychodynamic construct for the theoretical and clinical understanding of aggression, Meloy classified the aggressive actions of serial murderers based on object relations of victim-targeting. He defines object relations as the internalized representations of self and other, and their respective affective complexes as the cornerstone of object relations theory. This view of the self is similar to Sullivan's *personification* theory, which refers to a complex, organized cognitive template or pattern — a mental image — of a particular person, not necessarily a real one.[127] Here, the individual's mental image is constructed out of experiences, deriving from interaction with other persons.

Attachment in adulthood suggests proximity to other objects that carry a certain emotional valence for the individual. For instance, Meloy suggests that in social situations attachment can be observed in normal or pathological patterns of proximity-seeking toward the object, for example a victim.[60] Meloy further argues that in a psychological context, it is the mental representation of an object or individual that is imbued with certain affects and maintains an enduring and relational, but not necessarily reality-based, quality in the mind of the perpetrator. These actual representations, and their respective affects, are argued by some to be the products of early learning.[127]

Meloy further argues that by carefully studying the patterns or instances of victim selection, one can make reasonable inferences about the nature of the serial murderer's reasoning for targeting specific victims when purged by his most primitive and aggressive impulses. Meloy points out, for example, that the serial murderer's interaction with his victims can be used to explore how an individual has the capacity to utterly dehumanize another human, to project his internal representation onto a victim. This author concurs, and adopts the view that the killer's distorted relationships with others will be revealed in his crime scene behavior. Thus, Meloy suggests that the study of the pattern of victim selection will help improve law enforcement's response to serial murder, and also allow researchers to predict the size of future potential victim pools, and thus contribute to an assessment of the offender's dangerousness.

To that end, the attachment facet forms the second dimension of the Facet Model of Serial Murder, as shown in Figure 3.1. Characteristics for the first dimension run horizontally, while those for the second dimension run vertically. The attachment facet has two elements: victim as vehicle, and victim as object.

3.5.1   Victim as Vehicle Element

Research by Canter describes a style of offender-victim interaction where the victim is treated as a *vehicle*.[96] In his offender-victim interaction scheme it is suggested that, in terms of attachment, the offender has a mid-intimacy style of interaction with his victim. In other words, the individual attaches a certain degree of significance to the victim. In Canter's view, in normal life this type of offender possesses adequate social skills and the narrative account will reflect many episodes which may have acted as catalysts to offenses. Of importance to the offender of this type is the kind of person the victim is and what the victim represents in the offender's personal life.[96] According to Canter, the central theme to the stories of these offenders reflects how the offense may be borne out of anger with themselves and the fates that have led them to their desolate situations. Their narratives will often reveal an exploitative use of women, showing a lack of basic compassion. Canter's victim as vehicle classification appears similar to Meloy's predatory classification of serial murderers, where the crimes are planned and have a degree of organization involved in them.

However, the definition of victim as *vehicle* is different somewhat in this book than originally presented by Canter.[96] Rather, in the victim as vehicle context, the level of attachment the offender has with his victim is low and impersonal. For example, Shapiro suggests that voyeurism is a form of long-distance attachment that is impersonal, because the offender's proximity to his victim is at a distance.[128] Shapiro also argues that this form of behavior parallels fetishistic sadism.

It is hypothesized that serial murderers who view their victims as vehicles kill repeatedly to reenact impersonal, *fearful* attachment conflicts.[129] Fearful attachment occurs in individuals who exhibit an impersonal style. This type of person is seen as introverted, aloof, and socially avoidant.[122] The fearful attachment person is caught in an approach-avoidance conflict; he or she lacks social intimacy, and the prospect of vulnerability in intimate relations is anxiety provoking. The fearful attachment type of individual is prone to anxiety due to feeling rejected.[130] Variables that reflect fearful attachment will likely score low on intimacy with the victim and low on mastery of the situation, because crimes are more likely to have an emotional aspect to them. For example, a study by Miller found that killers who treat their victims in an impersonal way see themselves as powerful people with strong feelings of self-confidence during the murder, but who otherwise lead lives of unbearable shame.[131]

3.5.2   Victim as Object Element

Canter also describes a style of offender-victim interaction where the victim is treated as an *object*.[96] He suggests that the offender-victim relationship will have low intimacy, and the victim is seen as nothing more than a *thing* to be abused for pleasure. In his description of victim as object, Canter suggests that these types of offenders make contact with their victims in an opportunistic way rather than stalking or specifically targeting them. Personal relationships are difficult for this type of offender. Canter points out that in terms of interpersonal relations, the offender keeps himself separate, although he is not aware of his loneliness because he is so self-absorbed.[96] Canter's classification of vehicle as object is similar to Meloy's affective serial murderers, where the crimes are emotional and there appears to be no apparent pattern.

In contrast to Canter's definition of victim as object, in the present book it is hypothesized that the serial murderer who treats his victims as an object will have high personal attachment to his victims in the form of an object. The victim as object element involves various processes by which the offender expresses *dismissing* attachment.[122,129] Dismissing attachment is applied to individuals who are self-assured; they exhibit controlling and calculating behavior.[122] Offenders with dismissing attachment behavior appear to be able to isolate their affective reactions from their cognitive representations of early events and develop a view of themselves as impervious to future rejection. Dismissing attachment individuals have mastered the style of maintaining superficial relationships with others, which is why they are able to lure victims into their web using cons and ploys. The dismissing person holds a view of himself and others that downplays the importance of everyday attachment relationships. This form of depersonalization is carried over into murder. Research by Birtchnell points out that depersonalization in this regard is a way of denying the emotionality of the other person by treating her as though she were an object.[132] This type of behavior is what Laing refers to as reification, the ability only to look at a person as an object of interest.[133] For example, Gacono and Meloy argue that it is possible that most criminals are detached from their victims, and appear to have little capacity to form affectional bonds with others.[134] Also, Meloy points out that through sadistic identification, a cold and detached attitude can be maintained that transforms the seeking of relations based upon affectional need into relations based upon power gradients of dominance and submission.[60]

So, although in terms of his everyday behavior the offender who sees his victims as objects is dismissive of attachments with others, he actually displays a high degree of personal attachment in the way he deals with his victims. For example, he is likely to spend more time with the body. In other words, this type of murderer may select victims who fit a fantasized object, to satisfy his instrumental goal, for example, sexual gratification. Meloy argues that this fantasizing most likely occurs due to the need to control others, denigrate others, and render them available as prey.[60] For example, Guttmacher describes the sadistic serial murderer as one who derives sexual gratification from killing and who often establishes a pattern, such as the manner in which they kill or the type of victims they select, such as prostitutes, children, and the elderly.[44] However, Lester describes a type of serial murderer who selects victims who fit a fantasized object, but otherwise commit crimes of rage.[52]

3.6   Common Behavioral Actions

In addition to the Facets identified in Figure 3.1, it might be expected that serial murderers would display a number of crime scene actions in common. However, it is not possible to specify the actions at this stage in the book. For example, if the FBI claims are correct about the dominant focus of serial murder, then all crimes should display evidence of a sexual sadistic focus.

3.7   Summary

3.7.1   The Facet Model of Serial Murder

To summarize, the hypothetical serial murder model in Figure 3.1 is two-dimensional. The first dimension is the behavioral organizational facet, while the second dimension is the attachment facet. The behavioral facet consists of two elements: affective and cognitive. The affective element is located in the lower half region in Figure 3.1. The affective element region is defined by disorganized crime scene actions, low self-awareness, and expressions of rage. So, for example, in this sector one might expect to find evidence of forensic clues at the affective-type crime scene, which indicates low self-awareness. Likewise, one might expect to find the victim to be bludgeoned to death, with the weapon at the crime scene.

The next element is cognitive. The cognitive element is located in the upper half region in Figure 3.1. The cognitive element is defined by organized crime scene actions, and high self-awareness. In the cognitive element, one might expect to find little or no forensic clues at the crime scene, which indicates high self-awareness. Additionally, one might expect to find evidence of sadism; for example, intrusive acts such as the insertion of objects and exploration of the victim's body cavities.

The second dimension in Figure 3.1 is attachment facet. The attachment facet has two elements: victim as vehicle and victim as object, as shown in Figure 3.1. Characteristics that define the two elements run vertically. For example, looking at the bottom of the diagram in Figure 3.1, we see above the victim as vehicle element, impersonal attachment, which is listed in both the affective and cognitive categories. This suggests that different types of serial murderers who show impersonal attachment could display either affective or cognitive behavioral organization at the crime scene. For example, one might expect to find little or no evidence of contact with the victim's body in murders where the crime is impersonal and the victim is used as a vehicle. Various methods of killing the victim may also occur, such as a gun or poison, indicating minimal contact with the victim.

Similarly, serial murderers who show personal attachment could display either affective or cognitive behavioral organization at the crime scene. One might also expect to find evidence of antemortem and postmortem mutilation, postmortem sexual activities, and posing of the body, indicating that the killer tends to spend a considerable amount of time exploring the victim's body.

Research Objectives

4

The discussion in the previous chapters alluded to the weaknesses of current serial murder classifications and theories in the literature. For example, classification models of serial murderers have typically relied on speculation, as the focus of serial murder, that the offender is driven to murder due to his violent fantasies; suffers from some form of pathology; or kills due to narcissistic drives[13,17,51,59] Another focus on serial murderers that is propounded in the literature is that offenders kill to act out sexual perversions.[17,63] These types of crimes are defined as *lust* murders.[20] Given that the model of serial murder proposed in this book incorporates a number of forms of serial murder, the hypothesis that sexual gratification is the focus for serial murder is likely only to reflect a subsample of killers. While there are certainly sexual overtones to many serial murders, lust murderers may not be representative of serial murderers at large.

The Facet Classification Model of serial murder proposed in the book does not carry direct implications for the internal dynamics of serial murderers. Rather, the model proposes that more objective accounts of what really happens in the course of a serial murder will relate in part to the link between the offender and the victim. The objective is important from a practical point of view, because it allows the study of the material that is available in police records, which is within the realms of what is referred to as Investigative Psychology.[73] Investigative Psychology attempts to derive inferences about the characteristics of an offender from the actual details of the way in which his or her crime was committed.

The basis for developing a classification system of serial murder is the hypothesis that variables derived from a crime scene will not have random interrelationships, but rather will reveal a grouping of offenses that have consistently related actions. Classifying serial murderers requires the specification of the behavior and characteristics of those who might commit such

acts. This raises important research questions. Which behaviors and characteristics can be specified with any consistency, and of those, which are the
most useful to specify?

There are a number of ways in which such association between the crime
scene behavior can be established, but whatever methods are used, they will
be more powerful in their application if they are part of a logical explanatory
framework. The framework adopted in this book may be characterized as a
psychosocial behavioral approach, in which the offenders' interactions with
their victims may tell us something about how they carry out their crimes
and, subsequently, their background history. For example, knowing which
crime scene actions show associations between offenses and offenders can be
used to help classify behavior into common themes.

Implicit in the objective is the need to identify behavioral traces at a
crime scene which can be used as variables for this research. Such traces
of behavior may be seen as discrete acts, which constitute one part, one
element, or ingredient within a series of actions which combine to form
an underlying structure to a crime scene. It is proposed that such structures
will be identified in the offender's first, middle, and last murder series. It
is further proposed that if similar structures are found, which are common
to different crime scenes committed by different serial murderers, then
these will indicate common themes by which a crime scene can be typed
or classified. Clearly, a major objective of this research will be to identify
such behavioral themes.

The following objectives are further proposed: that the analysis of the
data will reveal the two facets identified earlier, behavioral organization and
attachment. The behavioral facet will have two facet elements: affective and
cognitive. As previously mentioned, affective behavior is hypothesized to be
manifested in the form of erratic, emotional rage resulting in the offender's
crime scenes being disorganized, while cognitive behavior is hypothesized to
be manifested in the form of organized, sadistic behavior. The second facet,
attachment, also has two elements: victim as vehicle and victim as object (see
Figure 3.1 in Chapter 3). Victim as vehicle is most likely to be impersonal,
suggesting that the offender's interactions with his victim is minimal, while
victim as object is most likely to be personal, suggesting that the offender
imbues his victims with acts that require the offender to spend long periods
of time interacting with the victim's body.

4.1   General Hypotheses

The general hypotheses central to the research in the book therefore are

1. there will be groups of serial murderers who will consistently display signature behaviors that are more typical than any other group, which will relate to background history, and;

2. that serial murderers will have certain crime scene behaviors that they share in common.

Implicit in the objectives listed above will be that by examining crime scene data on solved serial murders, an empirical classification model can be developed, which will lead to an investigative classification system by which unsolved serial murders may be analyzed, in order to predict the type of individual who would commit such crimes.

4.2 Research Conditions

Relating offender characteristics to offense is a multivariate problem that has generally been ignored in the literature on serial murder. It is appropriate to construe the relationships between offender characteristics and offense as the canonical relationship between two matrixes: the P matrix of offender characteristics and the Q matrix of offense behavior. The P matrix is derived from the vectors generated by the attributes that describe each offender (e.g., age and criminal history) and Q from the attributes that describe each offense (e.g., type of weapon used and type of sexual assault).

There are several inherent problems that could be encountered in trying to meet the research objectives. In a situation in which an offender carries out one offense, the P matrix is the same rank as the Q matrix and a direct mapping of one into the other may be empirically feasible. However, in a situation in which an offender carries out a series of murders, there is a one-to-many correspondence between the vectors of P and Q that could lead to behavioral inconsistency within an offense series and invalidate any extrapolation from offense to offender. To solve this problem, the potential indeterminacy in resolving $P > Q$, an iterative procedure, will be necessary whereby the empirical structure of the P and Q matrixes are established independently.

A further problem in the P and Q matrixes may occur when comparing certain offenders who carry out a large number of offenses and other offenders who commit relatively few offenses. To control for this problem, only the first, middle, and last murders in the series for each offender were used. Dividing the overall data sample into three subsamples allows for the exploration of consistency in offenders' crime scene behavior over time.

Because the crime is serial murder, not rape, there are no living victims for police to interview. In this study, information on the offenders' crime scene behavior, plus victim and offender background characteristics was gathered solely by examining police files, court transcripts, and medical examiners' reports.

4.3 Identifying Background Characteristics

The classification of crime scenes by reference to their underlying themes implies that for each different theme identified there will be a different type of offender, whose life experiences will likely be different within various themes. Serial murderers found within each theme will likely possess the same or parallel characteristics to those offenders committing similar offenses. This leads to another objective of the research: to identify which particular characteristics of serial murderers from each theme are important, including their likely criminal or sexual history; employment; education levels; and marital status, any and all of which are integral parts of the individual's life experiences. In this book, characteristics refer to an individual's criminal, sexual, and personal history.

To achieve the objectives set out above, attention was focused on the typical crime scene information recorded by the police during serial murder investigations. These data usually have no clear existing structures and may be rather high in noise. The noise inherent in real-world data stems from slight inconsistencies in the manner in which the data were eventually collected. For example, many different police forces, have no agreed convention for data collection, although with recent developments in computerized databases, the process of collecting and maintaining crime information has improved somewhat. Finally, although most of the information collected by the police is of a descriptive nature and not recorded in a quantifiable form, this type of data still does have some advantages. First, since it is collected by the police without any psychological hypotheses in mind, there could be less bias in the data. Secondly, as Webb and Weick point out in their paper on *Unobtrusive Measures*, this type of data has ecological validity; it can be seen in the context of the overall circumstances from where it was derived.[135,136]

Data Acquisition and Content Analysis

5

Details of offenders and offenses are generally found in written form in federal, state, and local police files; court records; and in the last few years, most of the police records are maintained and stored in computerized databases. Because serial murder cases often remain unsolved for months and even years, this makes the process of maintaining accurate information in police files problematic. This dilemma is further compounded by the fact that most data collected by police is not intended for research purposes, and therefore the information is not organized in an orderly fashion. In recent years, though, the management of case data for all crimes has greatly improved due to the increased use and development of computerized police databases.

5.1 Data Acquisition

5.1.1 Homicide Investigative Tracking System (HITS)

The data for this book were collected from various police departments throughout the U.S. However, 75% was collected by the author from making an on-site visit to the Homicide Investigation and Tracking System (HITS) unit located in Seattle, Washington.[137] Twenty percent of the research data were collected from other homicide database reports; for example, VI-CAP and HALT documents that were originally filed within the case files at the HITS unit. The remaining five percent of the data were obtained from court transcripts by accessing LEXUS and WEST LAW, the American online law databases.

To facilitate the data collection, the author was assigned a researcher from the HITS unit who initially guided him through the use of the HITS murder database for extracting the relevant information on solved serial murder cases.

The HITS system developed out of a research project funded by the U.S. National Institute of Justice.[137] Initially, as a part of the project, HITS investigators contacted each of the State of Washington's 273 police and sheriff's departments, as well as each of the 39 county medical examiner/coroner's officers, country prosecuting attorney's officers, and the Department of Vital Statistics. With the cooperation of all law enforcement agencies in the State of Washington, researchers eventually entered over 1309 murder files into the HITS computer system.

Taking into consideration that 75% of the research data were extracted from the HITS homicide computerized database, it was important to explore how their data originally were collected and coded. Any errors in the HITS data would likely be reflected in the current book unless the errors were discovered and corrected.

Originally, the HITS data collection instrument consisted of 54 pages and contained 467 fields. This instrument recorded information related to the quality of the murder investigation and its chances of being solved, in addition to the salient characteristics of the murder, the victim(s), and the offender(s). Initially, the HITS database comprised a sample of murders that totaled 1309 victims.[138] The HITS homicide data and data-collecting instrument were subjected to a series of inter-rater reliability tests lasting over a year, which used the experiences of detectives and academics to determine its reliability.[138] As a result of the inter-rater reliability tests, the data entered into the HITS computer system were made more accurate and reliable.[137] In addition, the revised HITS form allowed other police agencies to be more accurate in recording and reporting information about solved and unsolved homicides from their jurisdictions.

The new HITS variable coding instrument, and subsequently the information entered in the computer, detailed crime classification chronology on victim(s), offender(s), the offender's M.O. *modus operandi*, geographic locations, weapons, vehicles and any other pertinent information regarding solved and unsolved violent crimes, such as rape, arson, kidnaping, murder, missing persons, and serial murder. In addition to the original 1309 victims entered into the database, new information on various types of solved and unsolved crime is coded and entered into the HITS system each day.

The HITS database also stores information contained from 145,000 records maintained by the Department of Corrections in Washington State. One added feature in the HITS system is the ability to create a "time-line" file that records the chronological activities of known violent offenders, which was helpful in recording the sequence of the offenses for this research. Another aspect that sets HITS above other violent crime tracking systems in the U.S. is that the computer is linked to local, state, and federal law enforcement agencies in the States of Washington, Oregon, California,

Idaho, Kansas, and the nation of Canada. This allowed information on additional serial murders to be reviewed by this author for the possibility of inclusion in the research.

5.2 Type of Variables Identified

Generally, two types of variables were identified in the course of coding the data: thematic variables and category variables. The fully defined research content category protocol can been seen in Appendices A and B. As previously mentioned in Chapter 3, thematic variables represent a general description or title of a behavior or phenomenon that may cover many possible variations. For example, was a knife or gun used as a weapon in the murder, or what was the method of approaching the victim? Thematic variables were encountered when reviewing the actual police files and court documents. The documents were scanned using the pre-defined coding instrument in Appendices A and B for the presence or absence of thematic variables. Category variables were the next to be identified. Category variables represent a unique measurement of observation where each category is independent of others. In other words, these are variables not measurable on a linear scale and which have only discrete values; for example, age and race of the offenders and victims.

5.2.1   Content Categories

Prior to constructing the content categories for this study, a review of the relevant literature on serial murder was explored. It was determined that while the basic content categories in the HITS form detailed the possible actions that may occur in any given serial murder, the form lacked specific questions. The form did not include certain questions that focused on certain offender-victim interpersonal actions. For example, the act of *piqueurism*, which is short jabbing of a sharp instrument into the flesh for pleasure, was not included on the HITS form as a crime scene variable. Including this type of behavior in developing a model of serial murder is important, as it points to a signature aspect in the offender's behavior.

5.3   Reliability

The first step in building an empirical model of serial murder requires accurate development of categories with which others could readily work. The crime scene actions for this project were primarily drawn on a *post hoc* basis from the predefined HITS homicide data-collecting instrument. With new categories added to cover a broader range of behavior than the original (HITS) form, a modified data-coding protocol form was then used to collect the details. The category scheme used an interpretive system that allowed for the multivariate exploration of data. All the crime scene actions and background variables were coded dichotomously, except for the variables of age and race of the victims and offenders, on the basis of whether the behavior or characteristic was present "1" or not present "0" in the case file.

It has been demonstrated that with traditional methods of coding, increasing the number of possible responses within the category set decreases reliability.[138] Equally as important is the Holsti and Krippendorf argument that dichotomous decision-making in content analysis had the tendency to raise inter-rater reliability from around 60% to a figure above 90%.[100,140] For example, Krippendorf points out dichotomous decision-making has several advantages over traditional methods:

1. It permits the coder to focus on one simple decision at a time and to review the criteria for choice at each step;
2. Dichotomous decision-making is particularly useful when many categories are necessary.

The data for this study were collected and coded only by the author. During a three-week period, the author scanned the HITS homicide computer system and numerous case files for solved serial murder cases conforming to the definition of serial murder, which is defined in Chapter 6. The computer headed each offense by a HITS number and the reporting agency's case number, which included the investigator's name and contact details. These features were important because it allowed each case to be reviewed with ease at a later date.

Due to the sensitivity of the case materials, the majority of the data for this book could not be removed from the premises from which it was gathered, nor copied from the original case files. Less sensitive materials were either copied from the actual police files or printed directly from the HITS computer system. There were a few incidents where victims survived the attack, and their statements were referred to for collaboration purposes.

Research Design and Methodology

6

The research plan for this book focused on the crime scene actions of U.S. serial murderers and their background characteristics. This required finding out how offenders initially approached their victims and what behavioral actions were subsequently performed during the crimes. Briefly, serial murderer is defined here as any individual who murdered three or more victims, on different dates, and at different geographical locations.

6.1 Coding the Data Matrix

Details on 107 U.S. serial murderers who were responsible for 728 murders were collected and coded from the sources described in Chapter 5, using a modified version of the HITS form. Eleven of the 107 offenders were a part of a team; therefore they were collapsed, reducing the number of actual offenders or cases to 96, which was used in the facet analysis. The data that generated the Q matrix was derived from police records describing eyewitness accounts, including visual sightings and telephone conversations, police field reports, detective reports, and medical examiners' reports. As previously mentioned, independent corroboration with the investigating detective was used when necessary. The materials used to generate the P matrix were derived from detective reports, along with psychological and psychiatric records.

The Q matrix represented the offender population; that is, the offenders were represented as rows in the matrix, while the columns were formed by crime scene actions. Each variable was coded numerically to represent the absence or presence of predefined actions. Figure 6.1 below gives an example of how the Q matrix is formed where each row is an offender, and each column is represented as a number indicating the absence of such behavior, coded as "0," or its presence as "1."

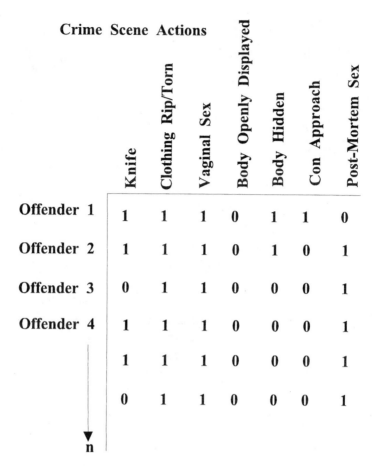

Figure 6.1 Part Data Matrix

In the sample data matrix in Figure 6.1, for example, the actions of Offender 1 can be interpreted as: the initial approach to the victim was through the use of a con; the victim was subjected to her clothing being ripped or torn, followed by vaginal sex, then being killed with a knife; and the offender hid the victim's body. The victim's body was not openly displayed and there was no evidence of postmortem sex.

Each row creates a unique numerical profile of the serial murderer's actions in each death. The Q matrixes for the first, middle, and last murders in the series each extended to 65 columns (i.e., crime scene behavior), by 96 rows or offenders. For each subgroup, the Q matrix exhibited the behaviors in all serial murders committed by a sample of U.S. serial murderers, which formed a rectangular raw matrix of the offenders' crime scene actions. A description of each crime scene behavior and background characteristics can be found in Appendices A and B.

6.2   The Initial Preparatory Stage

There are current validity problems with the analysis of data derived from archival sources, such as police and court records. The problem is the lack of a clear empirical definitional system when specifying the relationships between variables, as demonstrated in the FBI's classification of crime scene actions into the organized and disorganized dichotomy.

For example, to measure the significance between characteristics and crime scene actions, the FBI profilers typically take one offender feature at a time and attempt to relate it to one offense variable, typically using Chi-Square and 't' tests as their statistical procedures.[17] However, this process is likely to be unproductive. Guttman points out that the Chi-Square test, which is the basis of most inferences derived from frequency aggregates, has no particular alternative hypothesis.[141] Also, when trying to compare relationships between crime scene behavior where the variables have not been empirically derived, the variations that occur within a group of actions across a set of related offenders are hidden when comparisons between group averages are made. As Guttman further points out, grand theories about relationships are rather useless from a scientific point of view if they do not include an *a priori* definitional system for observations.[141]

What was necessary, therefore, was a formal system for representing sets of interrelated, multivariate hypotheses. The Facet Approach was considered the most appropriate procedure, because it places an emphasis on deriving interpretable patterns or relationships among variables that might not have high levels of measurement.

6.3   Mapping Sentence

One essential tool for constructing a Facet Model is known as a mapping sentence. A mapping sentence makes one focus on the relationship among relevant variables and the universe of possible observations in a study. Once the background, domain, and range facets have been identified, they are linked together in a mapping sentence.

A mapping sentence is defined as "A verbal statement of the domain and of the range of a mapping, including connectives between facets as in ordinary language." [88] A mapping sentence represents a definitional system and is open to empirical verification, but it does not represent a hypothesis or a theory; however, it does furnish the key concepts in the form of facets and facet elements for formulating hypotheses and theories.

There are many advantages to using a mapping sentence and some of these advantages have been outlined by several researchers, such as Brown,

Levy, and Guttman and Guttman.[89,142,143] A mapping sentence provides the following advantages:

1. A precise definition of the universe of content or observation, and a succinct statement of the research design;
2. An aid to the perception of systematic relationships;
3. A detailed definitional framework for the observation, such that theory construction is validated;
4. An aid to the development of comparable and cumulative research.

The mapping sentence structure is not fixed and can be modified after each level of multivariate analysis on the data.

In this book, the mapping sentence provided a precise and clear definition of the content universe (crime scene actions of serial murderers); and it helped define and set the boundaries of the offender's focus towards the victim in addition to his background criminal history. The general mapping sentence used to guide the collection of data for this book is described in Figure 6.2

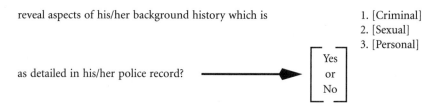

Does offender 'X' by his/her

BEHAVIORAL ORGANIZATIONAL FACET   **ATTACHMENT FACET**

1. [Affective] behavior and whose focus towards his victim is one of   1. [Object]
2. [Cognitive]   2. [Vehicle]

                                                          BACKGROUND FACET

reveal aspects of his/her background history which is   1. [Criminal]
                                                           2. [Sexual]
                                                           3. [Personal]

as detailed in his/her police record?   ⟶   Yes
                                                        or
                                                        No

Figure 6.2 General Mapping Sentence

6.3.1   Structuples in a Mapping Sentence

The basic contents of a mapping sentence is its structuples. A structuple is defined as an element of a Cartesian set; it is a profile composed by selecting an element from each facet.[88] Each structuple represents one possible item or observation in relation to the domain facet. A structuple is constructed by drawing one, and only one, element of each and all domain facets in the mapping sentence.

The general mapping sentence shown above has three facets:

1. The first content domain facet is the **Behavioral Organizational Facet**, which describes the offender's aggressive behavior as it is concerned with the individual and situational differences in relation to the victim;

2. The second content domain facet is **Attachment Facet**, which is the focus (instrumentality) of the offender's attachment towards his victim. The first two content domain facets are conceptualized as being represented in the Q matrixes for each of the sub-populations.

3. The third content domain facet is the **Background Facet**, P matrixes, which describes the offender's background characteristics and what was likely to be recorded as the antecedent histories. The facet of background was conceptualized as having elements of prior criminal offenses. For example, the structuple of violent criminal history included convictions for crimes against the person such as murder, attempted murder, rape and kidnaping, arson, burglary, fraud, and forgery. The structuples for the background facet also included sexual history and personal history, such as employment and educational levels.

6.3.2 Elements of the Facet

The mapping sentence aids in developing the universe of observations and the perception of systematic relationships. For example, there is one population facet **X** which are U.S. serial murderers; three content facets, **Behavioral (B), Attachment (A), and Background (B)**; and one common range facet (**R**) into which the contents of facets are mapped. The mapping sentence shows how the application of Facet Theory assists the researcher in generating all possible combinations of structuples which provide the content universe of a domain. For example, does offender **X** by his cognitive (**Structuple 2**) behavior and whose attachment towards his victim as a vehicle (**Structuple 2**) reveal aspects of a violent (**Structuple 1**) criminal history in their criminal police record (**R1**)? Yes.

The facet approach allows the researcher to visually inspect that all the possible relationships between the variables have been systematically accounted. It can be further used to make sure that all the comparisons between the variables are exactly comparable. This is an important aspect of generating serial murder types from crime scene actions that has typically been overlooked.

6.4 Nonmetric Multivariate Analysis

To empirically explore the relationship between the facet elements, the non-metric multivariate statistical procedure Smallest Space Analysis (SSA) was used to analyze the Q matrixes. Smallest Space Analysis is a robust procedure for revealing the structures inherent in complex qualitative data, which have low levels of measurement. The SSA makes only limited assumptions about the scalar qualities of the original data, unlike factor analysis.

6.4.1 Smallest Space Analysis (SSA-I)

Smallest Space Analysis is a structural hypothesis testing procedure that examines whether or not a content universe is ordered in a substantively interpretable manner. The hypothesized order may be quantitative, qualitative, or both, and can be specified through a mapping sentence. From this analysis, facets are then sought in the space.

The primary purpose of SSA is to investigate the content universe such that structural hypotheses about the order of variables in the content universe can be tested. SSA maps the columns of data matrix into a variable space in a similar way. SSA follows the *Principle of Contiguity*, such that variables which are conceptually related will be found close together when mapped into a conceptual space.[144] The SSA procedure is robust for many different types of data, encompassing categorical, ratio level, discreet, continuous distributions, and numerical data. SSA also has been successfully used for symmetric one-triangular matrices with geographical distances, as demonstrated in previous research by this author.[87]

6.4.2 Regions and Dimension Interpretation of SSA

Regional interpretation of the SSA space follows naturally from several features of the way the content universe is represented. The SSA space contains a map of the different variables, entered into the analysis as a triangular matrix under the *Principle of Contiguity*. As previously mentioned, this means that the closer any two variables are together in the SSA plot, the more conceptually related they are, since the program places highly correlated variables together. The plot can be rotated, stretched, translated, and reflected without any effect on the meaning of the solution, because the information is contained in the distances between the variables.[101] However, this is not the case for metric multidimensional scaling analysis. Therefore, the orientation of the axes in the SSA plot is not meaningful, although as an artifact of the program, the axes may correspond to the principal components of the correlation matrix. In this one sense, the fitting of the dimensions on the SSA plot does not really satisfy the conceptual requirements of the SSA space that continuous regions should be identified.

An additional way to interpret SSA plots is with dimensions and regression lines.[145] This is accomplished by putting perpendicular lines from the variables to the regression line and then seeing how well the interval scale thus derived would perform as a predictor on the response variable. However, this approach could be misleading since the distances are obtained from ranks of the inputs triangular matrix, which it is argued that the best information from the plot could be higher-ordered metric — not interval, which could threaten the validity of the regression.[146] A further problem is that dimensions may be moved to an infinite number of orientations; therefore, the regression line should be moved accordingly so as to maximize the predictive power. This practice tends to undermine the strength of the MDS procedures as a tool for finding structure and instead suggests heuristic solutions of one dimension, even though the SSA suggests more than one dimension.

Another feature of the SSA procedure that suggests regional rather than dimensional interpretation concerns any "empty" spaces between the variable points in the solution. Theoretically, this space is actually full of variables that are conceptually related to all the variables in the solution. For example, let us suppose that we have two variables, B and C, in the SSA space, and a third variable hypothesized to be between B and C. Conceptually, the third variable would appear as the midpoint between B and C if the hypothesized variable was put into the analysis. In this regard, the consequence of this principle is that "large" spaces in the SSA plot indicate an area of the domain which has not been examined with existing variables, and therefore gives an indication of what extra variables may be needed in future research. This is one example of the advantage that MDS procedures have over, for example, Cluster analysis. Cluster analysis would not be able to recognize such spaces in the sampling of the domain because it is a structure-imposing procedure. For example, no indication would be obtained by the Cluster analysis since the clustering solution is created by iteratively looking at each value in the association or correlation matrix in series, unlike the SSA solution which looks at them all in parallel. There is a final argument for regional rather than dimensional interpretation: regions may be hypothesized as *a priori* structures by Mapping Sentences in Facet Theory, while dimensions are far less testable as structural hypotheses.

6.4.3   Partial Order Scalogram Analysis (POSA)

The SSA scores subjects on conceptual attributes by producing statistical coefficients as indexes of similarities for the derivation of a attribute structure. Having grasped the attributes and their structure, our attention now turns to assessing each individual by the same attributes by focusing on the individuals. This is the purpose of POSA, which is a technique for measuring individuals with respect to a multivariate attribute. POSA is a structural hypothesis that individuals and attributes may be ordered along two dimensions of type and degree. In order to use POSA, Shye and Elizur point out that it is essential that all items in the scalogram have a common meaning, or more simply, a common range.[148] The issue of common meaning is substantive, and must be argued for each case. However, statistical methods such as Cronbach's alpha on the variables to be used in the POSA will give an indication of whether they can be viewed as partial measures of a concept, such as attitude towards an object or intelligence. The value of Guttman scaling by POSA has been noted by other researchers, such as Coombs, who suggests that "behavior is intrinsically partially ordered."[148] If behavior was not partially ordered, then it could be concluded that the structural hypothesis was not partially ordered. Equally as important, an experimental hypothesis that behavior may be represented by a two-dimensional partial order is a valuable hypothesis to be tested, rather than a sterile hypothesis of no difference or no structure that the researcher is not really interested in at all.

6.5 Summary

Before any robust serial murder classification model can be developed, it is essential to build an understanding of the ways in which variations between offenders relate to their victims and to each other. Rather than relying on a single behavioral characteristic as a means of decision-making, it is better to explore a combination of behaviors. This means that any error in one piece of information will have less impact on the decision process. Determining if a combination of crime scene behaviors are indeed measuring related phenomena has both theoretical and technical merit. The facet approach is a robust method for clarifying the research position and revealing the relationship between variables on an *a priori* basis rather than *post hoc.*

Descriptive Statistics of Victims

7

To have a fuller understanding and appreciation of the serial murderers and their victims with whom this book is concerned, some summary descriptive statistics are required.

7.1   Characteristics of Serial Murder Victims' Ages

In Figure 7.1 the percentages represent the distribution of the victims' ages at the time of their deaths. The under age 10 victim is, typically, a child who has not reached sexual maturity and remains immature in nearly all respects and situationally vulnerable. The victim age between 11 to 17 years is a person who is typically more sexually developed or developing. Most, but not all, are still living with their parents. There are, however, a few individuals who are married or living with a partner. The person is usually more financially independent if employed, which allows them to be mobile, thereby placing them in more vulnerable situations. The 18 to 50 years person will have a greater independence, reveal more maturity, and is usually married or living separately from their parents. This greater independence allows the individual to engage in the consumption of alcohol and drugs, thereby placing them in vulnerable situations. The person age 50 or over will usually, but not always, be retired. In many instances, this category includes elderly individuals who are often prone to vulnerable situations.

The percentages are based on 728 victims or cases in which the average number of victims per offender was 7.5. Looking at Figure 7.1, we see that serial murderers, at least in the U.S., prefer to target victims between the ages of 18 and 50 years (n = 483 or 67%). Similarities in victims' ages were found in a study of 169 male serial murderers.[20] In his study, Hickey found the

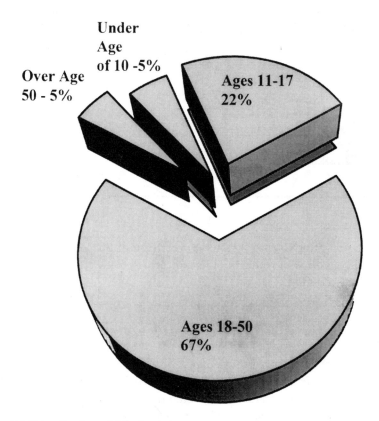

Figure 7.1 Distribution of Victims' Ages

highest proportion (48%) of victims were adults over the age of 18. In Figure
7.1, the next highest percentage of victims (n = 163 or 23%) was between
the ages of 11 and 17. This figure is higher than the percentage found in the
Hickey study. For example, Hickey found that only 3% of his male serial
murderers murdered teens.[20] The last two victim age groups, under 10,
(n = 37 or 5%) and over 50 (n=37 or 5%) had equal percentages. Hickey
found for his sample of male serial murderers the exact same percentage for
child victims (5%); however, he found that 16% of the killers had murdered
at least one elderly person.

7.2   Characteristics of Victims' Gender

Figure 7.2 shows the percentage differences in male and female as targeted
victims. In 728 serial murder cases (n = 492), 67% of the victims were females,
while (n = 236) 32% were males. This finding is similar to intersexual homicides which involve some degree of intimacy between the offender and victim.

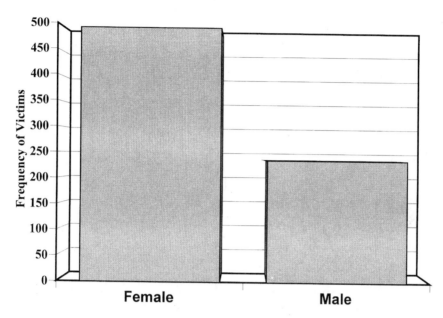

Figure 7.2 Characteristics of Victims' Gender

For example, the killing patterns in three cities in the U.S. research by Silverman and Mukherjee found that males killed females 76% of the time in stable-domestic relationships and 81% of the time in other suspect-victim relationships.[149] The findings also support Hickey's argument that serial murderers victimize females consistently more than males.[20]

In a study looking at the behavior of sexually sadistic criminals, Dietz found that 73% of the sadistic offenders victimized only females and 17% victimized only males. Ten percent of the offenders were found to victimize both males and females.[80] However, the figures differ from homicides in general; for example, in 1986 about 75% of approximately 20,000 murder victims were males.[20]

7.3 Characteristics of Victims' Ethnicity

Percentages given in Figure 7.3 show that the most likely victims of serial murderers are White (Caucasian). This finding is given importance when coupled with the fact that in this study of 107 serial murderers, 81% of the offenders were White. This finding supports the claims by other researchers that suggest that serial murder is primarily intra-racial.[4,20,50]

Looking at the figures in Figure 7.3, we see that the majority of the victims were White (n = 581 or 80%), while the next highest percentage of victims

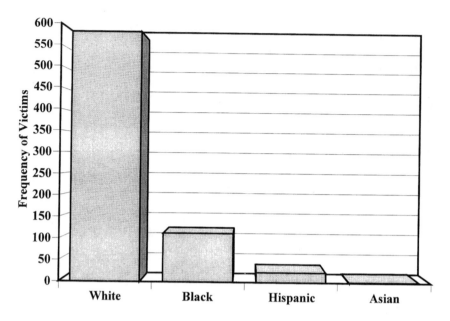

Figure 7.3 Characteristics of Victims' Ethnicity

were Black (African-American) (n = 113 or 16%), followed by Hispanics (n = 22 or 3%) and Asians (n = 1 or 0.1%). The finding that the majority of victim-offender relationships were White supports Wolfgang's premise that characteristics of homicide victims in general in many instances resemble those of their assailants.[24] However, a study on multiple-offender homicides by Cheatwood found that victim-offender relationships, with regards to race, were difficult to characterize by a single event.[150] The Cheatwood study emphasized the cross-race features in multiple-offender cases. Conversely, based on the results reported above, it can be said with some confidence that in a series of murders that are linked, where the victims are White, the offender is most likely going to be White. The same holds true for the Black victim-offender relationship.

7.4   Characteristics of Victim-Offender Relationships

Research on the crime of serial murder needs to place much more emphasis on the risk factors within a particular population, as suggested in a recent study by Godwin.[151] For example, Jenkins argues that only when law enforcement's emphasis on various populations are understood will we began to relate to the phenomenon of serial murderers and their victims.[152]

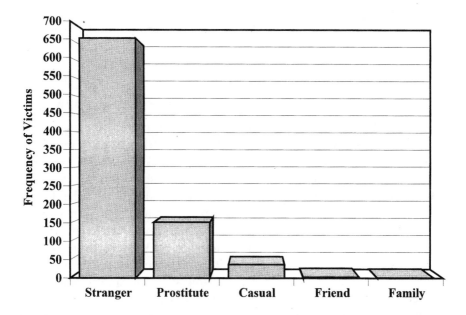

Figure 7.4 Characteristics of Victim-Offender Relationships in Serial Murder

The findings shown in Figure 7.4 support the contention that victims of serial murderers are more likely to be strangers (n = 652 or 90%). The next highest percentage of victim-offender relationships was casual (n = 37 or 5%), meaning that the offender and victim barely knew each other, seeing each other perhaps once in a year; this included one-way acquaintances. This was followed by the victim as a friend of the offender (n = 25 or 3%), meaning that both people saw each other on a regular basis. In just 1% (n = 10) of the cases, victims had a family relationship with their killer. The family relationship figure of 1% is contrary to the results on homicide reported by Wolfgang and Pokorny studies, where they found that most general homicides were usually family, relatives, or close friends.[24,153]

7.4.1   Stranger-to-Stranger

The fact that 90% of the victims were complete strangers to their killers is much larger than the figure reported in Hickey's study, where he found that of 203 cases, 62% were stranger related.[20] Beyond this one difference, however, Hickey's remaining victim-offender relationship figures were similar to this present study; family member (17%) and acquaintances (4%). A study that compared victim-offender relationships of 28 serial murderers found that 89% of the victims were not known by the attacker before the murder, while 29% of the serial murderers knew at least one of their victims.[154]

Echoing this book's findings on stranger-to-stranger encounters as the predominate offender-victim relationship is research carried out by the FBI on 113 victims of serial murders.[156] In that study, the FBI found that 81% were strangers to the offender, while 19% were known to the murderer.

7.4.2 Victim Worked as a Prostitute

The final victim-offender relationship shown in Figure 7.4 is where the victim worked as a prostitute. It is claimed by some researchers, notably criminologist Dr. Steven Egger, that many of the victims of serial murderers are prostitutes.[2] Egger points out in his recent book *The Killers Among Us* that "It would appear from the data available on serial murder investigations that the most frequent victim of a serial killer is the female prostitute."[2] Egger based his findings on a search of major newspaper reports of serial murders, either solved, unsolved, or under active investigation, between October 5, 1991 and October 5, 1993. He discovered during this two-year period a total of 198 prostitutes as victims of serial murderers, involving 21 different offender patterns. However, quite a different story is revealed in Figure 7.4. Looking at the percentage of victims found to be working as prostitutes at the time of their deaths, the results show that out of 726 solved cases only (n = 152) 21% were prostitutes. However, a straightforward comparison between Egger's findings and this study may not be possible because Egger's data includes unsolved murders, whereas the current study focuses on solved crimes. Nonetheless, Jenkins points out that prostitutes are clearly a high-risk victim population; however, he suggests they are by no means the only targeted group.[152] Jenkins found in his study that there are clearly other discernible areas that serve as major sources of victims. For example, he reviewed 52 cases of serial murder, containing no less than 10 killers or groups of killings, and found that at least eight of the extreme cases drew most of their victims from young male drifters, for example at homosexual pick-up points, while three cases targeted coeds at and near university campuses.[152]

7.5 Victim — Killer Relationships in Relation to Victims' Ages

The results shown in Table 7.1 indicate an apparent trend in stranger-to-stranger encounters in serial murders when the age of the victim is between 18 and 50 years. Various explanations can be offered for this finding. For example, murdering strangers is probably perceived by serial murderers as offering more anonymity because no previous relationship exists between

Table 7.1 Victim — Killer Relationship by Victim Age Group

	Under Age 10		Ages 11–17		Ages 18–50		Over Age 50	
Relationship	(N)	%	(N)	%	(N)	%	(N)	%
Stranger	(33)	5	(146)	20	(437)	61	(28)	4
Friend			(6)	.8	(18)	3	(1)	.1
Casual	(3)	.4	(9)	1	(21)	3	(4)	.6
Family	(1)	.1	(2)	.3	(4)	.4	(3)	.4

N = 716 Victims (12 victims' information unknown)

the two persons. Criminologist Elliot Leyton suggests that both anonymity and thrill is achieved by seeking out unsuspecting strangers.[7] Perhaps even more important, serial murderers can much more easily view strangers as objects to possess, dominate, and dehumanize compared to someone with whom they possibly have an relationship.

A recent study of offenders who abducted and murdered children found similar victim-offender relationships in 621 cases.[156] For example, 50% of the encounters were stranger-to-stranger when the victims' ages were between 10 to 12. When the victims' ages were between 13 to 15, the percentage of stranger-to-stranger encounters increased to 60%. However, the figure dropped slightly to 58% when the victims' ages were between 16 and 17 years.[156] In comparing serial murderers who claimed victims of various ages to those who exclusively murdered victims under 18 years, stark differences can be found. For example, Hanfland and his colleagues found in their child abduction-murder study that when the victims' ages were between 1 and 5, 64% of the encounters were stranger-to-stranger.[156] Likewise, when the victims' ages were between 6 to 9, 44% of the encounters were stranger-to-stranger. However, as we can readily see in Table 7.1, neither of the percentage levels for the stranger-to-stranger encounters even come close to those reported in the child murder study.

For example, in Table 7.1 we see that when the victims' ages were under 10 years only (n = 33), 5% of the cases were stranger-to-stranger encounters. When the victims' ages were between 11 and 17, the number of stranger-to-stranger encounters increased to (n = 146) 20%. Broadly, the findings show that for serial murderers who select strangers as their targets, the victim's age range is more likely to be between 18 to 50 years. Equally important, when the victim's age is over 50 years, the victim-offender relationship is still more likely to be stranger-to-stranger (n = 28 or 4%) and less likely to be a friend, casual, or family member. The percentages between age and victim-offender relationships — friend, causal, and family member — are relatively low.

7.6 Summary

The general findings of the present chapter confirm other serial murder research by suggesting that the crime of serial murder is predominately intraracial. Although victims of serial murderers were most likely to be females, the victims in this study were less likely to be prostitutes. Also stranger-to-stranger encounters were by far the most frequent type of victim-offender relationships, especially when the victim's age was between 18 and 50 years, which is similar to homicide victims in general.

Descriptive Statistics of Offenders

8

As mentioned previously, the descriptive statistics in this chapter refer to 107 American serial murderers. When possible comparisons are made with other similar serial murder studies, it is done so. In addition, the results are compared and contrasted with offenders who committed general homicides and child murders.

8.1 Characteristics of Offenders' Ages

The age distribution of serial murderers in Figure 8.1 refers to the recorded ages at the time of the offenders' arrests. The overall mean age was 30 years. The minimum age was 19 and the maximum was 50. Looking at the distribution of offenders' ages, we see that the largest group (n = 30 or 28%) was between the ages 26 and 31 years. This is followed next by offenders appearing in the age group between 37 to 42 years (n = 27 or 25%). Thus, the ages for most serial murderers in this sample of American killers range from their mid-twenties to late thirties. The next category of serial murderers was over the age of 42 (n = 19 or 18%). This is followed by the youngest age group, 18 to 25 years (n = 18 or 17%), which in turn was followed by the age group 32 to 36 (n = 13 or 12%). The average age of this study's sample is slightly higher than found in Hickey's study, where he found the mean age to be 28 years.[20] However, in his study of 28 serial murderers, James found that 50% of the offenders were in the age group between 28 and 38 years of age.[154]

When the mean age achieved for this offender sample was compared to serial murderers who predominantly targeted and murdered children, a similar picture emerges. For example, the mean age of child murderers was reported by Hanfland and his colleagues to be 27 years, a lower mean age

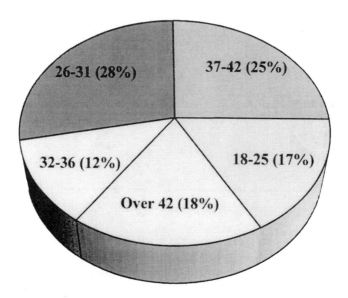

Figure 8.1 Distribution of Serial Murderers' Ages

than this study's sample of 30 years.[156] The mean age for the sample of child murderers is closer to Hickey's sample of serial murderers' mean age of 28. However, looking at individual age groups, similarities were found between ages 26 and 31 years. For example, in the study by Hanfland and his colleagues, 26% of the child murderers' ages ranged between 26 to 30, while this study found that 28% of the murderers' ages were between 26 and 31 years. However, the major differences become apparent once the age group exceeds 40. Hanfland's study found that only 9% of their child murderer population were over the age of 40, while this study found that 18% of the killers were over the age of 42.

The general findings indicate that there are little or no differences in age groups between serial murderers and individuals who murder only once. For example, using a bivariate analysis of homicides in nine cities, Zahn and Sagi found the mean age for family homicide was 33.[157] For homicides involving acquaintances the mean age was 30, while the mean age for stranger homicide was 29.[157]

8.2 Characteristics of Killers' Age and Victim – Offender Relationship

The results shown in Table 8.1 reveal some interesting trends between age and victim-offender relationships. All groups were more likely to be abducted

Table 8.1 Characteristics of Victim-Killer Relationship by Offender Age Group

Relationship	Age 18–25		Age 26–31		Age 32–36		Age 37–42		Over 42	
	N	%	N	%	N	%	N	%	N	%
Stranger	(25)	23	(37)	35	(17)	16	(6)	6	(11)	10
Friend	(3)	3	(2)	2	(1)	.9				
Casual	(1)	.9	(3)	3						
Family			(1)	.9						

N = 107 Offenders

by a stranger. These findings are similar to those reported by Hickey; he found that 62% of the male serial murderers killed strangers only.[20] In contrast, Hanfland and his colleagues found that for child murders only 53% of the encounters were stranger-to-stranger.[156]

8.3 Characteristics of Serial Murderers' Gender

The distribution of male versus female serial murderers shown in Figure 8.2 clearly indicates that serial murder is predominately a male phenomenon. One hundred and five (95%) of the offenders were males compared to only (n = 5 or 5%) of females. Other research on serial murder has found similar

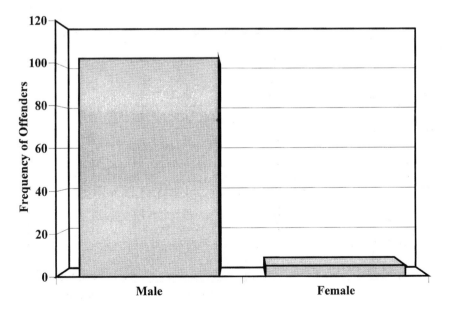

Figure 8.2 Characteristics of Killers' Gender

results.[20,52,64] For example, research by Hickey identified between 1795 and 1988 34 female serial murderers and 169 male serial murderers in the United States.[20] Briefly, the high percentage of female serial murderers in Hickey's study is due to his definition of serial murder. Hickey included females who murdered for profit and nurses who murdered patients. As previously mentioned, some of these women are referred to as *black widows*, because they primarily murder their husbands or boyfriends in order to collect on insurance money or Social Security benefits. Although the discussion of different types of definitions of serial murder is beyond the scope of this book, there is considerable debate among law enforcement and academics about the definition of serial murder. For example, what constitutes serial murder for some is the pathology shown by the offender at the crime scene, while others define serial murder based strictly on victim count.

8.4   Characteristics of Serial Murderers' Ethnicity

As shown in Figure 8.3 below (n = 88), 82% of the serial murderers in this study were White. In research by James, he found that 86% of his offender sample was White (Caucasian).[154] Also, in Hanfland's study of child murderers, 80% of the child killers were White.[156] The category of offender ethnicity, Hispanic, was found to be relatively low (n = 2 or 2%).

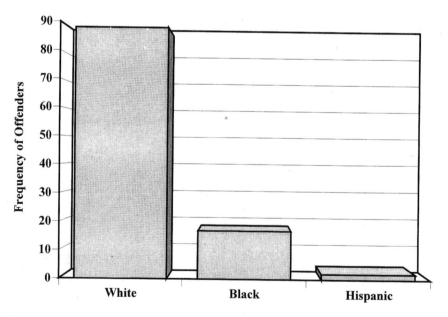

Figure 8.3 Characteristics of Killers' Ethnicity

Seventeen (or 16%) of the study's sample of serial murderers were Black (African-American), including one Black male-female team. This finding supports research by Jenkins.[158] Jenkins investigated the involvement of Blacks in serial homicide between 1971 to 1990 by scanning newspaper reports and secondary sources. Jenkins found, contrary to popular conception, Blacks represented a sizeable proportion of serial murderers.[158] In the period studied, there were approximately 100 cases of serial murder in the U.S., of which about (n = 13) 13% involved Black offenders.

Hanfland and his colleagues also found that 20% of the child murderers in their study were Black.[156] As Jenkins points out, the failure to draw attention to Black serial murderers might arise from a form of bias within the media and law enforcement.[158] Jenkins also states that underestimating minority involvement in serial homicide may lead to neglecting the protection of minority individuals and communities.

8.5 Serial Killers' Employment History

The sample of serial murderers in this study came from a wide variety of occupations. Offenders generally were employed by others (n = 54 or 51%), and the number of offenders who were self-employed was n = 18 or 16%. The notion that serial murderers are roaming the country abducting and

Figure 8.4 Serial Killers' Employment History

murdering victims during all times of the day and night is highly unlikely, considering the percentage of offenders who were employed by others at the time of their crimes. The fact that the majority of the offenders were employed by others reduces their chances of spending time looking for victims. However, looking at Figure 8.4, we see that (n = 18) 16% of the killers were self-employed. Being self-employed may be perceived by the offender as a way to maintain a steady cash flow while also freeing up his time to hunt for victims. A third of the serial murderers had no job (n = 35 or 33%). This is almost ten times the national unemployment average in the U.S.

Nevertheless, the results contrast somewhat with Hanfland's findings that 50% of the child murderers were unemployed at the time they committed murder.[156] The reason for the higher level of unemployment in the child killer group is probably due to difficulty in obtaining victims. To lure children to their deaths most likely requires the offender to stalk the victim; for example, by sitting outside an elementary school. Stalking requires the offender to be available during daytime hours; therefore, it would be difficult for him to maintain a daytime job. It is most likely that the remainder of his time would be occupied with carrying out the murder, getting rid of evidence, and disposing of the victim.

8.6   Serial Killers' Marital Status

The percentage figures in Figure 8.5 show that the majority (n = 63 or 59%) of the offenders were single at the time of their arrest. This figure is lower than that reported by the FBI in their study of serial murderers; they found that 80% of the offenders were not married.[155] The next most-frequent category was divorced (n = 30 or 28%). The percentage of offenders who were married was n = 18 or 17%. In Hickey's study on 34 female serial murderers, he found that the majority remarried several times in order to kill again and again.[20]

8.7   Serial Killers' Educational Status

The serial murderers in this study generally were not highly educated; (n = 60) 56% did not complete high school. A significant number of serial murderers, however, did complete high school (n = 47 or 44%). The level of education falls considerably after high school, as demonstrated by the small number of killers who had some college (n = 13 or 12%) followed by those who attained a Bachelor's Degree (n = 4 or 4%). None of the serial murderers in this study had postgraduate degrees. The findings accord with the FBI

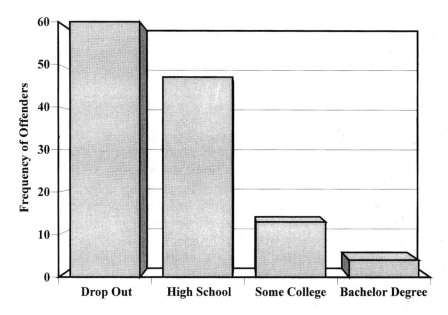

Figure 8.5 Serial Killers' Marital Status

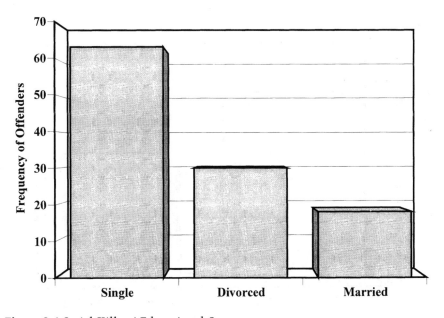

Figure 8.6 Serial Killers' Educational Status

study on serial murderer in which Burgess and her colleagues found that only one third of their offender sample did average or better in school, with 68% receiving a fair to poor academic rating.[18] These results support Hickey's contention that the serial murderer's ability to kill repeatedly without detection is more a function of cunning and deceit than intellectual ability or academic attainments.[20]

8.8   Serial Killers' Mental History

The variable, mental problems, was defined as any serial murderer in the sample who had a juvenile or adult recording as being treated for mental health problems. This included any reports which recommended or showed that the offender had been treated by a psychologist or psychiatrist for mental health problems other than alcohol or drugs. Thirty (or 28%) of the serial murderers in this study had a record of being treated for mental health problems; however, for the remaining offenders no specific information was available. The finding appears to support Lunde's finding of little evidence of mental illness in serial murderers.[159] In contrast, the FBI study on 36 killers found that 69% of their offender sample had some type of psychiatric assessment or confinement.[17] Hanfland and his colleagues found that for child murderers, 23% of their sample suffered from mental problems.[156] However,

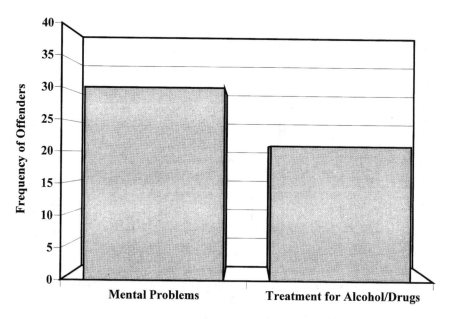

Figure 8.7 Serial Killers' Mental History

Fox and Levin suggest that "we must approach the neurological assessment of serial murderers with skepticism, pointing out that the distinction between explanation and prediction is crucial." [64]

Many people believe that alcohol and drugs are mandatory elements in the construction of a serial murderer. The report of alcohol and drug treatment in this study was taken from trial transcripts and police reports. Other instances of alcohol use came from court transcripts of surviving victims' accounts, i.e., that she or he could smell liquor or beer on the offender's breath, or that the offender consumed alcohol in the victim's presence. Twenty-one (or 20%) of the killers in this study had a record of being treated for alcohol and/or drugs. Not shown in Figure 8.7 is a similar percentage (n = 156 or 21%) of cases that involved offenders who used alcohol and/or drugs prior to committing their murders. Hanfland and his colleagues reported that 30% of the child murderers in their study had alcohol problems, while 27% had drug problems.[156]

8.9   Serial Killers' Sexual History

8.9.1   Offenders' Sexuality

Looking at Figure 8.8 we see that (n = 86) 80% of offenders in this study were heterosexual, while (n = 18) 17% were homosexual, and (n = 10) 9% were bisexual. These percentages suggest that most serial murderers are not that much different from the general population. Just one offender (or 0.9%) was a transvestite. However, (n = 25) 23% of the serial murderers were pedophiles.

8.9.2   Pornography

Pornography as a facilitator in serial murder was made popular by Ted Bundy's confession that pornography drove him to murder repeatedly.[64] In this sample of killers, it was found that (n = 68) 64% of the offenders consumed pornography. This variable was defined as any offender who read and/or collected a variety of pornographic materials. This was determined by information contained in police reports. Fox and Levin point out the role of pornography as a facilitator in serial murderers: "Violent pornography may not directly cause or inspire its consumers to develop into serial murderers, but it unquestionably provides a cultural context in which sexual homicide is encouraged." [64] For example, in the FBI study on serial murder, researchers found that 81% of their offenders in the study reported interests in pornography.[155] However, a study of child murderers found that only 4% of the offenders used pornography.[156] In

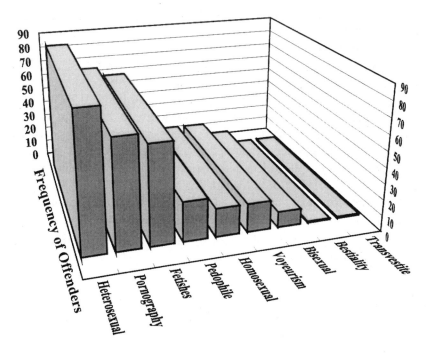

Figure 8.8 Serial Killers' Sexual History

that study, Hanfland and his colleagues explained that the exposure to pornographic materials was unnecessary in the process of getting motivated to commit murder. So, there is the question of just how influential pornography is as a motivational factor; however, it is quite apparent by the results reported above, that serial murderers do engage in viewing pornography on a regular basis.

8.9.3 Bizarre Sexual Activities

There does appear to be a certain degree of bizarre sexual background history in this sample of serial murderers, although it is not the dominant behavior that one might expect. For example, based on psychiatric records, while (n = 62), 58% of the offenders in this study engaged in using inanimate objects such as dildos and other sex toys as part of their fetish sexual activity, only (n = 18) 17% of the killers received sexual gratification by peeping through windows and so forth to watch people, and only one killer engaged in extreme bizarre behavior, such as bestiality. The latter finding is much lower than the one reportedly found by the FBI that indicated 23% of their sample had had sexual contact with animals.[155]

8.10 Characteristics of Serial Killers' Criminal History

8.10.1 Burglary Offenses

It is generally assumed by investigators that serial murderers have no criminal record, but rather embark on an unique form of criminal activity.[2] The present results shown in Figure 8.9 does not support this finding. For example (n = 65) 61% of the serial murderers had a prior conviction of burglary, theft, or robbery. Similarly, Hickey reported in his study on 169 serial murderers that 21% had a record for burglary, 23% robbery, and 24% for theft/stealing.[20] However, James found that 61% of his sample of serial murderers had some kind of criminal record.[154]

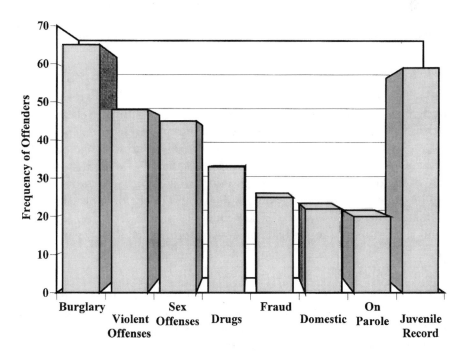

Figure 8.9 Characteristics of Serial Killers' Criminal History

8.10.2 Violent Offenses

The next highest occurrence of criminal history was violent offenses. This variable included convictions or charges that were later dropped for lack of evidence. Violent offenses included criminal acts such as murder, attempted murder, rape, attempted rape, kidnaping, and attempted kidnaping. There were (n = 46) 24% of such individuals. In contrast, Hickey's study found that only 7% of his 169 serial murderers had a prior conviction for homicide, while Hanfland and his colleagues found that 60% of the child murderers in their study had prior arrests for violent crimes; for example rape, murder, kidnap, and assault.[20,156]

8.10.3 Sex Offenses

It is a commonly held belief by investigators that serial murderers are likely to have a past history of some sort of sexual offenses.[17,51] Forty-eight (or 45%) of the offenders in this study had a prior record of sexual-related offenses. Again, this variable included convictions or charges dropped due to lack of evidence. Rape was not included in this category. This variable included offenses such as indecent exposure and crimes against nature; for example, fellatio and cunnilingus. It also includes the sexual abuse of children other than their own, and incestuous involvement with their own child.

8.10.4 Drug Offenses

The relationship between serial murder and past convictions for drugs is much lower than found in the homicides that occur in intimate relationships, such as those between husband and wife. For example, research by Silverman and Mukherjee found that 87% of the cases involved drugs, while only 13% of the events were drug-free.[149] Looking at Figure 8.9, we see that (n = 33) 31% of the killers in this study had past drug convictions. In a study by Dietz and his colleagues of sexual sadistic killers, 50% of the offenders had convictions for drugs.[80] However, Hickey found a much lower percentage (5%) of his serial murder sample had convictions for drugs.[20]

8.10.5 Fraud Offenses

Less than one quarter (or 24%) of the serial murderers in this study had convictions for fraud. In James' study of 28 serial murderers, 50% were involved in fraud of one form or another.[154] For example, the serial murderer Ted Bundy was clever at defrauding different businesses, including gas stations, by using his victims' credit cards.[115]

8.10.6 Domestic Offenses

Domestic violence included any criminal convictions, charges later dropped, or complaints filed which related to a history of domestic disturbances; for example, assault on a female. Only 22 (or 21%) of the killers in this study met one of the above requirements for domestically related crimes. Hickey discusses the relationship between domestic violence and females classified as serial murderers.[20] His comparisons between domestic violence and serial murder related only to whether females who were abused in the past go on to become serial murderers. This is obviously not related to this study, because males are the predominate gender in the present study.

8.10.7 Offenders on Parole or Probation

It is important for the investigator working on a series of killings to know if serial murderers are likely to be known by the police. Looking at Figure 8.9, we see that only 19% of the serial murderers in this study were currently on parole or probation during the time they committed their crimes. Hanfland and his colleagues also found that 27% of their child murderers were currently on parole or probation at the time of their arrest.[156] Having information of this sort is extremely important to a police investigation. Combined with other types of evidence, knowing that is it possible that some serial murderers are currently on parole or probation can help focus or refocus an investigation. For example, this finding suggests that a suspect could likely be found in the active files of the correctional or judicial system.

8.10.8 Juvenile Criminal History

In a study by Toch, he points out that people who were abused as children tend to manipulate others through violence in order to satisfy personal needs and tend to be violent whenever they feel threatened.[28] Sears points out that Toch's theory also applies to serial murderers.[161] Following Sears' line of reasoning, one would expect then that serial murderers would most likely have a history of juvenile delinquency. Looking at the last column in Figure 8.9, we see that 55% of the serial murderers in this study had a criminal record under the age of 18 years. This finding supports the FBI study on serial murderers, where they reported the following present in the childhoods of their offender sample: destruction of property (58%), arson (56%), and stealing (82%).[17] This finding should come as no surprise because, even as far back as the 1950s, research on 14 famous serial murderers from around the world found that many of the killers had engaged in theft and many other types of crimes — both as juveniles and adults — prior to committing murder.[161]

8.11 Miscellaneous Characteristics of Serial Killers' Background Histories

8.11.1 Military Record

Several additional background variables were also examined. A relatively low percentage (n = 29 or 27%) of the serial murderers entered the military. This

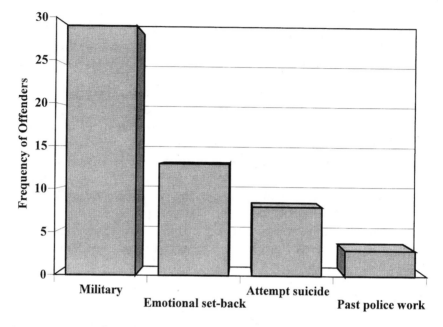

Figure 8.10 Miscellaneous Characteristics of Killers' Background Histories

is somewhat less than the 50% figure reported by the FBI's sample of serial murderers.[61]

8.11.2 Emotional Setback

In interviews with serial murderers, the FBI reported that many of the offenders revealed expressions of low self-esteem prior to the murders.[61] Information on whether an offender suffered an emotional setback prior to murdering was based on mental health records. Examples of the variable included breaking-up or arguing with a girlfriend or boyfriend. This includes a temporary or permanent separation from a spouse and any deaths within the immediate family. Thirteen (or 12%) of the offender sample were found to have suffered an emotional setback prior to embarking on murder. This finding suggests that there may be additional, deep-rooted psychological reasons for repeated killing, rather than some acute emotional shock which sets the killer into motion.

8.11.3 Offender Attempted or Committed Suicide

Research by Silverman and Mukherjee found that 13% of their offender sample committed suicide in domestic-stable marriages, while for domestic-unstable marriages the figure was 31%.[149] However, they found that when the victim-offender relationship was stranger-to-stranger, the figure reported was just 7%. A similar result can be seen in Figure 8.10. In only eight instances (7%) did the serial murderer kill himself or attempt to kill himself. However, compared to other types of homicides, committing suicide after murdering is rare.[52] The rate in American is about 0.2 per 100,000 per year, compared to a total murder rate of about 9.[52]

8.11.4 Prior Work in Law Enforcement

The literature on serial murder suggests that serial murderers are often preoccupied with a fascination about police work.[50,52,61,162] However, the results in Figure 8.10 tell a different story. Only 2% of the serial murderers in this book indulged in reading and procuring literature on police procedures, including collecting and wearing police paraphernalia.

8.12 Summary

The serial murderers in this study appear to be similar to other serial murderers reported in different studies in regards to background characteristics. For example, the mean age of the offender sample was 30 years, which is approximately the mean age reported in other serial murder studies.[20,50] In regards to offender age and victim-offender relationship, several important findings were reported that could be of investigative value. For example, it was found that offenders between the ages of 26 and 31 were more likely to target and abduct strangers than any other age group.

There was no surprise in the fact that males made up the sample population more than females. However, in regards to offender ethnicity, while White was found to be the dominant race, Black serial murderers accounted for 16% of the offenders in this study. This figure is somewhat higher than reported by the FBI's studies on serial murder; however, the percentage is similar to studies carried out by Jenkins.[158]

Another interesting finding was that the majority (51%) of the killers were currently employed at the time of their arrest, while 33% were unemployed. The remaining percentage of offenders were self-employed. Knowing this type of information is useful for investigators, because it could imply that in a series of murders occurring locally, the chances are that the suspect lives and works in the nearby area.

The idea that serial murderers are particularly intelligent and well-educated was not supported by the findings in this chapter. For example, over half (56%) of the killers did not complete high school. This finding does not mean that the offenders were not streetwise or cunning; however, it does suggest that they were most likely employed in blue-collar jobs.

The public's perception that serial murderers are different from people in the general population in terms of sexuality was generally not supported; 80% of this serial murderer sample was heterosexual and 17% were homosexual. However, the results do show that a quarter of the killers were pedophiles. In regards to criminal history, it is important to recognize that 61% of the offenders had a past conviction of burglary, theft, or robbery. Twenty-four percent of the killers had previous convictions of a violent crime, such as murder or rape. It seems, therefore, we may have failed in our criminal justice system to adequately deal with the *old criminal* before his career of serial murdering began.

Elements of Crime Scene Behavior

9

A full description of the crime scene variables can be found in Appendix A. Just to note, the frequency for each of the variables may equal more than the total number of victims due to some actions occurring more than once.

9.1 Elements of Killers' Method of Gaining Access to the Victim

9.1.1 Blitz, Cons, and Ploys

James' study of 28 serial murderers found that 68% of the killers used some form of a con game or ruse to lure their victims.[154] In Figure 9.1 we see that the majority of victims in this study (n = 390 or 54%) were blitz attacked, while only (n = 242) 33% of the victims were lured to their deaths through the use of a con. It can be noted that Hanfland and his colleagues found that 21% of their child killers used a con to gain control over their victims.[156] Con in this study means that the killer initiated contact with his victims by use of a verbal contact, questions asked, or story told. Ploy differs in that it requires the killer to use some form of subterfuge — a broken arm, stalled car, etc. — to lure victims to their deaths. In the present study, there were (n = 133) 18% of such cases involving a ploy to lure victims.

9.1.2 Solicited for Sex

The frequency with which serial murderers used sex as a ruse to gain access to victims was (n = 228) 31%. This variable includes offenders who made contact with their victims either as a prostitute or in a nightclub setting. For example, a recent study by this author on victim target networks in serial murder suggests that serial murderers regularly forage for potential victims in red-light areas.[151]

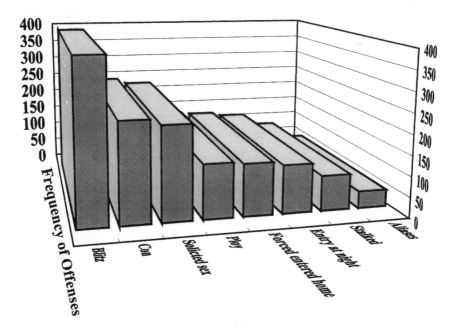

Figure 9.1 Elements of Killers' Method of Gaining Access to the Victim

9.1.3 Forced Entered Victims' Homes at Night

The literature of gaining access to a victim in serial murders by breaking and entering their home is virtually silent. However, in this study (n = 128) 18% of the victims were targeted in their homes, and in 119 instances 16% of the victims' homes were entered during the night.

9.1.4 Aliases

In order to gain the confidence of a potential victim, some serial murderers resort to the use of aliases. This variable involves the offender's use of names other than their legal name, including any nicknames or slang names. The variable also includes any forged names, via Social Security numbers and driver's license numbers. Approximately (n = 42) 6% of the serial murderers in this study used aliases.

9.1.5 Victim was Stalked

Eighty-seven (or 12%) of the victims in this study were stalked for a period of one day (24 hours) or longer by their killer. This includes any evidence of break-ins at the victim's home when the victim was absent.

9.2 Elements of Killers' Method of Controlling the Victim

Some researchers suggest that often it is control over a victim that serial murderers seek.[20,52] This study looked at eight methods that serial murderers used to control their victims. For example, one study points out that "binding a victim makes control easier and for uncooperative, strong victims, it may be absolutely necessary." [156] The methods of controlling the victim are shown in Figure 9.2 below.

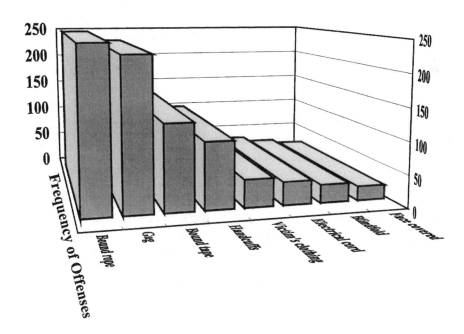

Figure 9.2 Elements of Killers' Method of Controlling the Victim

9.2.1 Victims Bound with Rope

Looking at the very first column in Figure 9.2, we see the frequency of victims who were bound with a rope, string, or twine is (n = 250) 34%. It can be noted that a recent study of offenders who murdered children found that one quarter bound their victims.[156]

9.2.2 Victims Gagged

In an effort to control the victim, serial murderers can use a gag. In 230 cases, 32% of the victims were gagged. This includes the use at any time during the attack of any physical article placed in or around the victim's mouth, but does not include manual gagging. In some instances, a gag may be used to prevent noise or be associated with sexual role-playing or bondage.

9.2.3   Victims Bound with Tape

This method of control includes victims who were found bound by tape or who showed evidence of being restrained by tape. One hundred and thirty-one (18%) of the victims were bound by tape. In a study by Holmes and Holmes, they elaborate on the serial murderer's use of tape, such as duct tape.[50] Holmes, in his interviews with imprisoned serial murderers, was informed by the killers that they learnt about the efficiency of using duct tape inside the prison walls. Holmes suggests that the increased use of using tape as a method to bind murder victims was borrowed from the movie *A Few Good Men*, when a young Marine was forcibly removed from his barracks and bound with camouflage-printed duct tape. Holmes points out that "when duct tape is used on a number of murder victims, it may be an indication that the perpetrator has been in prison at some time or a member of a special branch of the military" [50] Although Holmes' theory about the use of tape is speculative, it may have some validly.

9.2.4   Victims Bound with Handcuffs

Another method of controlling a victim is the use of handcuffs. This form of restraining the victim also suggests that the crime is preplanned. In 102 cases, 14% of the victims in this study were bound with handcuffs.

9.2.5   Victims Bound with Own Clothing

In contrast to the preselected restraint, such as a pair of handcuffs, some serial murderers may use an article of the victim's clothing as a restraint. The number of victims who were bound by their own clothing was relatively low (n = 43 or 6%). The use of a victim's clothing to bind might suggest that the crime was unplanned.

9.2.6   Victims Bound with Electrical Cord

Another method of controlling the victim that suggests the crime was unplanned is the use of an electrical cord to bind the victim. Thirty-six cases (5%) of the victims in this study were bound with an electrical cord. The presence of this variable occurs mainly in instances where the victim was murdered in their own residences.

9.2.7   Blindfold and Covering the Victim's Face

Another variable that dealt with the offender's use, at any time during the attack, was any item that physically interfered with the victim's ability to see. This included only the use of articles and not the temporary use of the offender's hands. In 28 cases, 4% of the victims were blindfolded. Contrary to the view of some investigators and researchers, a blindfold found at the crime scene does not necessarily mean that the victim knew her attacker. Rather, as one serial murderer states in his interview with criminologist Ronald Holmes, "I blindfolded my victims because faces scream at you." [50]

A similar variable to blindfold is the victim's face being covered. The variable, face covered, includes any physical article that was used to cover the victim's entire head, anytime during the attack or after the murder. In just 22 cases, 3% of the victims had their entire face covered during the attack.

9.3   Elements of Killers' Cognitive Planning

9.3.1   Weapon and Restraint Selection

Variables in Figure 9.3 indicate the extent to which serial murderers preplan their murders. The first column represents offenders who preselected their weapons. In 627 (or 86%) of the cases, the offender determined his weapon of choice. The next preplanning behavior is the offender preselecting a restraining device. In 356 (or 49%) of the cases, the serial murderer carried his own restraints to the crime scene. The evidence of these two behaviors clearly show that most serial murderers, at least in this sample, went to great lengths to plan their crimes.

9.3.2   Crime Kit

This behavior describes serial murderers who possessed a crime kit for torturing their victims. This includes any electrical devices, cutting tools, pliers, etc., for use in submitting the victim to sadistic torture. For example, the serial murderer Ted Bundy carried a kit that included handcuffs, an ice pick, a ski mask, a mask made of pantyhose, rope, black garbage bags, and a tire iron.[163] In 227 (or 31%) of the cases in this study, the serial murderer used a crime kit for torture. Although in slightly more than one quarter of the cases killers used a crime kit, the prevalence of a crime kit is not perhaps as dominant as one might expect based on reports often given in the media and true-crime publications.

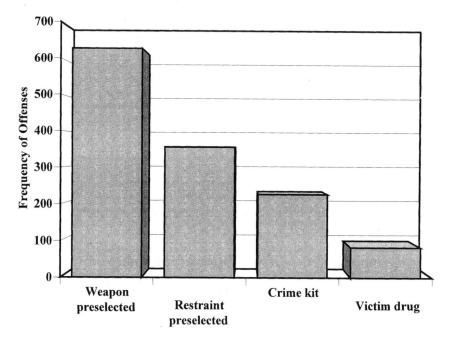

Figure 9.3 Elements of Killers' Cognitive Planning

9.3.3   Victim Drugged

This behavior describes victims who were neutralized by chemical soporifics. In 83 cases, 11% of the victims in this study were slipped a neutralizing drug in order to render them unconscious. For example, the serial murderer Randy Kraft consistently drugged his male victims in order to have complete control over their bodies.[164]

9.4   Killers' Methods of Death

9.4.1   Method of Death: Knife

Serial murderers select their weapons of death very carefully, according to research by Holmes and Holmes.[50] They suggest that serial killers use hands-on weapons for three reasons: (1) to touch the victim; (2) because the touch terrorizes the victim; and (3) because the touch degrades the victim. Looking at Figure 9.4, we see that the most frequent mode of death was by stabbing or some form of slashing (n = 335 or 46%). By way of comparison, Hickey's research on 169 male serial murderers found that 55% used one or more of the following: stabbing, hacksawing, axing, and throat-slashing.[20]

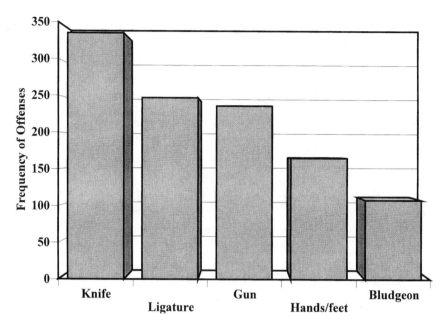

Figure 9.4 Killers' Methods of Death

9.4.2 Method of Death: Ligature Strangulation

Hickey found that 33% of his serial murder sample used strangulation as the method of killing.[20] However, Hickey did not differentiate between manual strangulation and ligature. With regards to the present sample of killers (n = 247), 34% of the victims were murdered by ligature strangulation, while (n = 165) 21% of the victims were killed by the offender's hands and feet. The variable, hands/feet, includes both manual strangulation and being beaten and stomped to death. While this does not specifically distinguish between ligature and manual strangulation, it does provide a clear division between the use of a ligature and the use of the offender's hands and feet as a weapon.

9.4.3 Method of Death: Firearm

Criminologists Fox and Levin argue that guns are rarely used in serial murders.[64] However, in Hickey's study he found that 19% of his serial murderer sample used a firearm exclusively, while 45% used some firearms.[4,20] Firearms in this study were defined as any type of gun: shotgun, rifle, handgun, etc. Out of 728 victims (n = 236) 32% were murdered with a firearm. This finding provides an indication that some type of firearm is not often the serial murderer's weapon of choice.

9.4.4 Method of Death: Bludgeon

Bludgeon is a method of killing the victim that requires hands-on touching by the killer. In a study of 30 male sexually sadistic criminals Dietz, Hazelwood, and Warren found that 60% of the offenders bludgeoned their victims to death.[80] In 108 (15%) of the cases in the present study, the victims were bludgeoned to death. Bludgeoning includes homicide that results from being beaten to death by any blunt instrument, for example a club or tire iron. In a study by Hickey, he found that only 3% of his male serial murderers bludgeoned their victims to death.[20]

9.5 Methods of Killers' Sexual Degradation of the Victim

In a study by Sears, he suggests that serial murderers are more likely to be sexual sadists.[160] However, a study by Rappaport disputed this view, arguing that neither sexual activity nor murder was the true motive for the serial murderer's behavior.[165] Rather, Rappaport points out, such murders are an attempt to cope with an internal conflict, a way to achieve relief from psychological pain, primarily by demonstrating power and mastery over others.

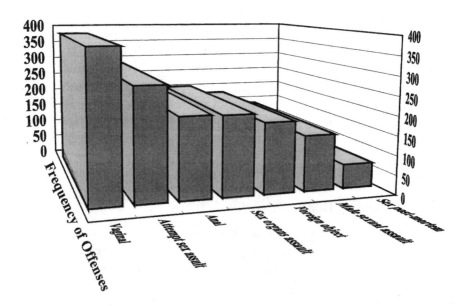

Figure 9.5 Methods of Killers' Sexual Degradation of the Victim

9.5.1 Vaginal Penetration

If the dominant focus of serial murderers is sadistic sexual activities, then one could expect that variables which have a sadistic focus occur most frequently. As shown in Figure 9.5, the most frequent type of sexual assault in the present sample was vaginal penetration (n = 379 or 52%). Similarly, Dietz and his colleagues found in their study of sexually sadistic killers that 56% of the offenders vaginally raped their victims.[30] The next most frequent form of degradation was attempted sexual assault (n = 286 or 39%). This variable includes incomplete or attempted sexual assaults.

9.5.2 Anal Penetration

According to forensic psychologist Richard Walter, anal rape is more degrading to the victim than vaginal assault.[166] The number of victims that were anally raped prior to being killed was (n = 208) 29%. Hazelwood and his colleagues noted that anal and oral rape is preferred over vaginal rape.[167] Oral sex was not included in this study due to the difficulty in determining if the act actually occurred or not, since the victim is dead. The availability of medical examiners' reports suggesting whether oral sexual activity had occurred or not was less than forthcoming. Nevertheless, the present results suggest that vaginal penetration was the preferred method of sexual degradation.

9.5.3 Sex Organs Assaulted and Foreign Objects

The remaining four types of sexual degradation involve more sadistic acts; for example, sex organ assault, and any assaults by hand or a weapon to the male or female genitals, breasts, and anal areas. Two hundred and six cases (28%) included this form of degradation. The number of cases where the killer exploited the victim's body by inserting foreign objects was (n = 183) 25%. This finding is somewhat lower than the one reported by Dietz and his colleagues, where they found that 40% of the killers penetrated their victims with a foreign object.[80] Moreover, the differences in these percentages may point to the fact that Dietz and his co-workers used a subgroup of sadistic offenders rather than individuals who are representative of serial murderers in general.

9.5.4 Male Sexual Assault

Research by Hickey found that a subsample of his serial murderer sample killed as a result of homosexual liaisons.[20] Looking at Figure 9.5, we see that (n = 144) 20% of victims in this study were males who were anally raped by their attacker prior to death. Dietz and his colleagues suggest that male killers anally assault male victims because of a common history of homosexual involvement, although they did not test this hypothesis on their sample.

9.5.5   Postmortem Sexual Activities

Necrophilia as a form of sexual deviation is posited as a common occurrence in serial murder.[20,168] Postmortem sexual act or necrophilia is defined as having sexual relations with dead bodies. In this sample of serial murderers (n = 63) 9% of the victims were sexually violated after death. This relatively low percentage accords with Lester's opinion that necrophilia is quite uncommon.[52]

9.6   Elements of Killers' Sadistic Behavior

9.6.1   Tortured Victims

De River defined sadist as any individual who exalts in the infliction of pain on his victims.[45]

Conversely, some researchers argue that a desire for power over others is the essential feature of sadism, and the subject of violence to power is more important than the infliction of pain.[191] The latter view raises important questions about an offender's control over a living victim being mutually exclusive, and whether his intrinsic rewards of sadistic actions can be achieved after a victim's death. Consequently, there lacks a clear and definable line about when the continuum of a killer's sadistic pleasures end.

The variable, tortured victim, describes sadistic acts performed on the victim while they were alive; for instance, electric shock, cutting, or flagellation. Also included was any mental torture, such as forcing the victim to write a letter to loved ones prior to death. Torture also describes victims who suffered multiple stab wounds of ten or more. As Figure 9.6 shows (n = 348) 48% of the victims in this study were tortured prior to death. In his study of serial murderers, Hickey found that the enjoyment of torture and killing was expressed most frequently by team serial murderers than by any other group, such as male serial murderers who acted alone.[20]

9.6.2   Dismemberment Postmortem

Dismembering a body could imply some forensic awareness on the part of the killer.[169] However, the action could also have some sort of psychological meaning for the offender. Looking at Figure 9.6, we see that a relevantly low number (n = 151) 21% of the cases involved killers who dismembered their victims. This finding suggests that the dismemberment of a victim's body is not as common as some investigators have suggested.

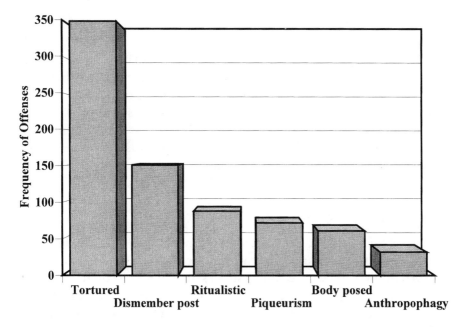

Figure 9.6 Elements of Killers' Sadistic Behavior

9.6.3   Ritualistic Acts

Ritualistic acts describe any evidence found at the crime scene that suggests the killer performed ritualistic acts on, with, or near the victim's body. For example, this would include evidence of candle burning, stacking of rocks, or dead animals found at the crime scene. In 88 (12%) of the cases, the offender performed some sort of ritualistic act at the crime scene. In a study by Hickey, he found that nearly one fifth of his 76 team killers were involved in ritualistic activities.[20]

9.6.4 Piqueurism

De River (1958) points out in his famous book, *Crime and the Sexual Psychopath*, that individuals who engage in piqueurism become sexually excited by the act of feeling the ripping and tearing of some sort of material or human flesh.[45] Although the act of piqueurism occurred in only (n = 72) 10% of the present cases, with the exception of a recent study by Keppel and Birnes on signature actions in serial murderers, piqueurism is rarely discussed in the serial murder literature.[170] Keppel and Birnes suggest that piqueurism is a unique signature in serial murder; it is a kind of psychological fingerprint.

9.6.5   Victim's Body Posed

In a study by Holmes and Holmes, they point out that the positioning of the victim's body can provide important information about the serial murderer.[50] The FBI notes that if the victim's body has been mutilated, it may be positioned in a special way that has significance for the offender.[61] Posing is not to be confused with staging, because staging refers to manipulation of the crime scene around the body.[170] This category describes the position of the victim's body when found. In 61 (8%) of the present cases, the victim's body was found to be posed by the killer. This finding supports Keppel and Birnes' opinion "that posing a murder victim's body is very rare; that only 1% of all murder cases have killers who posed the victims' bodies." [170]

9.6.6   Anthropophagy

Anthropophagy is defined as the eating of human flesh by slicing off body parts.[20] Several serial murderers have practiced this form of cannibalism; however, the occurrence of cannibalism in serial murder is still relatively low despite the media's hype surrounding a few cases that feature this type of behavior. Looking at the very last column in Figure 9.6, we see that in (n = 32) 4% of the cases in this study, the offender performed anthropophagy on his victims. For the investigator, finding evidence of anthropophagy in a series of murders could suggest that the act is a *calling card* of the killer.

9.7   Actions Indicating Killers' Psychological Reflection

9.7.1   Offender Retained Trophies

A trophy for the serial murderer is something taken from the crime scene that has some intrinsic value.[50] For example, some serial murderers have been known to remove their victim's breasts for later use. Others have saved victims' teeth or hair as part of their souvenir fetish.[4,20] However, retaining trophies is not as common in serial murder as one might expect. For example, in this study 173 cases (24%), just slightly less than one quarter of the 728 murders, involved a killer who retained body parts and other items of the victims as trophies. This percentage is lower than the one found by Dietz and his co-workers in their study on sexually sadistic killers (n = 12) 40%.[80] The differences in results could again be attributed to the fact that the Dietz study involved a subsample of sadistic offenders who are more likely to retain personal items belonging to the victim. The investigator who suspects that body parts or other types of items may have been taken by the killer should be put on alert that many times trophies, amongst other items, might be

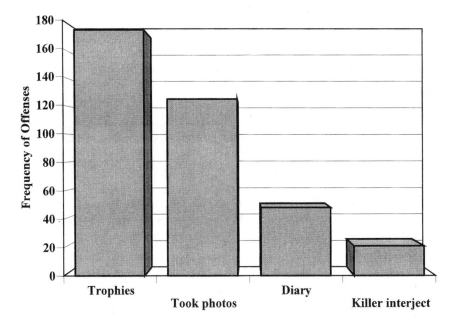

Figure 9.7 Actions Indicating the Killers' Psychological Reflection

found in the predator's car or home. In a study on 28 serial murderers, for instance, James found that 36% of the killers had kept items relating to the crimes in their homes, apartments, or cars.[154]

9.7.2   Photos

Serial murderers have been known to engage in photo-taking or videotaping their hedonistic acts. This category describes cases where the offender took photos and/or videos of the victim prior to or after death. In the present study, it was found that in (n = 124) 17% of the cases, the killer photographed or videotaped his crimes. This figure is slightly higher than the one reported by James in his study of 28 serial murderers. In his study, James found that only 11% of the killers visually recorded interactions with their victims.[154] However, Dietz and his colleagues found that 53% of his sexually sadistic killers recorded their offenses in either written form, photos/videos, or by collecting news articles about their murders.[80]

9.7.3   Kept Diary of Crimes

This variable describes cases where the killer maintained a diary or written account of his murders. This included any clippings of news stories about the murders. It was found that (n = 48) 7% of the cases involved a serial murderer who retained such details.

9.7.4   Offender Interjected Himself Into the Investigation

Media reports often portray the serial murderer as cunning and who returns back to his crime scene to participate in the investigation.[171] However, in the present results, in only a minority (n = 21) 3% of the cases did the killer interject himself into the criminal investigation.

9.8   Actions Indicating Killers' Forensic Disorganization

9.8.1   Semen Found at Crime Scene

From the very early beginnings of serial murder research, serial murderers have been labeled according to whether their crime scenes actions were organized or disorganized.[172] Seven variables showing aspects of the killer's disorganization are presented in Figure 9.8. The first variable, semen found at the crime scene, reflects a lack of awareness on the part of the killer. The present study found that in (n = 302) 42% of the cases the killer left semen at the crime scene. This finding suggests that most serial murderers are conscious of leaving forensic evidence behind at the crime scene.

9.8.2   Restraint Found at Crime Scene

The next variable that suggests a lack of forensic awareness is where the offender leaves a restraint at the crime scene. In 157 (22%) of the offenses, the killer left behind articles used to restrain the victim. This variable also shows that the crime was most likely unplanned.

9.8.3   Body Openly Displayed

The next variable describes how the killer left the victim's body after the murder. For example, if the victim's body could be viewed with ease and was not covered by trees or other barriers, then it was coded in this category. The number of victims' bodies that were found openly displayed was (n = 134) 18%. This is a fairly low frequency and may suggest that serial murderers spend considerable time hiding their crimes. In support of this finding, James found in his study of 28 serial murderers that 64% of the killers examined tried to conceal the bodies of their victims in a location where they would not be found immediately.[154] Interestingly, however, a study that looked at child murderers found that 17% of child killers openly placed their victims' bodies to ensure discovery.[156,169]

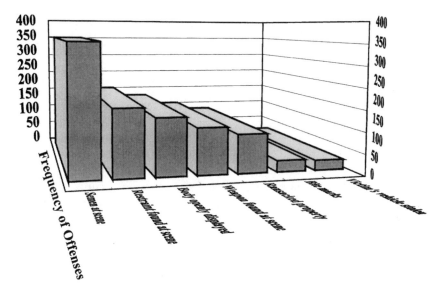

Figure 9.8 Actions Indicating the Killers' Forensic Disorganization

9.8.4   Weapon Found at the Crime Scene

One variable that is most likely to forensically link the killer to the murder is the discovery of a murder weapon. However, insofar as serial murder is concerned, offenders appear to be careful at not leaving their weapons behind at the scene. For example, only in (n = 109) 15% of the cases did the killer leave a weapon behind at the crime scene. This suggests that in incidences of serial murder investigators are unlikely to solve a series of murders by finding the murder weapon.

9.8.5   Ransacked Victim's Property

The next category focuses on the condition of the victim's property at the crime scene, whether indoors or outdoors. It also included personal items belonging to the victim found torn apart as if the killer was looking for something specific. The position or placement of the victim's clothing, for example piled neatly, was not included in this category. Ninety-one (or 13%) of the cases had incidences where the killer ransacked the victim's property.

9.8.6   Bite Marks on Victim

The next category includes any forensic evidence of bite mark(s) on the victim's body, including any evidence of chewing on a particular body part, which occured in 27 (4%) of the cases. This variable, if present in a series of murders, could forensically link the crimes to a suspect. For example, a bite mark was one of the key forensic clues that helped to convict the serial murderer Ted Bundy.[115]

9.8.7   Victim's Vehicle Stolen

Stealing the victim's vehicle was included in the forensic disorganization category because in most cases taking the victim's vehicle suggests that the crime is unplanned. Equally important, however, is the fact that chances are the killer will leave evidence in or on the vehicle, such as weapons or fingerprints, that could later be used to link him to the crime. In 24 (3%) of the serial murder cases, the offender stole the victim's car in order to escape the scene.

9.9   Actions Indicating Killers' Forensic Organization

9.9.1   Body Hidden

In a study by Gee, he discusses a type of serial murderer who secretly hides the victims' bodies and tries to conceal the crimes.[169] Gee suggests that the absence of the victims from the community is not noticed and their bodies are discovered by chance. This category included cases where the victim's

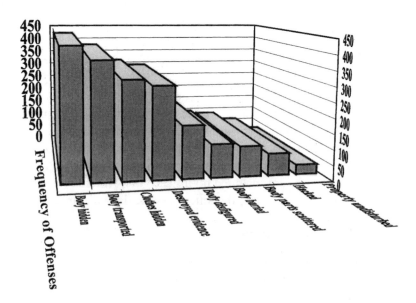

Figure 9.9 Actions Indicating Killers' Forensic Organization

body was found hidden. In other words, the body could not be visually seen with ease. This variable did not include victims who were buried. Looking at the first column in Figure 9.9 above, we see that in over half of the serial murder cases (n = 427 or 59%) the offenders hid their victims' bodies. One of the most common reasons for hiding the victims is that when they are found, it is often hard for pathologists to determine an identity because their remains have decomposed. According to a study by Holmes and Holmes, for the serial murderer, learning how to dispose of bodies takes the same form of any other social learning process; the offender personally learns the most beneficial manner of disposing of his victims.[50]

9.9.2   Body Transported

The next category includes cases where the victim's body was moved from the assault or murder site to the disposal site. This includes the offender either moving the body by foot or transport. The number of cases in the present study that involved killers who moved their victims' bodies was (n = 382) 53%, which is lower than that found in a study by James; he reported that of the 28 serial murderers in his study, 68% of the time the bodies were moved from the location where the women were killed.[154] Transporting the victim's body from the actual murder site to another location provides the killer with some comfort; traces of forensic clues that he might have left behind at the murder scene can no longer be discovered.

9.9.3   Clothing Hidden

The next variable describes an offender who intentionally hid his victim's clothing to avoid detection. This also includes any burning of the victim's garments. It was found in 321 (44%) of the cases the killer took forensic caution by hiding or destroying his victims' clothes. This act suggests that the offender is well aware that forensic clues, including hairs and fibers, can transfer from his body to the victim's clothing.

9.9.4   Offender Destroyed Evidence

The next category characterizes those serial murderers who have performed some act which can be interpreted as interference with the possible forensic examination of the crime scene or victim. This would not simply refer to wearing gloves, which is a common practice among most criminals, but rather would involve such activities as wiping and washing the victim, as well as removal from the scene of incriminating articles or other evidence. The number of cases where a killer took measures to destroy or attempt to destroy physical evidence was 301 (or 41%). Although less than half of the offenses involved killers who cognitively planned to hide their crimes by getting rid of evidence, the finding does provide a glimmer of hope to investigators; a possibility that traces of the killer's shadow will be left behind at the crime scene.

9.9.5   Victim's Body Disfigured

The next category describes the removal of body parts in order to hide the victim's identity and to destroy evidence. In 173 (24%) of the cases, this form of body disposal was used. The finding suggests that in some serial murders, the killer will go to extreme measures to hide forensic clues to avoid detection.

9.9.6   Victim's Body Buried

This variable describes cases where the victim's body was found partially or completely buried in the ground. This category does not include bodies that were completely or partially covered up by articles, materials, or brushes. In only 109, or 15%, of the serial murder cases in this study did the killer bury his victim. While this percentage figure is relatively low, considering the number of offenses (n = 728), the finding does support research by Gee that there is a subgroup of serial murderers who go to great lengths to conceal their victims' bodies.[169]

9.9.7   Body Parts Scattered

This variable describes offenses where the victim's body parts were found scattered away from the general area where the body was discovered. This category also includes any body part found at a distance from the crime scene area. For example, the serial murder team of Charles Ng and Leonard Lake buried some of their victims miles away from where they were murdered.[173] In the present study, (n = 99) 14% of the cases involved killers who scattered their victims' body parts. The low frequency may suggest to investigators that this action is a signature behavior.

9.9.8   Property at Crime Scene Undisturbed

The next variable describes cases where the victim's property at the crime scene was found in its original form. In other words, the property was left undisturbed. While this variable may appear out of place in the evidence of organizational category, it should be pointed out that usually in cases were the killer enters the victim's home, he tends to steal items. Therefore, cases where the offender does not disturb the victim's belongings could indicate that the murder per se was the most important goal. In 32 (4%) of the serial murder offenses in the present study, the killers left the victim's property untouched during the crime.

9.10 Summary

This review of the crime scene actions of serial murderers revealed some agreement with other researchers. However, there are several inherent weaknesses with many of the previous research studies on serial murderers. First, many of the researchers have grouped serial and mass murderers together. Secondly, most researchers have limited themselves to studying sexually motivated serial murderers, thereby omitting many other murderers whose killings may be expressive or out of rage. Thirdly, outside of Hickey's study of 203 serial murderers, there is no other study, other than the current one, that has looked into a range of different aspects of the serial murderer's crime scene actions. For example, in this chapter, it was found that blitz attack was the most frequent way of accosting the victim, compared to using a con or ploy approach.

Other findings indicated that the majority of serial murderers plan some aspects of their crimes. For example, in 86% of the cases, the offender preselected his weapon, and 49% of the time, his restraining device.

One of the more important findings was that there is a subset of serial murderers who primarily targeted and murdered their victims indoors. For example, in 18% of the cases the killer forcibly entered his victim's home, while 16% of the cases involved entries made at night.

Additional findings of the chapter were that the dominant method of sexual degradation of the victim was vaginal penetration. However, interestingly, in 48% of the cases the victim was subjected to sadistic torture. For example, consider the variable, piqueurism. There were 10% of the cases in this book which involved this form of aberrant behavior. Piqueurism has not been incorporated into one empirical study of serial murder until the present one, although it has been discussed on a theoretical level.[170]

Overall, the results suggested that generally serial murderers reveal organized behavior at their crime scenes. In 59% of the cases the killer hid their victims' bodies, and 44% the victims' clothing, while only 42% left semen at the crime scene. Broadly, the results of the chapter provided important relationships that could be essential to classifying the crime scene actions of serial murderers. This is the focus of the next chapter.

Smallest Space Analysis (SSA-I) of Crime Scene Behaviors

To reemphasize, there is a fundamental problem which handicaps our understanding of serial murder. This is the fact that serial murderers are an extremely heterogeneous population which has not on the whole been classified into meaningful groups. A serial murder, whether for sexual sadistic purposes or revenge, is just a label for what is in fact a quite complex behavior. These labels tells us little about the individual who carries out such behavior. Yet we tend to think of rapists, for instance, as members of a group more like each other, and researchers try to understand their behavior based on one aspect of that behavior: choice of victim. In other, nonsexual offenses, such as burglary or domestic homicide, no other consideration is given to such things as personalities of thieves or murderers, or a social psychology of stealing or killing. However, the literature often refers to sex murderers as if they can be distinguished by phrenology or some other aspect of their intra-psyche.

10.1 Modeling the Crime Scene Actions of Serial Murderers

To avoid the current difficulties with serial murder classification models discussed in the previous chapters, it is necessary to establish on the basis of empirical evidence the groupings of crime scene behaviors. The first stage of this is to identify the behaviors that distinguish offenders from each other. By assigning scores to individuals, using a combinations of facet scores, it should be possible to create an empirically valid classification model. Once the facets have been derived with some consistency, it should be possible to produce combinations of them so that a structured classification model can be prepared against which to establish offender themes and characteristics. To test the relationship between the crime scene actions requires systematic analyses of all the source materials. Facet Theory is a procedure especially appropriate for fields of research where there are no clear existing structures known to exist within the data.[90]

By applying Facet Theory to structure the Q matrixes, it is hypothesized that there are two faceted, mutually exclusive sets of items that make up an offender's interaction with his victims. The two facets and their elements, as discussed earlier, are

1. the behavioral organizational components (i.e., cognitive and affective)
2. the attachment components (i.e., object and vehicle)

It is therefore hypothesized that the analysis of the Q matrix will reveal four combinations of the two facets, termed "themes of behavior" which describe the serial murderers' modes of interaction with their victims.

10.2 Explanation of the Smallest Space Analysis Procedure

A brief description of the SSA procedure was outlined earlier in the methodology chapter. However, a more detailed description will be presented here. Smallest Space Analysis (SSA-I) is a nonmetric Multidimensional Scaling procedure, most frequently used in Facet Theory.[90,174,175] SSA enables explanatory models to be derived from data not readily amenable to conventional statistical analysis, because it imposes little *a priori* structure on the data, unlike Factor Analysis. SSA is appropriate in many psychological studies, such as the present one, as psychological hypotheses are usually about the relative associations between entities rather than their absolute differences.[87] SSA was used to determine the underlying structure in the crime scene actions of serial murderers, evolving them into specific hypotheses for close empirical testing.

The SSA representation of the coefficients matrix is nonmetric, meaning that no attempt is made to specify in advance a particular monotonic function that transforms the coefficients into distances. It is only the rank order of the coefficients, not their numerical values, that is preserved by the SSA mapping.[88] Other methods of showing relationships between variables of behavior could have been performed on the data in a process of variable to variable analysis. For example, cross-tabulation of every variable with every other would have found some co-occurrence, but the results would have been non-multivariate and very difficult to interpret. Also, qualitative, dichotomous data are not amenable to examination by methods which assume distribution and mathematically manipulate mean.[176] Rather, a multivariate analysis of the covariance between the variable behaviors is the most interpretable and robust method for data that are produced as qualitative, non-parametric categories in dichotomous form.

The SSA program computes iterations comparing the rank order between the correlation matrix and distance matrix, adjusting the spatial representation until the minimum of stress is reached within a designated number of iterations. The analysis provides a stress measurement called the Coefficient of Alienation, which is used to end the iterations. The Coefficient of Alienation gives a general indication of the degree to which the variables intercorrelate and are represented in the plot by their corresponding spatial distances. The smaller the Coefficient of Alienation, the better the fit. An acceptable Coefficient of Alienation level is 0.2 or below.[177] However, Donald and Canter argue that the most important principle of SSA is the interpretability of the structure. They point out that the Coefficient of Alienation is taken as an indication of goodness of fit between the correlation matrix and the geometric plot, the criterion for acceptability is most often taken to be the interpretability of the solution.

10.2.1 Preparing the Data for the SSA

As previously mentioned, variables selected for the analysis were written as dichotomous data, the score of "0" representing absence of the behavior in the crime, "1" representing presence of the behavior in the crime. Coding the data in dichotomous form enables a particular association matrix of co-occurrence to be produced, thus permitting the SSA program to construct the distance matrix from which geometric orientation or mapping is reproduced. Coding the raw data matrix in binary "0" and "1" format made the data amenable to a suitable association coefficient.

Sixty-five variables representing the crime scene behavior of U.S. serial murderers were drawn from a content analysis of police files, court transcripts, and the HITS database, as discussed in Chapter 5. Data from these sources formed the original numerical profile matrix. The thematic approach to modeling the behavior of serial murderers required assigning a score to the relevant variable, dependant on the offender having engaged in that particular action.

The variables were drawn from the list in Appendix A and directly related to the offender activity during the crime. Crime scene variables that the police would have no knowledge of prior to the case being solved were deliberately excluded from the analysis. For example, it is highly unlikely that police would know if the offender had used alcohol prior to committing the murder or whether the offender's vehicle was old or new.

Three sample raw data matrixes of 96 offenders and 96 offenses, first, middle, and last, formed the association matrix that was analyzed by SSA. The SSA program computes correlations, or in the case of this study, offense behavior of association coefficients of the co-occurrence of behaviors. The SSA then rank orders these correlations, transforming the original rectangular input data matrix to a triangular inter-variable distance matrix.

Data on 65 crime scene variables were analyzed by Smallest Space Analysis, employing a process of local monotonicity and Jaccard's coefficient of alienation within one to three dimensions. Jaccard's coefficient is the most appropriate association coefficient for dichotomous data. Research by Breakwell and his colleagues point out that Jaccard's coefficient is useful where the variables are derived from content analyses or where joint absence does not necessarily constitute agreement.[178] The association coefficient produced between each variable is simply a measure of co-occurrence. The co-occurrence measures the frequency of the "1" "presence." This process plays a major role in the SSA's Jaccard's association coefficient where the high frequency variables have the most likely chance to co-occur. In regards to the SSA configuration, this means that the very high frequency variables may appear close together in the plot. However, the co-occurrence of the variables in the plot remains subject to the rank order correlations of other variables included in the analysis. Low frequency variables are not constrained by the algorithm process.

The rank order of the distance between two points is inversely proportional to the rank order of strength or weakness of their original correlations. The SSA program then plots the variables as points in Euclidean space, in such a way that the higher the correlation between two variables, the closer the variables are in the geometric space.[179] The relationship between variables plotted in the geometric space is based on the assumption that the underlying structure will most readily be appreciated if the relationship between every variable and every other variable is examined.[174]

10.3 Procedure Rationale

Subjecting variables of a content universe to SSA has two major roles. The first role is exploratory in nature. In this role, prior to the formulation of facets, a content universe may be exposed to analysis to establish partitioning which then may be used to develop facets. The exploratory approach is appropriate when the subject matter is relatively new, or where there are no empirical studies arising from the literature. For example, in the serial murder literature, there is sufficient history to derive operational definitions concerning the crime scene actions of serial murderers. However, there are no empirical studies linking crime scene behavior of serial murderers or offense behavior to background characteristics. Therefore, it is important to establish that, on an empirical level, there are facet themes of behaviors in the crime scene actions of serial murderers.

For this book, one exploratory analysis was performed on the first murders in each offenders' series. The second role of SSA was confirmatory. In this role, the SSA was employed to confirm the facets and facet elements derived from the exploratory SSA. Two confirmatory SSAs were thus performed on the middle and last murders for each offenders' series. Both as an exploratory and confirmatory analysis, SSA has the ability to raise new hypotheses worthy of further examination.

The multivariate approach to modeling the behavior of serial murderers allows all the aspects of a particular domain, as in this study of crime scene actions, to be examined in context — revealing substantive and underlying structures. For example, in the case of serial murder, it would be anticipated that in accordance with the cognitive element, variables representing high self-awareness and personal attachment to the victim, such as postmortem sex and disfiguring the body, will be featured as neighbors in the spatial plot; while it would be anticipated that in accordance with the affective element, that those variables with low self-awareness and impersonal attachment to the victim, such as victim left fully dressed, incomplete sexual assaults, and leaving forensic clues behind at the scene, will tend to co-occur as neighbors in the SSA plot.

Facet Theory provides other MDS procedures which allow multivariate data to be further exposed and understood for their intrinsic structure. One such method is Partial Order Scalogram Analysis (POSA). An explanation of POSA and how it is used to explore the consistency of behavioral themes of serial murderers will follow later. For now, the application of SSA to a sample of 96 serial murderers and 96 offenses is presented to demonstrate both the exploratory and confirmatory possibilities.

10.4 Smallest Space Analysis SSA-I: Results

10.4.1 Interpretation of SSA Configurations

Figure 10.1 is a plot of the first by second dimensions of the three-dimensional solution. The numbers inside the squares correspond to the variable definitions, which are in Table 10.2. The SSA of offense behavior produced a coefficient of alienation as 0.26 in 6 iterations. The coefficient of alienation indicates how well the program represents the spatial distance and orientation of the variables to the association matrix. While the coefficient of alien-

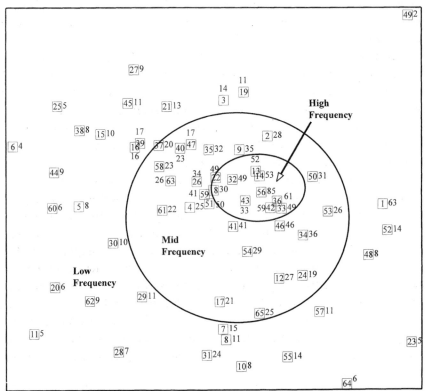

Two-Dimensional Plot
Coefficient of Alienation = 0.268
n = 65 Variables
n = 96 Offenses
n = 96 Offenders
Numbers in squares correspond to variable definitions in Table 10.2
Numbers outside of squares are frequency of crime scene actions

Figure 10.1 SSA Frequency Plot of Crime Scene Actions: First Murder in Series

ation is somewhat high, it is still within the realms of facet acceptability and may be due to the use of real-world data.

Regional hypotheses relate to several roles that the content facets of the variables can play in partitioning the SSA.[179] Regional hypotheses were used to provide statistically derived distinctions between offender activity in serial murder. The SSA configuration was examined to identify regions of the SSA plot in which crime scene behaviors appeared to have a coherent interrelationship, which is described by affective and cognitive element titles.

By examining the interrelationship of the variables in the SSA plot, regions were identified and partitioned by imposing boundaries which indicate elements of the facet. The partitions drawn on the SSA plot indicate conceptually distinct regions, or elements, that contain interrelated variables with a common theme. The boundaries imposed by interpretation of the plot relate to the role played by the facet. It should be noted that "regions" are not clusters.[147] Two facets describing four themes were identified as hypothesized, which are discussed in the following section.

10.5 SSA Results for the First Offense Series

The exploratory SSA, using the first offenses from each series, produced variables spread over most of the plot, with a central core of variables located in the middle, just to the right of the plot. From the central region, the crime scene variables spread out towards the edges of the plot, decreasing in number the further the distance from the central region. Analysis of frequency for the 65 variables, across the 96 offenses, indicates that this was the result of the presence of a modulating facet for frequency (see Figure 10.1). Briefly, a modulating facet is circular shaped with bands around a common origin.[179] Levy's research in discussing the modular role points out that a simple ordered facet can play a modular role; namely, have a correspondence with distance from the origin.[179]

10.5.1 Focal Aspects of Serial Murder

In Figure 10.1 the highest frequency variables located in the center region means that they have co-occurrence with each other and surrounding variables. Variables in the central core are thus items that are shared by the majority of the serial murderers in this study. As such, the variables were not likely to have a discriminating function in describing serial murderers by variations of behavior. The centrality of the highest frequency items is not a function of the coefficient; it simply means that the higher frequency variables have greater co-occurrence of common behavior in serial murder. The center of the innermost region can be thought of as the center point of the space, and intercorrelations between items in the innermost region will be higher than intercorrelations between items in outer regions.[180]

The layout of the variables in the center region gives an indication that those behaviors related to preplanning, control over the victim, and destruction of evidence are the most common in serial murders. For example, variables (V18) bound with rope, (V56) weapon preselected by offender, and (V33) clothing ripped/torn indicates control. Moving to the mid-band of frequency, we see behaviors that have to do with more involvement with the victim, either in a personal or impersonal way. For example, holding the victim captive (V27) is personal while blindfold (V5) is impersonal. The outer cord region consists of variables that involve acts with the victim after death. For example, (V25) anthropophagy and (V64) victim's vehicle stolen are actions preformed after death; however, anthropophagy is seen as personal, whereas stealing the victim's car is impersonal. The relationship that these actions have suggests that there is substantive order in the data.

The frequency plot is best understood by considering some variables in detail. Appearing very close to each other in the central region are variables (V33) clothing rip/torn, (V36) personal items stolen, (V42) vaginal penetration, (V43) anal penetration, and (V56) weapon preselected by offender. In the top band of the central region are variables (V13) victim's body hidden, and (V14) victim's body moved. Located on the left band of the central region are variables (V32) victim found nude, (V22) restraint brought to the scene by offender, (V18) victim bound by rope, and (V51) the type of weapon was a knife. Frequency for each variable in the central band region is plotted next to the variable square.

Several important relationships are revealed by the SSA analysis. For example, the act of removing personal items from the victim was found to be a common behavior in this sample of serial murderers, with a frequency of 61%. Variable (V36), personal items stolen from victim, is located in the central region, at the lower left side of the band. Stealing personal items from the victim's body could have distinct meanings. On the one hand, the action could reflect a killer who retains souvenirs for reflection about his murders. In this instance, the behavior is cognitive laden. On the other hand, the behavior could be affective laden, where the offender steals for profit.

There are two variables common in this sample of serial murderers that suggests preplanning, which is an organized feature. The first preplanning behavior is variable (V56), offender preselected his weapon. This behavior was found to be the highest frequency variable most common in this sample of serial murderers. Variable (V56) frequency is 85%. Preselection of a weapon shows planning and is more cognitive laden rather than affective. The behavior may also suggest an offender who has criminal experience, or that he has rehearsed the crime over and over in his mind, or both. The second preplanning behavior is variable (V22), offender preselected a restraining device. This variable does not imply a type of restraint, only that it was carried to the crime scene by the offender. The frequency for variable (V22) is 49%.

Three post-offense, forensic awareness variables found to be most common in this sample of serial murderers are (V13) victim's body hidden, (V14) victim's body moved, and to a lesser extent (V32) victim found nude. Frequency for the three variables are 52%, 49%, and 49%, respectively. The presence of these behaviors suggest that in addition to planning the murder, the offender is aware that leaving evidence behind could link him to the crime. For example, hiding the victim's clothing reduces the chances of leaving forensic clues at the crime scene. One variable in the central region,

(V33) victim's clothing ripped/torn, is the only behavior that involves initial contact with the victim. The frequency for variable (V33) is 49%. Ripping the victim's clothing reflects affective behavior.

Two variables in the central core have a sexual component: (V42) vaginal penetration, and (V43) anal penetration. The frequency for the two variables are 59% and 33%, respectively. This finding suggests that sex does play a role in serial murder; however, it is not as dominant a focus as suggested by Ressler et al.[17]

Moving out from the central region, is a mid-band of frequent variables (17 to 46%) that surrounds the central core. The large number of variables in the mid-band region (23 in total) indicates that there were many behaviors that occurred in a variety of offenses. This finding supports Canter's suggestion that offenders operate from limited narratives, contributing to consistent patterns in general behaviors, and their behavior at the crime scene.[96]

The SSA of offense behavior common in serial murder provides possibilities for heuristic interpretation that goes far beyond the general notion of routine criminal behavior. Except for the central core variables, weapon preselected by the offender, personal items stolen from victim, and vaginal penetration, all other behaviors occur in less than 53% of the serial murder offense sample.

The potential combinations, inherent in the radial order, derive from previous SSA and from the fact that serial murderers have a common focus but with different emphases. This focus and the referents that make it up are given clearer meaning by considering those items at the center of the plot for the first offense series. The central core actions are shared most with all the others around them, and so are both literally and metaphorically central to the issues being examined — the focus of serial murderers. The following variables or actions seem central:

Victim's body hidden
Body moved
Victim found nude
Offender preselected a weapon
Personal items stolen from victim
Victim bound by rope
Victim's clothing ripped/torn
Weapon: a knife
Anal assault
Vaginal assault

The ten behaviors listed above, all central to serial murder, give the likely indication that the main focus in serial murder has most to do with controlling the victim, planning the crime, and covering up forensic clues to hinder detection. It was expected that if the central focus in serial murder was sadistic sexual acts, as suggested by the current serial murder literature, then variables such as use of a foreign object, sex organs assault, and postmortem sexual activity would be plotted in the central region. However, in this sample of offenders, although sexual activity was a component in serial murder, it was not the dominant sadistic focus often propounded in the literature.[17,50,51] For example, moving the victim's body and hiding the body indicates that the offender is attempting to destroy forensic evidence. Bringing a weapon to the crime scene suggests that the offender planned his crimes, while the use of a rope is a means of controlling the victim. The focus of the variables in the central region certainly raises questions about the restricted view of *Modus Operandi* (M.O.), implying some signature method of operating.

10.6 Facets of Behavior in Serial Murder

One plane of the two-dimensional SSA space is shown in Figure 10.2. The exploratory stage of the SSA analysis produced a Jaccard's association coefficient of 0.26 in 6 iterations. A clean structure is apparent in Figure 10.2. The SSA plot relates to the behavioral organizational facet and its two elements, affective and cognitive, as hypothesized.

10.6.1 Affective Element

For clarity, it should be reiterated that each of the 24 points in this space is a dichotomous variable as applied to the 96 serial murderers across their first 96 offenses. If a diagonal line is drawn across the plot, sloping uppers from left to right, it could be argued that those variables relating to affective aggressive actions from the offender's emotional state appear to the right of the diagonal. This region is therefore seen to comprise the affective facet.

Five variables — use of hands and feet as a weapon, restraint found, weapon recovered, weapon of opportunity, and crime in victim's residence — are plotted in what we would term the affective region. The location of these variables, in the lower part region, suggests that serial murderers who attacked victims indoors did not plan their crimes. The location of these behaviors in the low region of the plot supports part of the Facet Model of serial murder described in Chapter 3: affective laden offenders with low self-awareness are more likely to be disorganized. The emotional aspect in the murder is revealed by the killer leaving his victim fully clothed. This supports the original hypothesis that affective actions are immediate gratifications, where the offender has little or no attachment to the victim and spends very little time with the body.

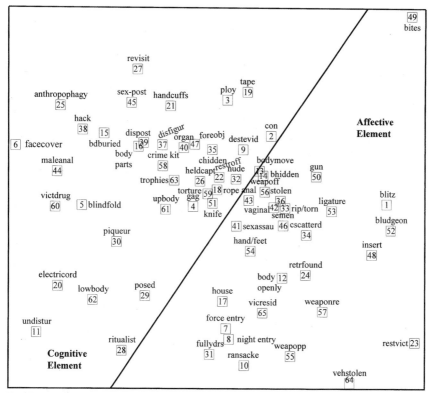

Two-Dimensional Plot
Coefficient of Alienation = 0.268
n = 65 Variables
n = 96 Offenses
n = 96 Offenders
Numbers in squares correspond to variable definitions in Table 10.2
and Appendix A.

Figure 10.2 SSA Configuration of Crime Scene Behaviors and Behavioral Organizational Facet Elements: First Murders in the Series

Six variables — blitz attack, bludgeon to death, attempted sexual assault, clothing scattered, clothing rip/torn, and semen found at crime scene — are found in the upper right region of the affective element. These behaviors further support the study's hypothesis that affective laden actions are disorganized, and displays evidence of rage.

Variables in the affective region thus support Meloy's opinion that affective violence is an immediate response to a perceived threat and results in a lowering of the sense of agency.[60] Meloy further points out that due to the low sense of agency, and the need to possess the victim's body, the focus on fetishistic behavior is relatively insignificant in the affective element.

10.6.2 Cognitive Element

It is argued that variables in the cognitive region are found to the left of the diagonal line in the SSA plot. Variables that could be seen as relating to control and sadism appear to be located here. Cognitive-laden behaviors were hypothesized as actions directed towards a goal rather than immediate gratification. Five variables — posing the victim's body, retaining trophies, ritualistic acts, postmortem sexual activity, and anthropophagy — suggest that murder is secondary to possessing the victim's body.

The hypothesis that cognitive-laden behaviors were more likely to reveal high levels of self-awareness (i.e.,organization) is supported by five variables — destroyed forensic evidence, crime kit, restraint preselected by offender, weapon preselected, and the use of a con or ploy to lure victims. These variables are located in the upper left quadrant of the SSA plot in Figure 10.2 and accords with the facet model of serial murder discussed earlier in Chapter 3. The co-occurrence of these variables in the same region supports Kopp's contention that offenders with a greater sense of agency during a crime are more likely to have control over their behavior.[162]

Seven variables — victim held captive, face covered, victim drugged, blindfold, victim gagged, bound with handcuffs, and bound with electrical cord — imply the offender is attempting to control his victim. This lends support to Meloy's proposal that offenders who plan their crimes also show high levels of organization and control during their crimes.[107]

Five variables — disfigured body, body parts scattered, body buried, body hacked, and victim's clothing hidden — suggest that the offender is destroying or attempting to destroy forensic clues that could eventually link him to the crimes. It is also worth noting that these variables co-occurred with those variables that showed preplanning and organization. The relationship between these actions departs significantly from the FBI findings on serial murderers who dismember their victims. Ressler and his colleagues suggest that serial murderers who dismember and mutilate have disorganized crime scenes.[17] However, as revealed by the SSA, serial murderers who destroyed evidence tended to have cognized actions, such as using a ruse to lure their victims, which are behaviors that indicate organization and high self-awareness.

Three variables particularly relating to some form of sexual activity are male sexual assault, anal penetration, and postmortem sexual activity. These behaviors suggest a sadistic fetishistic focus. These cognitive laden behaviors consistently co-occurred with variables that were high on mastery, such as preplanning and taking extreme measures to get rid of forensic evidence. This finding is somewhat different from previous studies on serial murderers who performed postmortem sex and retained trophies. For example, in their study on convicted serial murderers, Ressler and his colleagues and Douglas and his colleague argue that serial murderers who engage in postmortem sex are disorganized.[17,59] Clearly, in the cognitive region there are variables high on organization, such as con approach and crime kit, nested in with organized behaviors; for example, destroying forensic evidence, postmortem sex, and retaining trophies. The co-occurrence of behaviors such as postmortem sex, retaining trophies, and inserting foreign objects with evidence of cognitive planning and control variables certainly opens the debate on the FBI's organized and disorganized model as a profiling tool.

10.7 Attachment to Victim Facet

10.7.1 Victim as Vehicle Element

Again, one plane of the two-dimensional SSA space is shown below in Figure 10.3. If we draw a diagonal line sloping downwards, going from left to right, the actions below the diagonal line could be construed as representing the attachment facet element of victim as vehicle.

The act of blindfolding the victim suggests the offender may be fearful of directly facing his victim. *Fearful* attachment behavior is impersonal; the offender appears to show an approach-avoidance complex. This agrees with the hypothesis that the individual may have difficulties with social intimacy and is vulnerable in intimate relations.

Two variables in the SSA plot, semen found at the crime scene and body openly displayed, suggest the offender is not forensically aware and therefore disorganized. Five additional variables — ransacked, weapon hands/feet, weapon of opportunity, victim's vehicle stolen, and restraint found at crime scene — also give a likely indication that the crime was unplanned. However, three variables — face covered, victim drugged, and blindfold — also indicate that serial murderers who view their victims as vehicles could equally display organized-type behavior that suggests planning. This suggests that, as the model predicts, the victim as vehicle may include both affective and cognitive offenders.

10.7.2 Victim as Object Element

The actions above the left to right downwards sloping diagonal could be construed as describing the victim as object element. It was hypothesized that serial murderers who viewed their victim as objects display self-assurance and exhibit an ability to control their behavior during the crime. Two variables, con and ploy approach, suggest the individual has mastered the style of maintaining superficial relationships with others. This process, discussed in Chapter 3, comes from *dismissing* attachment behavior. *Dismissing* attachment involves personal attachment to the victim as though he or she is

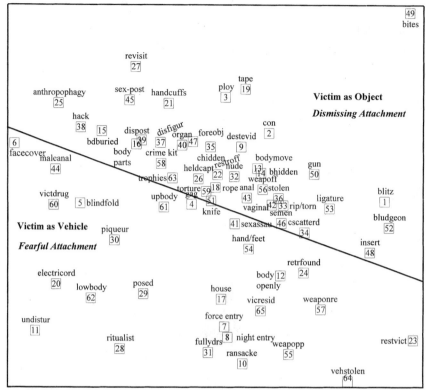

Two-Dimensional Plot
Coefficient of Alienation = 0.268
n = 65 Variables
n = 96 Offenses
n = 96 Offenders
Numbers in squares correspond to variable definitions in Table 10.2
and Appendix A

Figure 10.3 SSA Configuration of Crime Scene Behaviors and Attachment Facet Elements: First Murder in the Series

nothing more than a prop to be exploited. For example, the variables anthropophagy and postmortem sexual activity indicate high personal contact with the victim.

Correspondingly, the victim as object element appears to have other actions that indicate personal attachment to the victim as a symbolic object. Four variables — victim tortured, dismembered body, foreign object inserted, and sexual organs assaulted — show this apparent trend. Also, the co-occurrence of these sadistic behaviors with destruction of forensic evidence is a further indication that the killer has the ability to maintain control while performing acts of degradation. This finding echoes Terr's theory that individuals who perform morally repugnant acts have the ability to maintain their sadistic thoughts in tasteless chucks so they can tolerate them.[181] Similar behaviors were found in Meloy's predatory serial murderers classification scheme. Meloy discovered in the most sadistic serial murderers that their crime scene behaviors were organized.[107] The victim as object formulation for the serial murderer is to create an identity for the self. The act of establishing an identity through murder is described as *transcendence*.[75] Here, the offender creates a self through his crimes by creating dread in others, and by controlling life and death. However, in accordance with the two-faceted model, there are also variables in the victim as object element that indicate a lack of organization. For example, blitz and clothing ripped/torn, suggest that the murder is opportunistic and could appear to indicate a lack of planning.

10.8 Regional Themes in Serial Murder

Analysis of the first 96 offenses for 96 serial murderers found that, arguably, all four of the possible themes were present as hypothesized. The two-dimensional solution for the first offense series had a Guttman-Lingoes' coefficient of alienation = 0.26 in 6 iterations as previously mentioned. Figure 10.4 below shows the SSA configuration of offense behavior with the crime scene themes Affective-Vehicle (AV), Affective-Object (AO), Cognitive-Vehicle (CV), and Cognitive-Object (CO) transposed. Variables definitions are listed in Table 10.2. SSA of the data produced a configuration where the two facets created four structured regions, surrounding a central region of highly frequent variables. To repeat, the central region indicates behavior most frequent in serial murders, with the addition of a modulating facet of frequency. The SSA configuration in Figure 10.4 below is defined as a radex model.[101]

The descriptions assigned to each region express a common origin of the element items. The thematic titles are descriptions indicating a general underlying structure of the data. The thematic titles refer to the degree of control the offender has over his aggression during the crime and attachment the offender has with his victim. It should be emphasized, however, that the thematic approach to classifying the crime scene actions of serial murderers may be seen as behavioral and does not necessarily infer personality traits.

10.9 Cronbach Alpha Analysis

It is common in psychological research to attempt the measurement of variables for which there is no universally agreed measure. Any variable measurement, but especially data open to different interpretations such as crime scene actions, must be queried as to its reliability in terms of producing the same results on different occasions.

In order to establish on an empirical level that crime scene variables are structured into meaningful themes with similar psychological meanings, it is necessary to determine that the variables are indeed measuring related phenomena within each theme. Selecting items to form an appropriate scale is therefore a very important step that is both theoretically and technically sound. An appropriate test for measuring related phenomena is Cronbach's Reliability Alpha Scale.[182] A moderate Alpha scale score is .60.[182] Variables in each theme were submitted to Cronbach's Alpha Analysis. A total of 55 crime scene actions were analyzed. Variables from the SSA central region were not included in the analysis because the actions occurred most frequently; therefore, they would not be distinctive enough to classify the offenders. Alpha results for each behavioral theme are given in Table 10.1 below. All Alpha scores were acceptable.

Table 10.1 Cronbach's Alpha Reliability Analysis of Crime Scene Actions Comprising of Four Behavioral Themes

	CO Theme	CV Theme	AO Theme	AV Theme
Scaled Items N = 55 Crime scene actions	Held captive	Gag	Weapon gun	Weapon hands/feet
	Clothes hidden	Tortured	Ligature	Body openly
	Bound tape	Trophies	Bludgeon	displayed
	Crime kit	Upper body	Object found	Attempted
	Sex organ assault	stabs	inserted	sexual assault
	Disfigured victim	Ritualistic	Bite marks	Restraint came
	Foreign object	Piqueurism	Blitz	from victim
	Dismemberment	Lower body		Restraint found
	postmortem	stabs		Crime victim's
	Body parts	Body posed		residence
	scattered	Bound electric		Crime in house
	Body buried	cord		Ransacked
	Destroyed	Male anal rape		Forced entry
	evidence	Victim drugged		Night entry
	Con approach	Face covered		Fully dressed
	Ploy	Property at		Weapon
	Handcoffs	crime scene		recovered
	Sex postmortem	undisturbed		Weapon of
	Revisted crime	Blindfold		opportunity
	Hacked			Victim's vehicle
	Restraint			stolen
	preselected			Semen
	Anthropophagy			Clothing
				scattered
	n = 19	n = 14	n = 6	n = 16
∝ score	.9025	.6849	.6381	.6351

Let us consider these regions again in a little more detail.

10.10 Classifying Crime Scene Actions into Themes

10.10.1 Affective-Vehicle (AV) Theme

Sixteen behaviors in particular seem to indicate that the serial murderer attempts to commit, or at least is not deterred from committing, a completely emotional and unplanned murder where the victim is treated as a vehicle, to express their anger and rage. The following affective-vehicle thematic variables which co-occurred in this region are:

Weapon hands/feet
Victim's body left openly displayed
Attempted sexual assault
Semen found at crime scene
Victim's clothing scattered
Restraint found at crime scene
Restraint victim's clothing
Crime at victim's residence
Crime occurred in a house
Victim's property ransacked
Forced entry
Entry made during the night
Victim found fully dressed
Weapon found at crime scene
Weapon of opportunity
Victim's vehicle stolen

The affective-vehicle theme is distinguishable by the disarray in the crime scene. Out of all the facet themes, the AV seems to be the most unstructured. The victim is viewed as nothing but a vehicle on which to vent the offender's rage. Interestingly, the AV theme also reveals a subset of serial murderers who target, murder, and leave their victims' bodies in the same location, such as the victim's residence.

For example, in preparation for the crime, the AV offender may stake out a particular house where he will then break and enter to canvass for photos, names of children, and to get a feel for the general layout of the scene. He then will use force (V7) to enter the victim's home, usually during the night (V8). These actions suggest preplanning; however, the offender's actions during and after the murders are completely disorganized. The disorganization is demonstrated by the offender's use of a weapon of opportunity (V55) that is recovered (V57) at the crime scene, and restraint found at the crime scene (V24). Variables (V17) and (V65) certainly appear to support the hypothesis that there is a subset of serial murderers who attack victims

Table 10.2 Crime Scene Actions

Variable Number in SSA	Crime Scene Actions
1.	Blitz — Offender Initiated Contact with the Victim by Use of Blitz
2.	Con — Offender's Method of Attack was a Deception Or Con
3.	Ploy — Offender Initiated Contact with Victim by Use of Subterfuge
4.	Gag — Victim Gagged
5.	Blindfold — Victim Blindfolded
6.	Facecov — Victim's Face Covered
7.	Forced — Offender Gained Entry to Victim's Residence by Force
8.	Night — Offender Gained Entry to Victim's Home in the Night
9.	Destevid — Offender Destroyed/Attempted to Destroy Evidence
10.	Ransacke — Property At Crime Scene was Ransacked
11.	Undistur — Property at Crime Scene was Undisturbed
12.	Bdopenly — Offender Openly Displayed Victim's Body
13.	Bdhidden — Victim's Body Concealed, Hidden, Placed to Prevent Discovery
14.	Bodymove — Victim's Body Moved From Assault/Death Site to Disposal Site
15.	Bdburied — Victim's Body Buried Completely
16.	Bodparts — Victim's Body Parts Scattered
17.	House — Victim's Body Discovered in Building/House
18.	Bounrope — Body Bound by Rope
19.	Bountape — Body Bound by Tape
20.	Electricord — Bound Bound by Electrical Cord
21.	Bouncuff — Body Bound by Handcuffs
22.	Restroff — Restraining Device(s) Brought to the Crime Scene by Offender
23.	Restvict — Restraining Device(s) Victim's Clothing
24.	Retrfoun — Restraining Device(s) Found at Crime Scene by Offender
25.	Anthropophagy — Offender Engaged in Cannibalism/Drinking Blood
26.	Heldcapt — Victim Held Captive Prior to Being Killed
27.	Revisit — Offender Revisited the Crime Scene
28.	Ritualsc — Evidence at Crime Scene Suggested a Ritual Act on, with, or near the Body
29.	Bodposed — Victim's Body Intentionally Posed
30.	Piqueur — Jabbing Sharp Implements for Sexual Gratification
31.	Fullydrs — Victim's Body was Fully Dressed
32.	Nude — Victim's Body, When Found was Completely Nude
33.	Riptorn — Victim's Clothing Ripped or Torn by Offender
34.	Scatterd — Victim's Clothing (not on Body) Found at the Body Dump Site
35.	Chidden — Clothing (not on Body) Found at Body Dump Site was Hidden
36.	Stolen — Offender Took from Victim After Death Personal Items, e.g., Purse or Jewelry
37.	Disfigur — Offender Disfigured Victim's Body
38.	Hacked — Dismemberment Method was Hacked/Chopped Off
39.	Dispost — Dismemberment was Postmortem
40.	Sexorgan — Victim's Sexual Organs or Body Cavities Assaulted
41.	Sexassau — Offender Sexually Assaulted, or Attempted Sexual Assault on Victim

Table 10.2 (continued) Crime Scene Actions

Variable Number in SSA	Crime Scene Actions
42.	Vaginal — Type of Sexual Assault was Vaginal Sex
43.	Analsex — Type of Sexual Assault was Anal Sex
44.	Maleanal — Male Sexual Assault
45.	Sexpost — Sexual Assault was Postmortem
46.	Semen — Offender's Semen was Found on and/or in or Around the Victim
47.	Foreobj — Sexual Insertion of Foreign Object(s) into Victim's Body
48.	Insert — Victim on Discovery had Sexually Inserted Foreign Object(s)
49.	Bitemark — Bite Mark(s) were found on Victim's Body
50.	Firearm — Type of Weapon Used by Offender was a Firearm/Shotgun/Rifle
51.	Knife — Type of Weapon Used was Stabbing or Cutting
52.	Bludgeon — Type of Weapon Used was Bludgeon or Club
53.	Ligature — Method of Strangulation was Ligature
54.	Handfeet — Type of Weapon Used was Hands/feet
55.	Weaponop — Weapon of Opportunity was Used
56.	Weaponoff — Weapon was Preselected and/or Brought to Crime Scene by Offender
57.	Weaponre — Weapon was Recovered at the Crime Scene
58.	Crimekit — Offender Possessed a Crime Kit
59.	Tortured — Tortured Victims
60.	Victdrug — Victim Neutralized by Chemical Soporifics
61.	Upbody — Stab and Cutting Wounds Upper Body
62.	Lowbody — Stab and Cutting Wounds Lower Part of the Body
63.	Trophies — Offender Kept Victim's Items for Personal Gratification
64.	Vehstole — Victim's Vehicle was Stolen by Offender
65.	Vicresid — Abduction Site, Death Site, and Body Disposal Site Victim's Home

indoors. This finding contributes to the literature on serial murder, because currently there is no serial murder research that discusses issues related to offenders who primarily attack victims in their residences.

Three variables in the AV theme — attempted sexual assault (V41), body openly displayed (V12), and used victim's clothing as a restraint (V23) — are actions that appear to indicate low self-awareness, as well as impersonal attachment to the victim. Similar behaviors have been found in power reassurance rapists.[183] Often in crimes of this type, the offender's original intent is rape. However, during the attack the victim blocks the offender's advances; consequently, he reacts by killing the victim. Due to the emotional component, the preferred weapon is the offender's hands and feet. Other opportunistic behaviors in the AV theme are: scattering the victim's clothing, ransacking the victim's property, and stealing the victim's vehicle. These actions show that the crime is expressive where death is immediate and

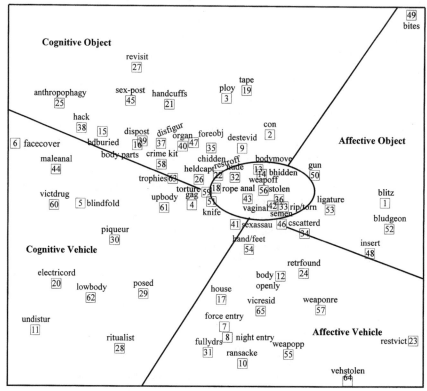

Two-Dimensional Plot
Coefficient of Alienation = 0.268
n = 65 Variables
n = 96 Offenses
n = 96 Offenders
Numbers in squares correspond to variable definitions in Table 10.2
and Appendix A

Figure 10.4 SSA Configuration of Crime Scene Behaviors: First Murder in the Series

stealing the victim's vehicle, variable (V64), provides a quick getaway. The AV theme thus agrees with Meloy's contention that affective violence results in low mastery and confusion at the crime scene.[60]

10.10.2 Affective-Object (AO) Theme

Of the two affective themes, the affective-object theme presents the more structured crime scene. Variables in the affective-object theme are located in Figure 10.4 in the upper right quadrant of the SSA plot. It is notable that there are few variables in this region. As previously mentioned, areas in a SSA plot which contain little or no points indicate weak areas in the data —

or in fact, missing facet elements. However, subsequent research on a different sample of serial murderers could be carried out to test for the existence of these missing elements. As it is, six crime scene variables seem to relate to the aspects of the AO theme:

Blitz attacked
Weapon a gun
Ligature
Bludgeon
Object found inserted in victim
Bite marks on victim

These six crime scene variables describe actions which appear to indicate that the offender possibly has an attachment to his victim as an object. For example, behaviors that indicate personal attachment to the victim are bite marks and object found inserted. These actions show the offender's callous disinterest in the victim as an actual person. Rather, the focus is on degradation of the victim's body; that is, the body has personal symbolic significance. Even so, the crime remains affective as some variables indicate that the offender is less than forensically aware; for example, he may leave an object inserted and bite marks on the victim. The emotional component in the AO theme also manifests itself by the victim being blitz attacked (V1).

A rage component in the AO theme is possibly revealed by the victim being bludgeoned to death. Excessive blunt trauma, usually in the face area, possibly indicates that the victim knew her attacker.[17] The variables bludgeon and blitz, nested together on the plot, suggest that offenders whose method of approach is blitz attack are more likely to kill their victims by bludgeoning them to death.

There are two distinct methods of killing the victim found in the AO theme. The first is the use of a gun (V50), an impersonal method of killing, because injury can be accomplished while maintaining a distance from the victim. The second method of death is personal, where the offender has more contact with his victims, i.e., ligature strangulation (V53) which requires more involvement and time spent with the victim, often a slower method of death.

A personal attachment variable that suggests the victim is used as an object to be exploited is (V48), evidence of a foreign object being inserted in the body cavities. Although foreign object is plotted on the boundary line in the AV theme, it has a higher association (.44) with bludgeon than it does with any of the variables plotted in the AV region. Therefore, it was decided to include the variable in the AO region because it helps define the theme more clearly. Some literature on serial murder suggests that inserting objects in the victim is a form of degradation.[17] The act could be considered a form of rage against the victim.

The AO theme seems to reveal a killer whose desire is expressive rage, but one that has a personal focus towards the victim. In this sense, the victim may hold a symbolic importance for the killer. The killer assigns his victims a more active and brutal role in the violent drama.[96] Similar behaviors have been found in anger-retaliatory rapists and signature serial murderers, where victims are blitz attacked, and the rapes and murders involved little planning.[50,170]

10.10.3 Cognitive-Vehicle (CV) Theme

The clinical literature on serial murder sees the main focus of serial murder as having sadistic sexual components mixed in with impulsive irrational behavior.[17,51,184] However, serial murderers who control their aggression while also committing sadistic acts seem to be relatively ignored. Fourteen variables found in the low left-hand quadrant of the SSA space, however, seem to deal directly with controlled aggression, planning, and torture of the victim; that is, they seem to represent the cognitive-vehicle theme. These are:

Blindfold
Trophies
Victim gagged
Victim tortured
Upper body stab wounds
Lower body stab wounds
Ritualistic activity
Piqueurism
Victim's body posed
Victim bound with electrical cord
Male sexual assault
Victim drugged
Victim's face covered
Property at crime scene undisturbed

Although the CV thematic behaviors seem to indicate more of a personal attachment to the victim than either of the affective themes, the focus is still impersonal. For example, (V30) piqueurism is small jab wounds made to the victim's body. Piqueurism is described as a sadistic act of feeling the ripping and tearing of flesh.[45] The stab wounds are usually found in the lower (V62) and upper (V61) regions of the victim's body. However, upper stab wounds plotted near the center region suggest that the victim's chest and facial areas were attacked most often. Stab wounds, in excess of ten or more, are indicated by variable (V59) victim tortured to death. The position of lower stab wounds (V62) in the SSA plot indicates that the stabbing of the victim below the waist is more a discriminating behavior. Other research on serial murder found lower stab wounds often occur in the form of mutilation to the victim's sexual organs.[63]

Although the CV theme suggests an offender who preplans certain aspects of his crimes, there appear to be some actions that are purely opportunistic. Thus, variables such as victim being drugged (V60) and property at the crime scene not being disturbed (V11) could be seen as organized actions. The disorganized actions are using an electrical cord (V20) and performing ritualistic (V28) acts on or around the body. The use of an electrical cord could be considered an opportunistic action because the weapon is usually obtained at the crime scene, while ritualistic acts have a greater possibility of evidence contamination, linking the offender to the murder. Several actions in the CV theme also appear to indicate an impersonal attachment to the victim, including blindfolding, face covering, and posing the victim's body. In interviews with imprisoned serial murderers, criminologist Ronald Holmes suggested that the offenders reported that the impetus to blindfold and cover their victims' faces was because faces screamed with terror.[50] As a result, the offenders sought to distance themselves from their victims.

Another important feature of the CV theme is that more of these offenders murder males. This is indicated by the presence of (V44) male sexual assault. The relative closeness of this variable to blindfold (V5) and victim drugged (V60) emphasizes Cartel's position that homosexual murderers achieve euphoria through torturing and killing people without experiencing reality disassociation, which accounts for their organization at the crime scene.[185]

Serial murderers with behaviors from the CV thematic region can be distinguished from other killers in that the central focus of the attack seems to be to maintain control over the victim. The power-assertive rapist has similar behavior to those found in the CV serial murderer. In particular, the rape is very brutal, and the rapist often blindfolds and gags his victims.[183] Most interesting is the relationship between gag and torture, which indicates that the CV type of murder is likely to be associated with controlled aggression and possibly sadistic behavior.

The trophy variable (V63), is also found in the CV region; this action appears to be one way in which the killer reflects psychologically about his or her crimes. The souvenirs may be body parts or in the form of small, personal items or clothing of the victim. The souvenirs retained by the offender are usually hidden in a private chamber of horrors along with various devices for torture and murder. For example, the location may be the offender's basement, attic, or an outside storage building.[56]

10.10.4 Cognitive-Object (CO) Theme

Nineteen variables possibly relative to the CO theme are to be found in the upper left-hand quadrant of the SSA. These behaviors are:

> Victim held captive
> Victim's clothing hidden
> Victim bound with tape
> Crime kit
> Restraint preselected by offender
> Sex organs assaulted
> Disfigured victim's body
> Evidence of foreign object being inserted
> Dismemberment postmortem
> Body part scattered
> Victim's body buried
> Evidence destroyed
> Con approach
> Ploy approach
> Handcuffs
> Sex postmortem
> Revisited crime scene
> Body hacked
> Anthropophagy

The variables show a sample of serial murderers who seem to distinctly plan and engage in the most sadistic forms of behavior, while being forensically aware that clues left at the crime scene may link them to the murders. A number of variables relate to the CO-type offender planning his crime and performing what could be construed as sadistic acts. For example, the actions sex postmortem, sex organs assaulted, and anthropophagy, embedded with behaviors such as crime kit and con approach, all indicate that the offender's actions are well thought out and cognized.

The cognitive-object theme is characterized by behaviors such as prolonged and bizarre assaults on the victims. The drive of serial murderers found in the CO theme seems to be to possess the victim's body; consequently, postmortem sex (V45) is the preferred choice of sexual activity. Research by Balint found a high order of mastery in his description of the qualities of a personal fetish.[186] Here, the victim is viewed as a worthless object raised to the dignity of a fetish, a lifeless thing that can be easily taken and possessed.

Other evidence of sexual exploration is revealed in the CO theme, such as in localized areas of the body in the form of skin tears or inserted objects (V47).

There are also a number of other variables that show the offender's fetishistic focus for sadism, including postmortem sexual activity (V45), victim's sex organs assaulted (V40), anthropophagy (V25) (i.e., cannibalism and drinking blood), and evidence of an object being inserted (V47), which all indicate personal attachment to the victim as an object. In this regard, the victim appears to be nothing more to the killer than a symbolic object with which to carry out his sadistic acts. Perhaps there is an implicit mastery of the victim in the form an object which is fueled through reenactment due to past traumatic experiences. Katz points out that reenactment to master negative life experiences is not only to triumph over the object but, like the sacrificial practice it is, to destroy flesh to restore the proper order of being.[75] The proper order of being is the illusion that there is no difference between reality and imitation.[187] This statement is best summed up by a convicted serial killer's personal perception of all future victims; each one is nothing more than a mere object, depersonalized in advance, with each existing only for himself and only to be seized and used as he sees fit.[50]

Other evidence suggests the view that the CO offender is organized in his behavior. For instance, several variables which indicate the offender is attempting to destroy forensic clues are: evidence destroyed at scene (V9), hacking the body (V38), burying the body (V15), and scattering body parts (V16), all actions which show forensic awareness.

The CO offender can also be distinguished by his ability to lure victims to their deaths using his charm while, at the same time, he is capable of showing sadistic behavior. Two variables in particular, con (V2) and ploy (V3), reflect the killer's ease in luring victims. The finding that more sadistic, organized serial murderers employ a ruse to trap their victims accords with James' study on 38 serial murderers, in which he found that 68% of the killers used some form of a con game to get the victim at a location where the killer then believed it was safe for him to carry out his assault and murder.[154] Likewise, Groth and his colleagues found similar behavior for the anger-excitation rapist.[183] Groth and his colleagues classified the anger-excitation rapist as an individual who finds pleasure, thrills, and excitation in the suffering of his victim. The killer's actions are sadistic and his aim is to punish, hurt, and torture his victim. Likewise, research by Holmes and Holmes describes the anger-excitation rapist as an organized offender who stalks his victims, and uses gags, bonds, and handcuffs.[50]

Using a plan of action, CO killers may equip themselves with a crime kit (V58) for torturing victims. The victim's body will subsequently exhibit signs of methodical mutilation in the form of antemortem and postmortem cutting, slashing, and stabbing. In these type of crimes, the victim may also be held captive (V26) for a time prior to the murder. It is also interesting to note that several other variables reflect the high degree of control that the CO-type offender has over his victims. Two variables in particular are bound with tape (V19), and handcuffs (V21).

Restraints and weapons are preselected and taken from the crime scene. Not leaving a restraint and weapon behind at the scene also suggests the offender is forensically aware. In sum, the CO theme reflects a serial murderer who is methodical, calculating, and cunning in the way he carries out his crimes.

10.11 Confirmatory SSA Results

The fact that some serial murderers commit a series of offenses introduces technical difficulties in developing classifications. One hypothesis explored in the present book is that the structure of the crime scene behavior found by SSA for the first offense series is similar for the middle and last offense series. In other words, it may be possible that offenders who change their actions in response to the reactions of the victim are not the same in different offense series. To examine this hypothesis, the offenders' crime scene actions for their middle and last offenses were analyzed.

Figures 10.5 to 10.8 show the SSA plots for the middle and last offenses. Figures 10.5 and 10.6 show the differences in the frequency for each variable, which are highlighted with a band separating the most frequently occurring variables, followed by the mid and then the lowest frequency variables plotted on the outer edge of the SSA. For clarity, each point is a variable describing offense behavior. The numbers refer to the variables as listed in Table 10.2 and Appendix A. The closer any two points appear, the more likely are the actions they represent to cooccur in offenses than in comparison with points that are further apart.

Again, a SSA was carried out on an association matrix of Jaccard coefficients, these being the most appropriate measures of association for this type of binary data. The two-dimensional solution for the middle offense series (Figure 10.7) has a Guttman-Lingoes' coefficient of alienation of 0.265 in 22 iterations, while for the last offense series (Figure 10.8) the coefficient of alienation of 0.268 in 23 iterations.

Looking at the SSA plots for the middle and last offense series, the configurations turned out to be very similar to the regional structure found for the first offense series, indicating that crime scene behavior, for at least this set of serial murderers, appears to be fairly consistent from one offense to the next.

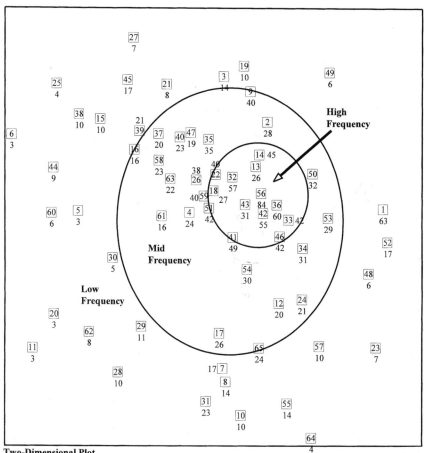

Two-Dimensional Plot
Coefficient of Alienation = 0.265
n = 65 Variables
n = 96 Offenses
n = 96 Offenders
Numbers in squares correspond to variable definitions in Table 10.2
and Appendix A

Figure 10.5 SSA Frequency Plot of Crime Scene Behaviors: Middle Murder in the Series

10.12 Summary

The sequence of variables in the SSA plots that make up a serial murderer's crime scene behavior can now be seen to form a radial order. Equally as important is the fact that across the three offense series — first, middle, and last — behavior appears to remain consistent from one offense to the next.

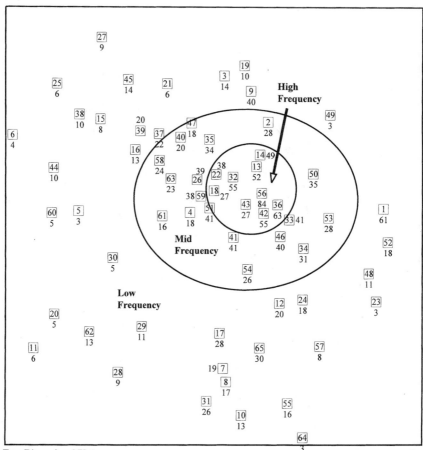

Two-Dimensional Plot
Coefficient of Alienation = 0.268
n = 65 Variables
n = 96 Offenses
n = 96 Offenders
Numbers in squares correspond to variable definitions in Table 10.2
and Appendix A

Figure 10.6 SSA Frequency Plot of Crime Scene Behaviors: Last Murder in the Series

The SSA results suggest that it is possible to classify serial murderers' aggressive behavior into two distinct facets as identified in Chapter 3. The first facet is behavioral organization which has two elements: affective and cognitive, describing the killers' aggression at the crime scene. The second facet is attachment, which also has two elements, victim as vehicle and object. These two facet elements describe the killer's personal and impersonal attachment to his victim, and the importance that the victim's body has for the offender.

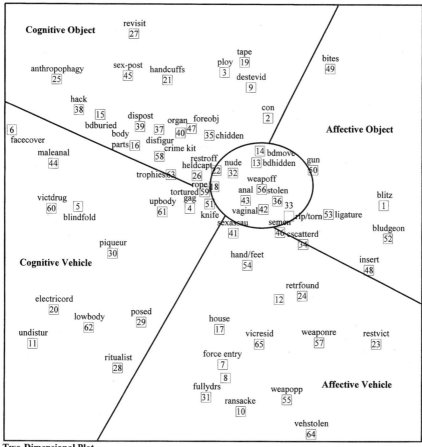

Two-Dimensional Plot
Coefficient of Alienation = 0.265
n = 65 Variables
n = 96 Offenses
n = 96 Offenders
Numbers in squares correspond to variable definitions in Table 10.2
and Appendix A

Figure 10.7 SSA Configuration of Crime Scene Behaviors Describing Four Themes: Middle Murder in the Series

The closeness of the activity in the central region, notably actions that showed preplanning, control over the victim, and destruction of evidence was noted as the central focus in this sample of serial murderers. This finding has considerable investigative weight, because traditionally the serial murder literature suggests that serial murderers who mutilate, perform postmortem sex, and indulge in cannibalism are disorganized and careless at their crime scenes, and that little preparation goes into planning their crimes.[17] However,

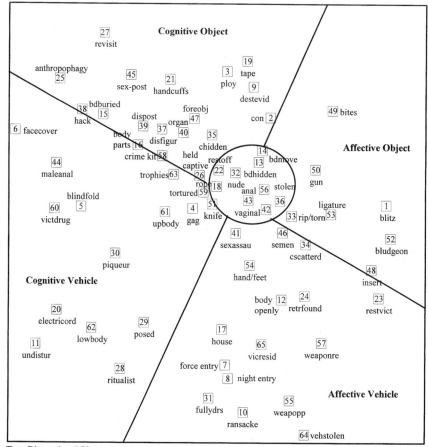

Two-Dimensional Plot
Coefficient of Alienation = 0.268
n = 65 Variables
n = 96 Offenses
n = 96 Offenders
Numbers in squares correspond to variable definitions in Table 10.2
and Appendix A

Figure 10.8 SSA Configuration of Crime Scene Behaviors Describing Four Themes:
Last Murder in the Series

the SSA results clearly point to a totally different reality. For example, the
cognitive-object thematic behaviors that indicate planning, such as using a
con approach and destroying forensic evidence, were consistently plotted as
neighbors with such behaviors as postmortem sex, inserting objects, disfiguring the body, and anthropophagy. Similar behaviors were plotted as neighbors in the cognitive-vehicle thematic region. For example, drugging the

victim and the use of a blindfold plotted together in all three offense series. These actions suggest preplanning.

Several important relationships were recognized that are currently not discussed in the serial murder literature. For example, behaviors that form the affective-vehicle thematic region suggest that there is a subset of serial murderers who primarily targeted, attacked, and murdered their victims indoors. In the affective-vehicle region, we saw behaviors consistently co-occurring, such as forced entry in the victim's residence during the night, and the victim left fully clothed. These actions appeared in the same region for all three offense series, indicating that there is likely a distinct group of serial murderers who entered victims' houses and carried out murders; they are quite different from those offenders who used a con approach and sadistically tortured their victims.

The results also found a subset of serial murderers, mainly those with AO thematic behaviors, who show a callous disinterest in their victims as persons. The killer's focus was on degradation of the victim's body and its symbolic significance. However, the crime remains affective due to variables that suggest the offender was less than forensically aware; for instance, he may leave an object inserted and bite marks on the victim. The analysis also found a third subset of serial murderers, mainly those with CV thematic behaviors. The CV crime scene seems to reflect an emotional component and an impersonal focus towards the victim. The central issue of the attack for the CV killer was to maintain control over his victims. For example, evidence that some victims were tortured and their bodies posed are two examples of control. The final subset of serial murderers was cognitive-object. CO offenders can be distinguished by their ability to lure victims to their deaths by using charm and, at the same time, exhibit the most sadistic behavior. The CO theme reflects serial murderers who are methodical, calculating, and cunning in the way they carried out their crimes. Also, forensic awareness is a strong attribute of CO serial murderers.

Partial Order Scalogram Analysis of Crime Scene Behaviors

11

SSA focused on the crime scene behavior of the offenders and preserved the similarity ranking among all pairs of behaviors; this was in accord with the hypothesized four types of crime scene themes. Having identified four theoretical behavioral themes in the SSA, the next step involves testing the hypothesis that there is an order in the crime scene behavior of serial murderers. Partial Order Scalogram Analysis, (POSA) is a technique for measuring individuals — serial murderers, in this book — with respect to a multivariate attribute. An appropriate procedure in this phase of the analysis, the substantive rationale of POSA is that it seeks to uncover structural relationships between crime scene behavior and facet themes, as revealed by the SSA.

11.1 Selecting Behaviors for Partial Order Scalogram Analysis (POSA)

The criteria for selecting behaviors to use in the POSA involved using most of the mid-frequency variables in the SSA having a frequency range between 17% and 50%. The mid-frequency actions are positioned to be more robust for depicting the overall crime scene behavior of serial murderers.[188] However, there were several variables from the mid-frequency region that were excluded from this analysis due to their ambiguities, such as upper and lower stab wounds; these actions are just as likely to occur across a variety of serial murders. The most frequently occurring actions in the SSA were also excluded in the present analysis. The reason for excluding the most common behaviors is they would not be representative of a theme and be unlikely to discriminate between different cases. The most frequently occurring actions are plotted in the central region of the SSA configuration, while the mid-frequency actions are located in the band surrounding the central region. An example of the frequency plots are given in Figure 10.1 in Chapter 10. Likewise, variables with low frequency, for instance those plotted on the peripheral edge of the SSA, are not likely to be representative of a theme either.[147] However, in addition to the mid-frequency variables, a few actions plotted on the peripheral edge of the SSA were included in the analysis. Although these variables have low frequency, they nonetheless play an important role in defining a theme. For example, the variable bite marks, from the affective-object theme, was included as being a part of the AO theme, even though the variable is plotted on the outer edge of the SSA. This is because bite marks indicate a personal attachment to the victim. This resulted in 38 crime scene variables.

The next step in the classification process involved determining whether the 38 crime scene actions have a linear structure. This was an important step in the study, because if the actions within each theme have no linear association, they are not likely to have a common order and will be unproductive for defining a theme. To test for linearity, a separate SSA was run on the behaviors that define each of the four themes. The results and SSA geometric plots are given below. Broadly, the plots suggest that there is linearity between the variables because they tend to form a straight line or group together. The SSA plots to follow are two-dimensional. However, if the plots were one-dimensional, if such an analysis were possible, the relationships between the variables may suggest linearity and could therefore form a Guttman Scale.

11.2 Linear Structure Between Variables in the Affective-Vehicle Behavioral Theme

Broadly, the SSA plot in Figure 11.1 shows that there is a moderate linear structure in the variables that make up the affective-vehicle theme. This finding does not negate the linearity, but it does suggest that there may be a second dimension. The seven variables that appear to form the linear structure are semen, weapon of opportunity, fully dress, clothing scattered, restraint victim's clothing, restraint found, and attempted sexual assault, with coefficients of .42, .44, .43, .42, .41, .40, and .40, respectively.

The remaining variables — ransacked, forced entry, body openly displayed, hands/feet, and weapon recovered — have associations of .35 and under, indicating that their relative geometric positioning is at some distance from those variables forming the central linear structure. Psychologically,

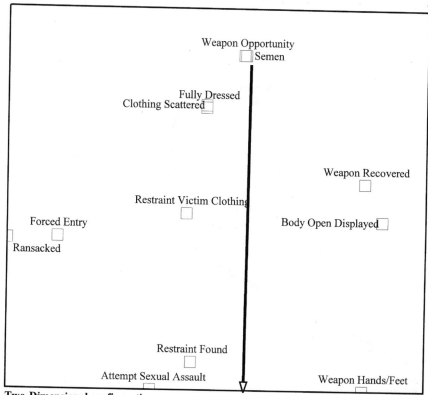

Two-Dimensional configuration
Coefficient of Alienation = 0.163
N = 12 variables

Figure 11.1 SSA Plot Showing Linear Structure Between Variables in the Affective-Vehicle Behavioral Theme

these four behaviors still play an important role in defining the AV theme; therefore, they remain a part of the theme.

11.3 Linear Structure Between Variables in the Affective-Object Behavioral Theme

The structure in Figure 11.2 forms more of a U-shape. In Facet Theory terms, this shape is indicative of variables that are quantitatively and qualitatively different.[188]

Nevertheless, the U-shaped pattern suggests in a broad way that the variables are linear. Note that two variables, ligature and gun, plotted toward the left-hand region, have coefficients of .40 and .41. Two variables, blitz

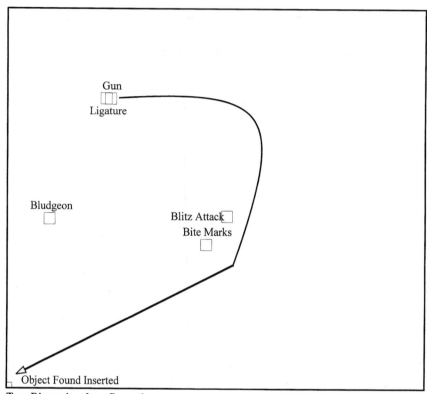

Two-Dimensional configuration
Coefficient of Alienation 0.10
N = 6 variables

Figure 11.2 SSA Plot Showing Linear Structure Between Variables in the Affective-Object Behavioral Theme

attack and bite marks, have associations of .34 and .35, respectively; however, they have a low association with the variable object found inserted, .12 and .14, respectively. One variable, bludgeon, plotted towards the left edge of the SSA, is not a part of the structure with a association of .10; however, it was decided to keep bludgeon as part of the AO theme.

11.4 Linear Structure Between Variables in the Cognitive-Vehicle Behavioral Theme

As in the previous SSA, a U-shaped configuration was found for the CV theme. This suggests that the variables are quantitatively and qualitatively different. Eight of the variables inside of the U-shaped have associations

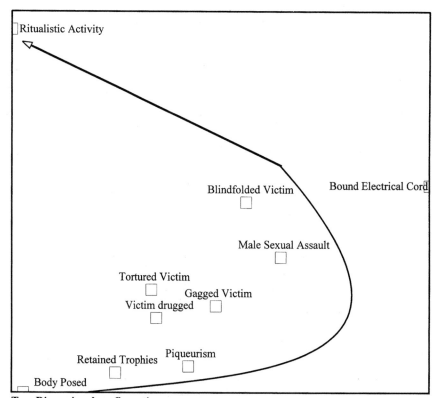

Two-Dimensional configuration
Coefficient of Alienation = 0.11
N = 10 variables

Figure 11.3 SSA Plot Showing Linear Structure Between Variables in the Cognitive-Vehicle Behavioral Theme

of .45 or higher, with one relatively high association for the variable tortured (.58).

The remaining two behaviors, ritualistic and electrical cord, are plotted on the edge and have low associations of .16 and .17. Although ritualistic was plotted on the outer edge, the action was instrumental in defining the CV theme.

11.5 Linear Structure Between Variables in the Cognitive-Object Behavioral Theme

As in the two previous SSAs, the structure for the cognitive-object theme is U-shaped (see Figure 11.4). The majority of the variables plotted have an

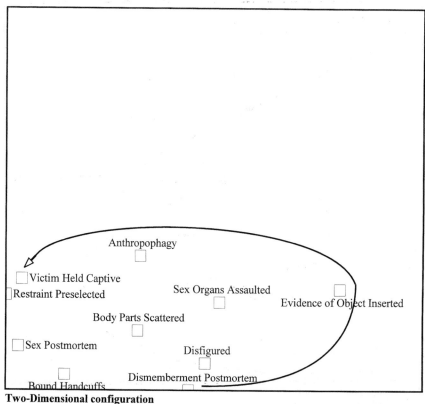

Two-Dimensional configuration
Coefficient of Alienation -= 0.09
N = 10 variables

Figure 11.4 SSA Plot Showing Linear Structure Between Variables in the Cognitive-Object Behavioral Theme

association of .52 or higher with the exception of one variable, bound with handcuffs, which has a low association of .33. This finding suggests that the variables appear to be reasonably linear and define the CO theme.

Broadly, the SSA results show that there are both qualitative and quantitative differences underlying the crime scene behavior of serial murderers. The findings also show how an empirical process was employed for selecting the variables used in classifying each theme. The general indication given by the SSA results shows that each group of behaviors that make up the four behavioral themes have a meaningful order to them, which does form a conceptual scale. The next step in the study was to employ Partial Order Scalogram Analysis (POSA) to test for a common order in each of the behavioral themes.

11.6 Scaling to Order the Crime Scene Behavior of Serial Murderers

Partial Order Scalogram Analysis (POSA) attempts to structure offenders according to fewer scales than the original number of variables used in the SSA. POSA empirically reduces the high number of profiles to an appropriate subset describing the dominant behaviors having the most influence in each crime scene theme. Research by Shye points out that "When empirical observations result in many profiles that are mutually incomparable, scales can often be found which reveal something about the structure of the concept being measured." [189] Shye goes on to argue that through POSA scaling, every individual can be assigned a new and shorter profile which lists his or her scores on the derived scales. The procedure provides the researcher with an opportunity to create fewer and possibly more fundamental variables for the contents investigated.

POSA has a structural hypothesis that individuals and attributes may be ordered along two dimensions of type and degree. POSA is a two-dimensional extension of the unidimensional Guttman Scale. It is a nonparametric multiple scaling method to measure individuals with respect to a multivariate attribute; in this analysis, crime scene behavior. This scaling process involves ordering elements on the basis of magnitude; for example, ordering serial murderers according to the extent to which they possess a particular behavior. However, multivariate attributes cannot often be scaled on a purely one-dimensional quantitative basis. Therefore, POSA provides a partial order scale in which qualitative variations in the data are represented in addition to quantitative variations.

POSA is a particularly fruitful approach to utilize in classifying serial murderers. In this book, the POSA procedure treats each offender as a profile of scores on a number of prescribed variables that describe each of the crime scene themes found in the SSA. In other words, mathematic scores of each offender are regarded as the profile of that individual. The application of the POSA procedure maximizes the underlying purpose of this study, by testing for order in the thematic behavioral variables shown to co-occur in the SSA.

The scaling procedure works by taking the profiles generated by each case for the selected thematic variables and scales them in relation to their overall cumulative scores across all the variables. The cumulative scores are a measure of the "quantitative" variation between the cases. This is regarded as a one-dimensional scale by common order, which is the same as the Guttman scale. In the cumulative scale, the profiles display complete order and are all comparable to one another. It can be stated that one profile is said to be greater than another only if it is larger or equal to the other in each and every score.[189] However, such a restrictive profile pattern is rarely produced when working with real-world data commonly found in police reports.

It is more common that the POSA profiles will display qualitative distinctions as well as quantitative ones rather than a complete order. To try this theory, let us consider two offenders' profiles, A and B, derived from the cognitive-object theme, which describes the most sadistic killer. Say that offender A has the mathematical profile 222221, which equals 11, while offender B has a mathematical profile of 111222, which equals 9. Briefly, as previously mentioned, "1's" indicate that the action is not present in the offender's profile, while "2's" indicate that the action is present. A serial murderer with profile A, 222221, has clearly been more sadistic in his murders than that of profile of B, 111222, in the sense of having committed more sadistic acts. However, comparing a serial murderer with a profile of 222111 with one whose profile is 111222 is more difficult. In the latter profile, we can see that both offenders have performed the same number of different types of behaviors, but they are qualitatively different. In terms of having a common order, the range of crime scene behaviors in the POSA plot must be meaningfully ordered with respect to a common content criterion. For example, in the cognitive-object theme, the ordering should be constructed in such a way so as to represent what is referred to as differing levels of personal attachment to the victim as an object; an offender with a high level of self-awareness who is sadistic in his crimes.

The POSA structure is interpreted diagonally, with the quantitative variation displayed along the two-dimensional "J" axis, and the qualitative variation along the "L" axis. Figure 11.5 shows the relative position of the "J" axis and "L" axis.

The advantage of POSA is that it facilitates the identification of the underlying themes found in the SSA, along a quantitative dimension as well as reflecting qualitative differences between the offenders' profiles. For example, one hypothesis is that serial murderers in the cognitive-object theme are likely to be sadistic and show organization at their crime scenes. If the analysis supports this hypothesis, then it is most likely that the POSA will plot sadistic and organized attributes in various high positions on the "J" axis. In contrast, a second hypothesis is that serial murderers in the affective-vehicle theme are more likely to commit emotional murders and show disorganization at their crime scenes. If the analysis supports this hypothesis, then it could be expected that behaviors indicating disorganization would be plotted high on the "J."

To that end, POSA is chiefly concerned with the problem "Given a set 'A' of observed profiles in N variables (Facet Themes) can we assign two scores — that is, a point in the coordinate plane — to each profile in 'A' so that for

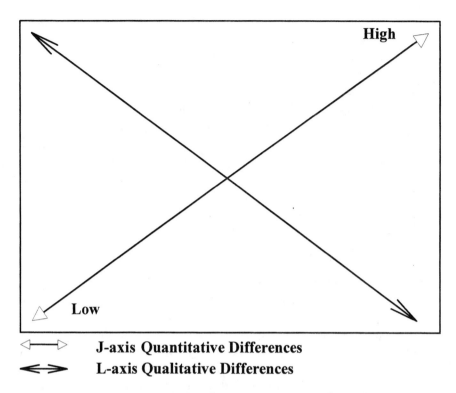

<table>
</table>

⟨————▷ **J-axis Quantitative Differences**
◀———▶ **L-axis Qualitative Differences**

Figure 11.5 Two-Dimensional Plot Showing POSA "J" and "L" Axes

two observed offender's profiles, their observed relationship would be correctly represented by their corresponding two-coordinate profile (i.e., one
quantitative and one qualitative)." In regards to this study it is then possible
with the minimal two-coordinate system to know the score for each serial
murderer and how each scored on a set of predefined behaviors in each theme
used by this empirical approach. It is also possible to explore in more detail
behavior that directly influences each one of the crime scene themes. This is
because of the knowledge that is acquired through the uncovering of the facet
co-relationships in the SSA. Therefore, this enables us to better understand
the complex interweaving of the interplay between the two facet elements,
affective and cognitive, and the four thematic classifications, affective-vehicle,
affective-object, cognitive-vehicle, and cognitive-object.

11.7 Individual Item Diagrams Partitioning

In interpreting a POSA plot, one is attempting to uncover groups of individuals who have a profile of behaviors in common. Thus, one considers

the distribution of offenders throughout POSA in relation to the "joint" and "lateral" axes. If a group of serial murderers who are located similarly on the POSA plot have characteristics in common, which can differ from the characteristics of offenders located on different parts of the POSA space, it can be suggested that particular behaviors are related to different types of offender characteristics.

Profiles are located according to the principle of contiguity. Thus, the more similar two profiles are, the closer they are in the POSA space. A plot is provided for each crime scene behavior, which is called an item plot. The individual item plots show the score of each offender's profile on that behavior. Also, the position of the points in the POSA space remains constant throughout all of the plots.

The individual item diagrams for each crime scene behavior are then partitioned in such a way that the regions of the space contain profiles with the same score on that item. With dichotomous data, these item plots are partitioned into two regions. First, a region that contains the majority of profiles where the particular behavior was present is represented by "2's"; the other region contains profiles where the behavior was absent, represented by "1's." The partitioning of the plots for each item may then be compared with the partitioning of each item diagram in order to reveal the relationships. For example, if two crime scene behaviors partition in the same direction, they can be thought of as both measuring a similar dimension or concept.

The role played in each item plot is discerned by the shape of the partition line. There are five main roles or types of partitioning the individual item plots; however, these are not always found in the analysis. The five types of partitions are shown in Figure 11.6.

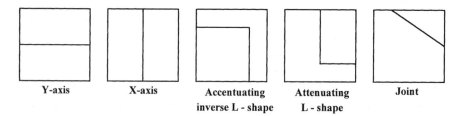

| Y-axis | X-axis | Accentuating inverse L - shape | Attenuating L - shape | Joint |

Figure 11.6 Five Types of POSA Item Partitions

The shape of line that divides the item regions for each type reflects the contribution that behavior makes toward shaping the main POSA space. The partitioning effects could be either polar, accentuating, or attenuating. The "X" axis runs vertically, and this type of partitioning constitutes one of two ideal poles of the scalogram. Profiles with this type of partitioning define the qualitative or lateral axis. The "Y" axis runs horizontally, and it provides the second of the ideal scalogram poles. This partition is orthogonal to the vertical partition and represents an independent or qualitatively different dimension. The inverse L-shaped partition is found with items playing a role of polarizers in the scalogram. This means high values on this item are associated with the extreme values on the lateral axis.[147] The L-shaped partitions are moderators of the scalogram. This means that high scores on this item are associated with middle values of the lateral axis.[147] The final partition is called a "Joint" and represents a quantitative distinction, so it is not qualitatively meaningful.

11.8 Coding the Data for POSA

Data coding for the POSA consisted of creating a new data matrix from the original data matrix of 96 offenders and 65 crime scene variables. The numerical categories were changed from "0's" to "1's" and from "1's" to "2's." The new coding allowed the data to meaningfully represent "1's" indicating that the behavior was not present in the crime and "2's" that the behavior was present. The next step involved taking each of the 38 crime scene variables and creating individual data matrixes. The task involved creating one matrix for each of the four behavioral themes for the first, middle, and last offenses. In all, 12 data matrixes were created for the POSA analysis. The rows represented the offenders or cases, and the columns each of the crime scene variables. Table 11.1 shows the variables associated with the four thematic regions taken from the SSA and subsequently used in the POSA.

For each of the four themes shown in Table 11.1, one POSA was run on each theme across the first, middle, and last offenses. The POSA results are discussed in the next section.

11.9 POSA Results for the Affective-Vehicle Theme

POSA results for the affective-vehicle theme are given in Figures 11.7 to 11.9. To facilitate the reader's understanding of the relationships between each of the themes, the POSA main item plots are grouped according to theme and offense series. For example, Figures 11.7 to 11.9 are POSA plots for the affective-vehicle theme as measured over the first, middle, and last offenses. Just to note here, in the POSA main item plots, variables printed in bold letters are associated with the solid lines, while variables that are not bold are associated with the broken lines. Variables with the broken lines indicate that they are a subset of the variable or variables that relate to the polarized solid lines.

Table 11.1 Four Thematic Regions and Crime Scene Antecedents Used in the POSA Analysis

	Affective Vehicle	Affective Object	Cognitive Vehicle	Cognitive Object
1	Forced Entry at Night	Blitz	Gagged Victim	Body Parts
2	Ransacked Property	Object Inserted	Blindfold	Handcuffs
3	Body Openly Displayed	Bite Marks	Electrical Cord	Restraint Offend
4	Restraint Victim	Weapon Gun	Ritualistic Activity	Anthropophagy
5	Restraint Found	Bludgeon	Body Posed	Held Captive
6	Fully Dressed	Ligature	Piqueurism	Victim Disfigure
7	Sexual Assault		Male Sex Assault	Dismember Postmortem
8	Weapon Hands/Feet		Victim Drugged	Sex Organs Assault
9	Weapon Opportunity		Tortured Victim	Sex Postmortem
10	Weapon Recovered		Retained Trophies	Object Inserted
11	Semen			
12	Clothing Scattered			

38 Crime scene variables

All POSA plots for the four behavioral themes across the first, middle, and last murder series show a substantial reduction of the potential profiles. For instance, for the cognitive-vehicle and cognitive-object behavioral themes, the potential number of profiles was 1024 or 2^{10}. For the affective-object theme, the potential number of profiles was 64 or 2^6, while for the affective-vehicle the potential number of profiles was 4096 or 2^{12}. The POSA substantially reduced all potential profiles to between 38 and 48 empirical profiles, showing that the combination of behaviors was far from random. In other words, there is a substantial order to the variables, meaning the behaviors are measuring similar intensity.

For purposes of understanding the interpretation of Figures 11.7 to 11.9, it is first necessary to understand that each point represents a profile describing a type of serial murderer. Where a number of offenders have identical profiles, then they are all represented by one point in the POSA space. For the AV theme, there were 12 crime scene variables used in the analysis. In the present set of 96 serial murderers, there were 45 different profiles for the first offense series, and 48 different profiles for the middle and last offenses. How well the profile coordinates in the POSA plot reflects the relative order of the empirical profiles is measured by the Correspondence Coefficient (*Correp*). An acceptable goodness of fit is approximately .90, signifying that 90% of empirical profile relations are reliably represented by the relative distances plotted. For example, the *Correp* for the affective-vehicle theme across the first, middle, and last offenses is .76, .72, and .74, respectively. The low *Correp* is most likely due to the use of real-world data.

The interpretation of the horizontal and vertical axes is derived by examining how each of the existing thematic behaviors relate to them. This is done in two ways. First, the main item plots are space diagrams in which the points are labeled according to the subject profile represented. The frequency of that profile is listed separately in the analysis. The POSA program also produces a subsequent set of plots called individual item plots. These profiles are spatially identical to the main item plots, but with differing labels at each point. Secondly, the statistical relationship of the offense variables to the vertical "X" axis and the horizontal "Y" axis can be gauged by examining the coefficient of weak monotonicity between the variable and the axis. The relationship between the crime scene behaviors in the affective-vehicle theme for the first, middle, and last offenses can be seen in more detail and more graphically by examining the distribution of the categories for each variable across the POSA space. The individual item plots for the AV theme across the first, middle, and last offenses are presented, along with their respective coefficients of weak monotonicity between each variable and the "X" and "Y" axes.

In examining the POSA plot in Figure 11.7, it is worth noting that the diagonal axis that runs from the bottom left to the top right reflects the overall quantitative order of the profiles. This is known as the joint "J" axis because the total scores added together have a meaning along this axis. For example, offenders that performed all 12 crime scene actions in the affective-vehicle theme would be plotted in the very top right-hand corner, having a profiling of 2222222222, while offenders that had none of the AV actions would be plotted in the far left-hand corner, having a profile of 1111111111.

The other diagonal axis, the "L" axis from the bottom right to the top left, is the qualitative direction. This diagonal axis is known as the lateral axis. For example, offender profile 10 is 2212112111, and offender profile 22 is 221111211, and both are located on the "L" axis. The similarities in the two profiles are appreciated by examining the placement of three variables: forced entry, ransacked victim's property, and victim found fully dressed. Looking at Table 11.2, from left to right, are the following variables: forced entry in the victim's home in the first column; ransacked property in the second column; and fully dressed in column six. The position of profiles 10 and 22 suggests that they are quantitatively similar, but qualitatively different from the likes of profile 15, 2111121112, which is located in the upper left region of the POSA plot. Although profile 22 and 15's total scores are the same — 13 — the variables they scored on are different.

On examining the POSA plot Figure 11.7 for the first offenses, we see that the profiles are mainly plotted along the "J" axis in the middle of the POSA space. Broadly, the POSA plots for the first, middle, and last offenses are very similar. Overall, the middle and last offense plots are similar to the first offenses in that all three, more or less, have a mixture of profiles that fall along the "L" (Qualitative) axis rather than the "J" axis. However, located in the middle and last offenses POSA plots, there are more distinct profiles falling along the "J" axis, indicating that serial murderers are performing similar behaviors and those behaviors are increasingly becoming stronger in magnitude.

The main item plots are best understood by considering that profiles located from the middle of the plot, spreading towards the right-hand region of the plot, are quantitatively different than those offenders' profiles located in the upper left-hand corner of the plot. So, for the affective-vehicle theme, this means that profiles appearing in the upper right and left-hand regions of the POSA space are said to be high on affective behavior and low on personal attachment. Profiles in the bottom left-hand corner of the POSA space score low on affective behavior, while profiles found in the right-hand corner of the plot indicate a high personal attachment or involvement with the victim.

Because the "J" and "L" axes are fixed in relation to the quantitative and qualitative properties of the data, the horizontal and vertical axes are therefore open to interpretation. However, the axes do provide an indication of the underlying themes that structure the affective-vehicle theme.

11.9.1 Interpreting the POSA Individual Item Plots for the Affective-Vehicle Theme

The "X" and "Y" axes have two different behavioral processes underlying the affective-vehicle theme. One process derives from the offender's attachment to the victim. For example, based on the definition of victim as vehicle that was defined in Chapter 3, individuals who fit this type of crime scene are considered as having *fearful* attachment, or impersonal attachment. To repeat, *fearful* attachment is where the individual has a fear of intimacy and is socially avoidant. Profiles of offenders with low impersonal attachment are found in the upper left-hand corner of the POSA plot. The second process is regarded as behavioral organization or degree of self-awareness. The AV crime scene is defined by a lack of organized behavior, sadistic actions, and personal attachment to the victim. In other words, the offenders' crime scene actions appear as though the killers spent a relatively short time with their victims, such as victim was left fully dressed and incomplete sexual assaults. As a result, the killers' interactions with their victims are impersonal.

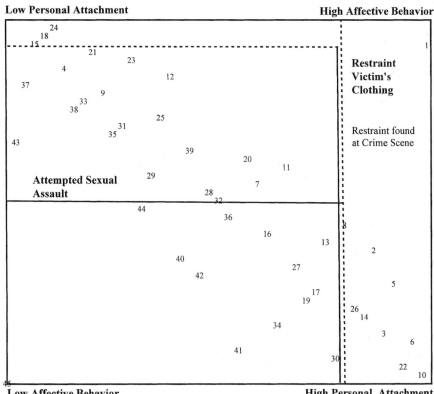

Figure 11.7 Main Item POSA Plot Configuration for the Affective-Vehicle Behavioral Theme: First Murders in the Series

The direct implications of the two distinct axes for the classification of serial murderers is readily appreciated by reference to Figure 11.10. This figure represents individual item plots of the 12 crime scene behaviors that define the AV theme for the first murder series. The plot shows a simplified summary of the partitioning of each variable on the POSA main item space shown in Figure 11.10. The relative position of the profiles for the first murder series, in relation to the "X" and "Y" axes, is found in the first two columns in Table 11.2. For example, one variable, restraint found at the crime scene, runs vertically and relates to the "X" axis for the first offenses, showing that those offenders who left a restraint at the crime scene are located in a rectangle in the bottom right-hand side of the plot.

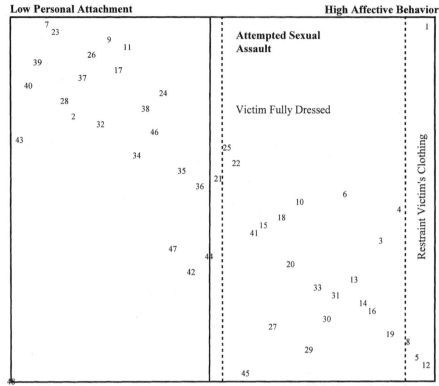

Figure 11.8 Main Item POSA Plot Configuration for the Affective-Vehicle Behavioral Theme: Middle Murders in the Series

Another interesting variable in the AV theme is victim's clothing used as a restraining device. The partition for the clothing as a restraint is called an accentuating inverse L, because the scores cross the lateral axis at the two outermost points, thus indicating the existing differentiation between the polar items. This suggests that restraint found and restraint as victim's clothing are statistically similar. The loadings of the coefficients of weak monotonicity in Table 11.2 between restraint victim $(X = .36)$ $(Y = .34)$ and restraint found $(X = .36)$ $(Y = .16)$ shows this apparent relationship. These two crime scene behaviors define the affective behavior. Referring to the description of the AV theme in Chapter 3, the presence of these two behaviors reflect a killer whose behavior is expressive, and the crime appears to be unplanned. The

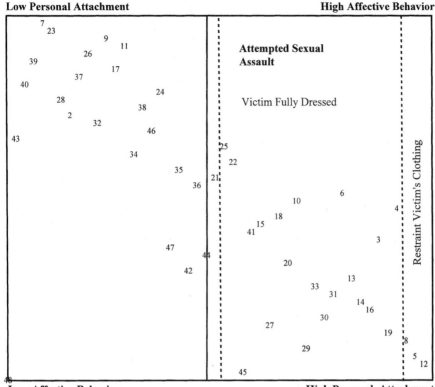

Figure 11.9 Main Item POSA Plot Configuration for the Affective-Vehicle Behavioral Theme: Last Murders in the Series

relationship of these two actions also gives a likely indication that the offender lacks forensic awareness by leaving the restraint behind at the crime scene. This finding agrees with Meloy's description of affective serial murderers.[60]

The variable that defines victim as vehicle is attempted sexual assault. Profiles with this variable are strongly associated with the "Y" axis, as demonstrated by the coefficient of monotonicity .98 as seen in Table 11.2. This variable is located horizontally on the "Y" axis, in the individual item plots for the first murders. Serial murderers who attempt sexual assault are found in a rectangle at the top left-hand corner of the main item plot for the first murders. The finding that serial murderers with impersonal attachment are less likely to remove the restraint from the crime scene is most interesting.

Table 11.2 POSA Coefficients of Weak Monotonicity Between Each Crime Scene Variable and the "X" and "Y" Axes for the Affective-Vehicle Theme

	Crime Scene Variables	X Axis First	Y Axis First	X Axis Mid	Y Axis Mid	X Axis Last	Y Axis Last
1	Forced Entry at Night	0.56	−0.21	−0.02	0.55	−0.02	0.55
2	Ransacked Property	0.64	−0.32	0.42	0.20	0.42	0.20
3	Body Openly Displayed	0.59	−0.08	0.40	0.21	0.40	0.21
4	Restraint Victim Clothing	0.36	0.34	1.00	−0.43	1.00	−0.43
5	Restraint Found at Scene	0.36	0.16	0.50	−0.02	0.50	−0.02
6	Fully Dressed	−0.80	0.99	0.99	−0.80	0.99	−0.80
7	Sexual Assault	−0.77	0.98	1.00	−0.85	1.00	−0.85
8	Weapon Hands/Feet	0.15	0.32	0.36	0.12	0.36	0.12
9	Weapon Opportunity	0.23	0.38	0.22	0.23	0.22	0.23
10	Weapon Recovered	−0.02	0.47	−0.32	0.71	−0.32	0.71
11	Semen	0.28	0.48	0.58	0.08	0.38	0.21
12	Clothing Scattered	0.30	−0.21	0.42	−0.15	−0.75	0.32

This occurs most likely because serial murderers who engage in affective rage have less contact with their victims, which could result in non-completed sexual assaults. In contrast, offenders high on personal attachment are more likely to engage in behavior requiring longer periods of time with their victims, as in using the victim's clothing as a method of strangulation. It is also worth noting that in the remaining crime scene behaviors, for the first murder series, no partition was possible due to a mixture of "1's" and "2's." The mixture of "1's" and "2's" in the POSA space means that the profiles, on those variables, were not rated similarly by all offenders.

In comparing the AV-theme individual item plots for the first murder series to the middle and last murder series, we see another development. Because the profiles for the middle and last murder series are almost identical, this suggests that serial murderers who perform certain behavior in the middle of their killing series are most likely to perform similar behavior towards the end of their killing career. This finding seems to indicate that serial murderers develop a consistent behavioral style after their first murder and also perform similar actions in their middle and last murders. How consistent these behaviors are will be tested in a later chapter. For now, though, we need to examine the differences in the underlying behavior for the middle and last murder offenses.

Overall, serial murderers in the AV theme, for the middle and last murders, appear to focus more on personal involvement with the victim. Offenders who attempt sexual assault are found in a rectangle, in the right-hand region of the main plot. The attempted sexual assault variable is strongly related to the "X" axis as demonstrated by the coefficient scores of 1.00 for

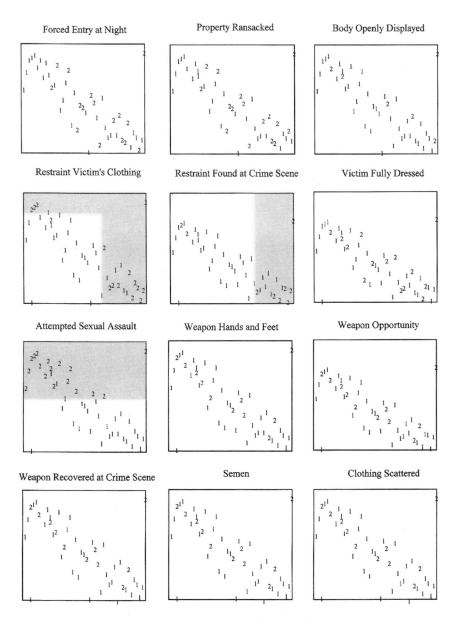

Figure 11.10 Individual POSA Item Plots for Affective Vehicle Thematic Variables: First Murders in the Series

the middle and last series. The coefficients are shown in columns three and five, scanning from left to right, in Table 11.2.

Another variable strongly relating to the "X" axis is victim fully dressed, having coefficient scores of .99, respectively, in the middle and last series.

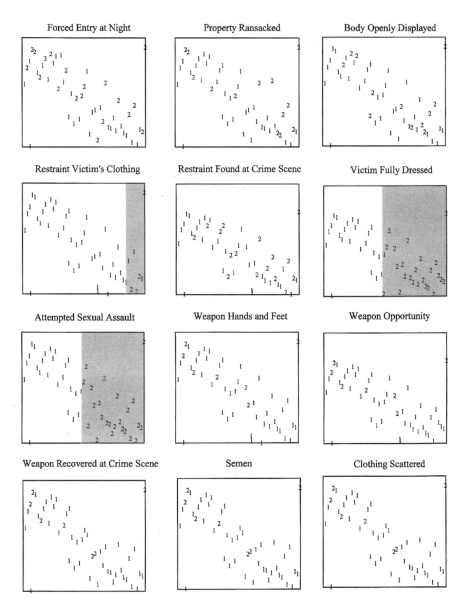

Figure 11.11 Individual POSA Item Plots for Affective Vehicle Thematic Variables: Middle Murders in the Series

The relationship that these two behaviors have to each other suggests that serial murderers who attempt a sexual assault on their victims are more likely to leave the victim fully dressed, meaning that the victim's clothing will likely not be removed from her body. However, intuitive investigators would expect

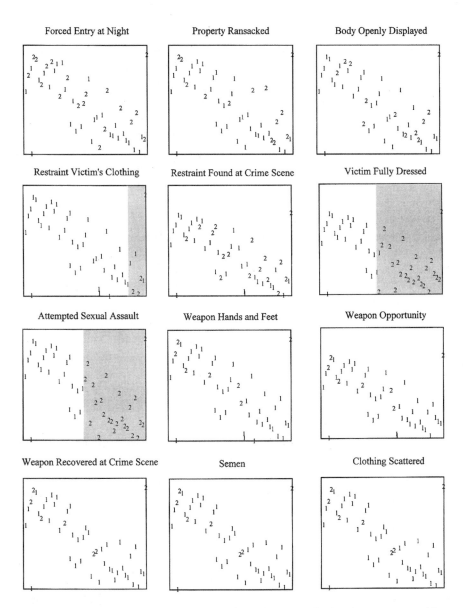

Figure 11.12 Individual POSA Item Plots for Affective Vehicle Thematic Variables: Last Murders in the Series

the victim to be unclothed. Leaving the victim fully dressed was not a significant variable in the first murder series; no clear partition could be drawn between the "1's" and "2's."

To understand the individual item plots, it is necessary to point out that victim's clothing as restraint is a subset of the variables sexual assault and fully dressed. This relationship forms what is known as a Guttman scale. The general finding is that serial murderers who attempt sexual assault on their victims and leave them fully clothed are more likely to use an article of clothing from the victim as a restraint. In the remaining seven crime scene variables, no partition was possible.

Both the POSA main plot and individual item plots provide a visual representation of the interaction between the offenders and their victims. The procedure is also a robust way to see the underlying behaviors that have the strongest influence in the affective-vehicle theme. The dominant behaviors found in the individual item plots for the AV theme suggest that the killer is emotional during the murder and the degree of planning is minimal.

11.10 POSA Results for the Affective-Object Theme

A graphic representation of the POSA results for the AO theme is shown in Figures 11.13 to 11.15. The AO theme was described earlier as being similar to the AV theme; however, they differ in terms of their level of behavioral organization and degree of personal attachment to the victim. The AO theme describes a crime scene where the offender is slightly more organized than the AV offender, and displays behavior that suggests he is attempting, or is not deterred from having, a personal attachment with his victims.

The basic structure of how POSA works was defined in the previous section. Figure 11.13 is a two-dimensional POSA main item plot for the AO theme in the first murder series. For the AO theme, six crime scene variables were used in the analysis. Analysis of 96 serial murderers using actions from the AO theme produced 43 different profiles for the first murder series, 41 different profiles for the middle murder series, and 44 different profiles for the last murder series. Looking at Figure 11.13, there appears to be a mixture of profiles plotted on both the "L" and "J" axes. The *Correp* for the affective-object theme across the first, middle, and last offenses is .80, .81, and .74, respectively.

Figures 11.14 to 11.15 are the middle and last murder series for the affective-object theme. A similarly distinct line of profiles are plotted, beginning in the middle of the plots and moving up the "J" axis to the upper right-hand corner. Profiles were similarly distributed in the first offense series. The location of these profiles suggest that these serial murderers scored high on variables that define the affective-object theme. Profiles found in the lower left-hand corner are offenders who scored low on the AO behaviors or do not possess any of the AO behaviors at all. This finding suggests that there is a greater joint spread reflecting greater extremes in relation to the set of variables. Serial murderers sharing the AO thematic behaviors are found in

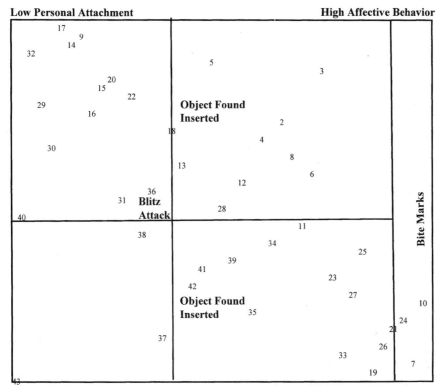

Figure 11.13 Main Item POSA Configuration of Affective-Object Behavioral Theme: First Murder in the Series

a rectangle on the right-hand region of the POSA space. At this juncture, it is necessary to consider the individual item plots for each offense series.

11.10.1 Interpreting Individual POSA Item Plots for the Affective-Object Theme

The "X" and "Y" axes have two different behavioral processes underlying the affective-object theme. The first process derives from the offender's personal attachment to the victim as an object for sadistic pleasures. Serial murders in AO theme have dismissing attachment attributes. The picture of this type of individual is that he is cold and introverted.[190]

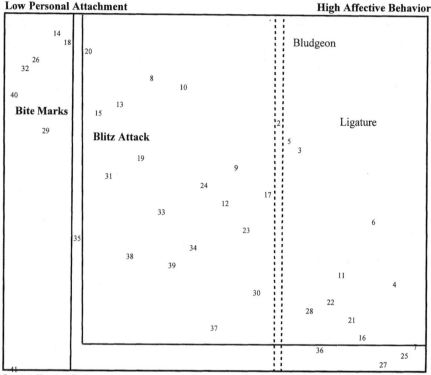

Figure 11.14 Main Item POSA Configuration of Affective-Object Behavioral Theme: Middle Murders in the Series

Profiles that relate to the offender treating the victim as an object are found in a rectangle in the right-hand region in Figures 11.16 to 11.18. Profiles found in the upper right-hand corner reflect killers' profiles that contain organized type behavior. Likewise, profiles plotted in the lower right-hand corner of the POSA space reflect offenders whose behavior is high on personal attachment to the victim. The affinity that these behaviors have with the AO theme seems logical, because sadistic acts require a personal involvement with the victim as an object. Briefly, just to reiterate, profiles in the individual item plots are plotted in the same positions as the main item profiles. The only difference is, in the individual item plots, the "1's" represent that the behavior was not present in the offender's profile, while the "2's" represent that the behavior was present.

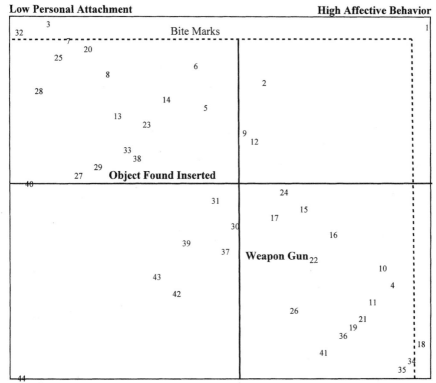

Figure 11.15 Main Item POSA Configuration of Affective-Object Behavioral Theme: Last Murder in the Series

Table 11.3 POSA Coefficients of Weak Monotonicity Between Each Crime Scene Variable and the "X" and "Y" Axes for the Affective-Object Theme

	Crime Scene Variables	X Axis First	Y Axis First	X Axis Mid	Y Axis Mid	X Axis Last	Y Axis Last
1	Blitz Attack	−0.71	1.00	−0.08	0.68	0.48	0.06
2	Object Found Inserted	0.42	0.14	0.63	0.22	−0.15	0.63
3	Bite Marks	0.99	−0.16	−0.02	0.62	0.59	0.07
4	Weapon Gun	0.00	0.60	−0.78	1.00	0.99	−0.76
5	Bludgeon	0.54	0.04	0.97	0.37	0.43	0.18
6	Ligature	0.69	−0.18	0.99	−0.77	−0.13	0.71

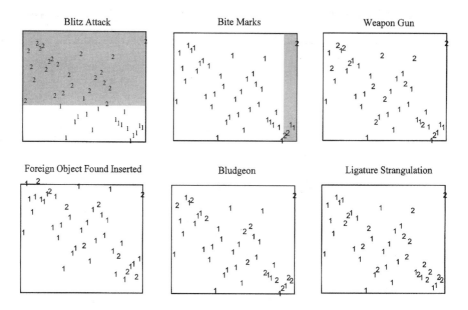

Figure 11.16 Individual POSA Item Plots for Affective Object Thematic Variables: First Murder in the Series

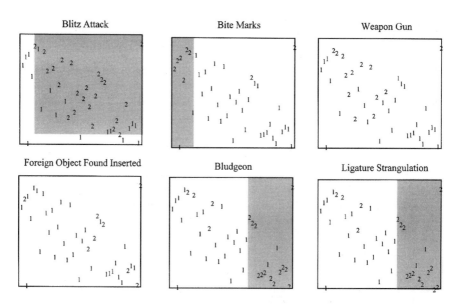

Figure 11.17 Individual POSA Item Plots for Affective Object Thematic Variables: Middle Murders in the Series

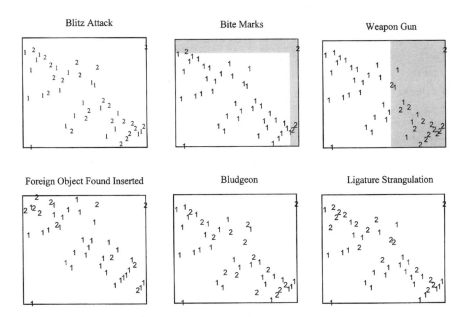

Figure 11.18 Individual POSA Item Plots for Affective Object Thematic Variables: Last Murders in the Series

Two variables, blitz attack and bite marks, are the main underlying behaviors in the affective-object theme for the first murder series. The profiles of the individual item POSA plots are shown in Figure 11.16. The variable blitz attack, has a loading of 1.00 on the "Y" axis. The coefficients are given in Table 11.3. The variable bite marks has a loading of .99 on the "X" axis. Blitzing the victim suggests the crime is opportunistic and likely to be unplanned. Blitz attack defines the affective element for this particular theme. Blitz attack for the last murder series played a lesser role in defining the AO theme, and could not be partitioned due a mixture of "1's" and "2's." This finding is logical if we assume that serial murderers become more organized over time and often change their method of approach.

The victim as object element is defined by the variable bite marks. Biting the victim is personal attachment and requires the offender to be close to his victim. Biting the victim may also reflect a rage component. No similar personal attachment behavior played a significant role in the affective-vehicle theme. The presence of bite marks has a statistical relationship on the "X" axis of .99. The intercorrelation between blitz attack and bite marks suggest that serial murderers who bite their victims do not blitz attack their victims, because the two behaviors are plotted on different axes.

There are different emphases between crime scene behavior in the first, middle, and last murder series. There also are different emphases in behavior between the middle and the last offenses. For example, the variable blitz attack is an underlying behavior in the AO theme for the middle series. Profiles with blitz attack are plotted on the "Y" axis for the first offense. The structure of the partitioning for blitz attack, for the middle murder series, is referred to as attenuating.[189] Attenuating partitions divide the higher profiles across the more central portion of the lateral axis, moderating the polar extremes and reducing the lateral spread. The variable blitz attack, for the middle offense, makes it possible to surmise that there is some progression in a serial murderer's aggression and rage. This finding is important from an investigative standpoint, suggesting that offenders refine their behavior from one murder to the next and become more forensically aware over time.

Two variables, bludgeon and ligature strangulation, partitioned in the middle series but not for the first and last murder series. The finding that these methods of killing the victim occur in the middle offense and not the first and last suggest that serial murderers who bludgeoned their victims and used a ligature were less likely to blitz attack and leave bite marks. The intercorrelation between bludgeon and ligature is .97 and .99, respectively. The remaining crime scene variables were too diffuse with "1's" and "2's"; therefore, no partition could be drawn.

In the last murder series, a gun was the preferred method of killing. Serial murderers who used a gun are plotted on the "X" axis. The changing of weapons in later murders has several implications. First, shooting is a quick method of death and requires less direct involvement with the victim. Second, the offender could be trying to alter his *Modus Operandi* (M.O.) in order to confuse the police investigation, thereby reducing the possibility of being apprehended. Serial murderers who used a gun are plotted in a rectangle in the lower right-hand corner of the POSA space in Figure 11.18.

The variable bite marks for the last offense series partition is called an accentuating inverted "L" as shown in Figure 11.18. The inverted "L" partition suggests that serial murderers whose profiles are high on personal attachment are associated with offenders on the "L" axis. Profiles that contain the variable bite marks are plotted on the very right edge of the POSA plot. This variable also has some association with the variable gun. Profiles with the two behaviors are plotted on the "X" axis, and their loadings are .99 and .59, respectively, as shown in Table 11.3. There seems to be two emphases in the AO theme. One is an offender who shows rage against his victims by leaving bite marks. The other is the use of a gun, which possibly demonstrates the offender's need to keep a distance from his victim.

11.11 POSA Results for the Cognitive-Vehicle Theme

A two-dimensional representation of the POSA results for the cognitive-vehicle theme is given in Figures 11.19 to 11.21. A total of 10 crime scene variables were used in the analysis. In the present set of 96 serial murderers, for the CV theme, there were 44 different profiles for the first murder series and 41 different profiles for the middle and last murder series. The goodness of fit (*Correp*) coefficients for the cognitive-vehicle theme across the first, middle, and last murder series are .68, .70, and .70, respectively.

The POSA main item plot in Figure 11.19, for the first murder series, illustrates a notable distribution along the Joint axis, suggesting a quite strong quantitative scale to the CV behaviors. The location of the profiles in the

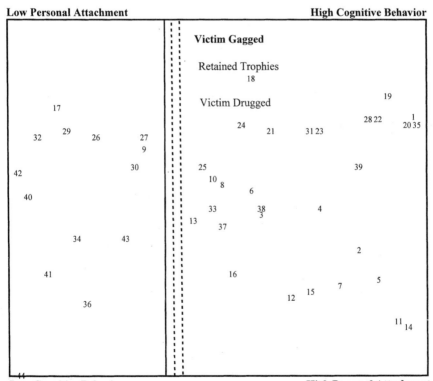

Correp Coefficient = .68
44 Individual profiles
10 Variables
N = 96 Offenders

Figure 11.19 Main Item POSA Configuration of Cognitive-Vehicle Behavioral Theme: First Murders in the Series

POSA space shows that the plots divided into two distinct regions. The majority of the profiles are plotted in a rectangle in the right-hand region of the POSA space, while a smaller portion of profiles are plotted in a rectangle in the left-hand region of the POSA space.

The main item plots for the middle and last murder series, Figures 11.20 and 11.21, show a similar profile distribution along the "J" axis. In addition, both the middle and last offense series are very similar to the POSA plot found in the first murder series, except that a few profiles in the middle and last series are distributed along the "L" (qualitative) axis. These profiles are located in the upper left-hand corner of the POSA space. As with the previous POSA main item plots, the profiles are best understood by examining the individual item plots for each murder series.

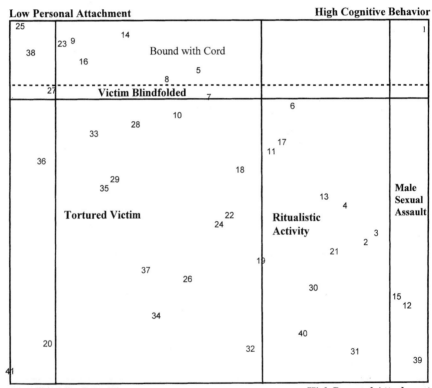

Correp Coefficient = .74
41 Individual profiles
10 Variables
N = 96 Offenders

Figure 11.20 Main Item POSA Configuration of Cognitive-Vehicle Behavioral Theme: Middle Murders in the Series

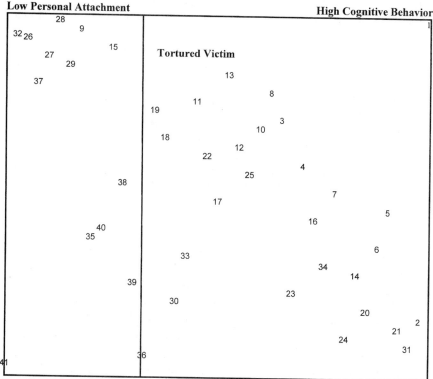

Figure 11.21 Main Item POSA Configuration of Cognitive-Vehicle Behavioral Theme: Last Murders in the Series

The process of developing an empirical classification model of serial murder is to consider which of the crime scene antecedents are most closely related to the "X" and "Y" axes. The inter-correlation coefficients showing this degree of relationship for the CV theme are given in Table 11.4. To repeat, the cognitive-vehicle theme is defined by its lack of behaviors that were emotionally charged and dominated by actions related to the instrumental gain of the killer, such as sadistic rewards and impersonal attachment to the victim.

11.11.1 Interpreting the POSA Individual Item Plots for the Cognitive-Vehicle Theme

The coefficients shown in Table 11.4 relate to the 10 individual variable plots shown in Figures 11.22 and 11.23. For seven of the crime scene behaviors in

Table 11.4 POSA Coefficients of Weak Monotonicity Between Each Crime Scene Variable and the "X" and "Y" Axes for the Cognitive-Vehicle Theme

	Crime Scene Variables	X Axis First	Y Axis First	X Axis Mid	Y Axis Mid	X Axis Last	Y Axis Last
1	Victim Gagged	0.65	0.13	−0.62	0.96	0.45	0.24
2	Blindfold	−0.48	0.98	−0.02	0.97	0.51	0.68
3	Bound with Cord	−0.17	0.91	−0.46	0.99	−0.49	0.99
4	Ritualistic Activity	0.91	−0.43	0.88	−0.30	0.98	−0.62
5	Body Posed	−0.25	0.79	−0.22	0.83	−0.39	0.89
6	Piqueurism	0.97	−0.24	1.00	−0.53	0.71	0.03
7	Male Sexual Assault	0.83	−0.06	0.85	−0.37	0.28	0.34
8	Victim Drugged	0.50	0.46	0.65	0.17	0.80	0.27
9	Tortured Victim	0.85	−0.14	0.78	−0.06	0.89	−0.51
10	Retained Trophies	0.70	0.02	0.16	0.57	0.38	0.75

the CV theme for the first murder, no partitions could be drawn due to a mixture of "1's" and "2's." Three variables — gag, victim drugged, and trophies — are the underlying behaviors in the CV theme for the first murder series. Profiles that include these behaviors are located in the main item POSA space, in a rectangle on the right-hand side of the plot.

The variable victim drugged has a loading of .50 on the "X" axis, trophies .70, and gag .65. The distribution of the profiles on the "X" axis, although their coefficients are low, is similar. This suggests that serial murderers in their first offense who drugged their victims are most likely to retain parts of the body or personal items as trophies for psychological reflection about the murder. Another interesting crime scene behavior is torture. Torture could not be partitioned, although it does appear to have some structure.

In the middle and last murder series, we see a refinement from the first murder series, with four additional behaviors playing a role. The introduction of four variables — bound with an electrical cord, ritualistic activity, male sexual assault, and tortured victim — agrees with the study's Facet Model that the CV theme is defined by organized behavior and impersonal attachment. It is also similar to Meloy's predator type serial murderer.[60]

Looking at the middle series, we see that the offender's method of controlling the victim changes from gagging to binding. Serial murderers who use an electrical cord to bind their victims are plotted on the "Y" axis, and has a loading of .99. The change in methods of controlling the victim suggest that the offender's actions are spontaneous and impersonal. Hence, the victim is treated as vehicle. Also, the role played by the variable trophy is not as dominant in either the middle or last murder series. This provides an indication that in the first offense the killer is concerned with various ways to control his victim, while in the middle and last offenses his focus is on an impersonal attachment to the victim. For example, retaining trophies is

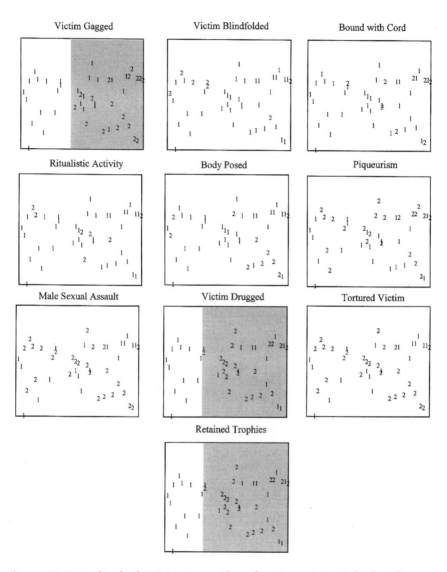

Figure 11.22 Individual POSA Item Plots for Congnitive-Vehicle Thematic Variables: First Murders in the Series

impersonal because the killer relives the interaction with his victims at a distance. Control is still present in the middle series; however, it is less a factor in the last offense series. In the middle and last offenses, it appears that attachment to the victim in the form of ritualistic activity, male sexual assault, torture, etc., is personal. This finding may suggest a refinement in the killer's attachment to his victims over time.

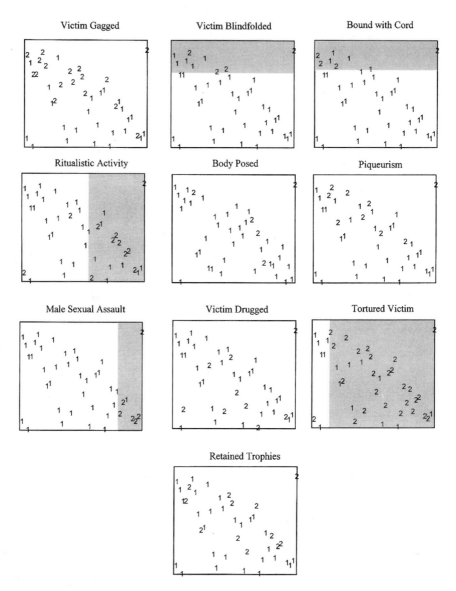

Figure 11.23 Individual POSA Item Plots for Congnitive-Vehicle Thematic Variables: Middle Murders in the Series

To reiterate, profiles plotted in the lower right-hand corner of the POSA space indicate high personal attachment. For the middle and last murder series, three crime scene behaviors show this trend. The first of the three variables is ritualistic activity, which did not factor in the offender's behavior in the first series. Profiles that contain ritualistic activity for the middle and

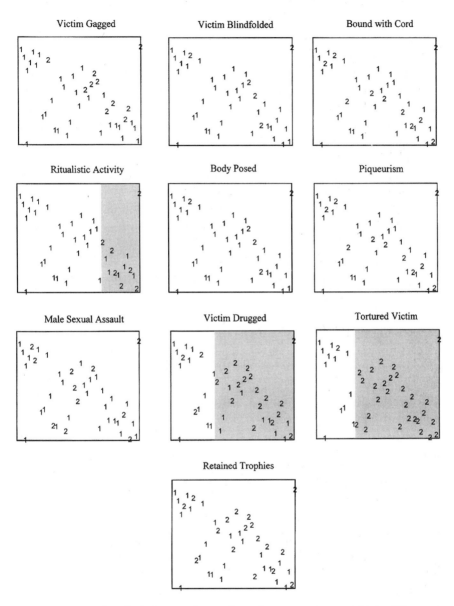

Figure 11.24 Individual POSA Item Plots for Congnitive-Vehicle Thematic Variables: Last Murders in the Series

last offense series are plotted vertically on the "X" axis, in the lower right-hand corner of the POSA space. Ritualistic activity has a loading on the "X" axis of .88 for the middle offenses and .98 for the last offense. The coefficients are shown in Table 11.4.

The second personal attachment behavior is male sexual assault. Profiles for this variable are found in the middle series only, and are plotted vertically on the "X" axis, in the lower right-hand corner as shown in Figure 11.23. The third personal attachment behavior is torture. Profiles for this variable are found in both the middle and last series, and are also plotted vertically on the "X" axis, in a rectangle in the lower right-hand corner of the POSA space. The loadings for torture are .78 for the middle series and .89 for the last murder series. The finding accords with studies cited earlier that suggest that homosexual killings are often sadistic, and the victims are often tortured to death.[17,80]

An impersonal attachment variable is victim blindfolded, which partitioned in the middle offenses but not in the first and last offenses. The variable blindfold has a loading of .97 on the "Y" axis. Blindfolding the victim has several implications: it gives a likely indication that the offender is attempting to disguise his identity; also the victim could be blindfolded for psychological reasons only known to the killer. Another interesting controlling behavior is victim drugged. Victim drugged is not as dominant in the middle series as in the first and last series. The methodical behavior of drugging the victim demonstrates preplanning.

Looking at the offender's behavior for the last murder series, there appears to be some refinement. For example, attempts to control the victim are more dominant in the middle offense, while the focus on personal attachment to the victim increases in the last offense. Offenders who perform ritualistic activity and torture are located high on personal attachment in the POSA space for the middle and last murder series, but not for the first offenses. This shows that although serial murderers are performing similar behaviors, they attune certain behaviors as they develop their criminal careers. The coefficients in Table 11.4, between ritualistic activity and tortured victim for the middle and last series, show this apparent significance.

The general finding for the cognitive-vehicle theme is that serial murderers' behaviors are organized and impersonal in their first offenses; however, attachment becomes personal in their middle and last offenses. One difference in the CV theme, compared to the other three themes, is the selection of male victims. This leads to an interesting find: serial murderers who select male victims are also sadistic. This finding lends weight to the hypothesis proposed earlier, that individuals with dismissing attachment behavior show hostility and coldness while also processing the ability to maintain some organization in their crime scenes. It also supports Terr's contention that sadistic individuals with dismissing attributes have the ability to compartmentalize their personalities while performing sadistic acts on their victims.[181] In addition, the significant crime scene behaviors that partitioned in the POSA supports the study's hypotheses that the CV theme is both expressive and instrumental. This finding agrees with research by Cornell and his colleagues' view that the distinction between instrumental and reactive violence is not absolute.[43]

Broadly, the results for the CV theme show that behavior is refined from one murder to the next. Similar assumptions on refinement of signature behavior of serial murderers, although not empirically supported by research, have been put forth in the literature.[59,170] The POSA results also show that, although a serial murderer's M.O. is likely to change, his signature theme, over time, becomes refined as he gains experience in his criminal career.

11.12 POSA Results for the Cognitive-Object Theme

A two-dimensional representation of the POSA results for the cognitive-object theme is shown in Figures 11.25 to 11.27. A total of 10 variables were used in the analysis. In the present 96 serial murderers, for the CO theme, there were 38 individual profiles for the first, middle, and last murder series. The goodness of fit (*Correp*) coefficients for the CO theme across the three offense series are .72, .76, and .77, respectively.

The "X" and "Y" axes in Figures 11.25 to 11.27 have two different behavioral processes underlying the cognitive-object theme. One process evolves out of forming pseudo-relationships with women, which is an attribute of dismissing attachment, or personal attachment. Profiles of serial murderers who display personal attachment are plotted in the lower right-hand corner in the POSA space. The second process derives from the offender's degree of control over his victim and high self-awareness.

Examining the POSA main item plot for the first murder series in Figure 11.25, we see that the majority of profiles have no systematic structure. This is an important finding because it does demonstrate that serial murderers, in the CO theme, have no particular pattern to their first offenses. However, the POSA main item plots for the middle and last murder series, although distributed in a much wider space than the first offense series, are structured — indicating that offenders have a common content criterion in their crime scene actions. This suggests that there are two major ways in which serial murderers differ from each other in the CO theme over the first, middle, and last murder series.

The monotonicity coefficients are given in Table 11.5 as a contribution to the first stage in interpreting Figures 11.25 to 11.27. The partitioning of the POSA space for the individual crime scene behaviors for the three offense series are given in Figures 11.28 and 11.29.

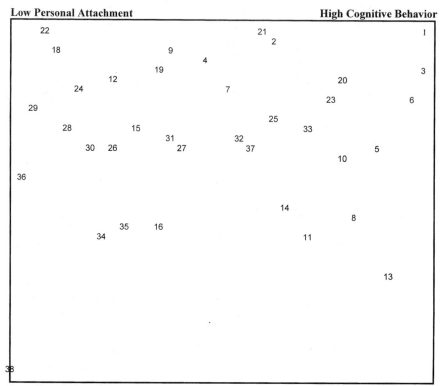

Correp Coefficient = .72
38 Individual profiles
10 Variables
N = 96 Offenders

Figure 11.25 Main Item POSA Configuration of Cognitive-Object Behavioral Theme: First Murders in the Series

11.12.1 Interpreting the Individual POSA Item Plots for the Cognitive-Object Theme

Each of the 10 individual item plots in Figures 11.28 to 11.30 is a simplified summary of the partitioning of each variable on the POSA main item space shown in Figures 11.25 to 11.27. Looking at the POSA plots for the first murder series, there were no crime scene behaviors that could be partitioned. This suggests that no partial order or common theme in the crime scene behaviors for the first murder could be found. This is a very important finding for two reasons. First, Ressler and his colleagues argue that serial murderers who leave sadistic crime scenes start their killing careers much later in life.[17,71]

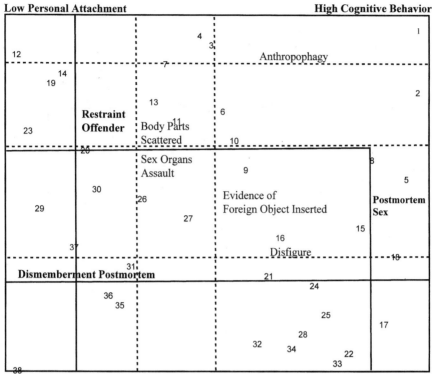

Figure 11.26 Main Item POSA Configuration of Cognitive-Object Behavioral Theme: Middle Murders in the Series

The fact that there are no clear divisions between the "1's" and "2's" for the first murder could suggest that the offenders have little criminal experience, but this was not a factor in the other thematic types: affective-vehicle, affective-object, and cognitive-vehicle. The finding that there is no structured order in the most sadistic killer's first offenses indicate that this occurrence is most likely unique only to sadistic serial murderers. Second, it demonstrates an important fact from an investigative standpoint that, although the CO crime scene has organized features, there is a combination of behaviors that could occur in the first murder with no particular order. However, looking at the middle and last murder series, we see the killers' behaviors start to become refined and, consequently, more organized and sadistic. As

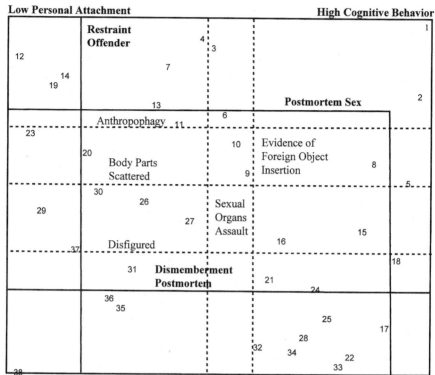

Figure 11.27 Main Item POSA Configuration of Cognitive-Object Behavioral Theme: Last Murders in the Series

noted previously, this finding is contrary to the FBI assumptions that serial murderers who mutilate, perform postmortem sex, and assault the victim's sexual organs leave their crime scenes in disarray, and are not forensically aware.[17,163] It also demonstrates the robustness of using a large sample size when building an empirical classification model of criminal behavior.

The distribution of profiles in the middle and last murder series mirror each other. The serial murderer's focus toward the victim as an object becomes refined, controlled, and sadistic. The level of personal attachment to the victim increases, as well as the level of organization. One variable, restraint preselected by offender, particularly supports this hypothesis. Bringing a restraint to the crime scene suggests preplanning. Serial murderers who

Table 11.5 POSA Coefficients of Weak Monotonicity Between Each Crime Scene Variable and the "X" and "Y" Axes for the Cognitive-Object Theme

	Crime Scene Variables	X Axis First	Y Axis First	X Axis Mid	Y Axis Mid	X Axis Last	Y Axis Last
1	Body Parts	0.41	0.93	0.12	0.94	−0.35	0.99
2	Bound with Handcuffs	0.27	0.82	0.30	0.62	0.43	0.77
3	Restraint Offender	0.40	0.72	0.77	0.27	0.70	0.50
4	Anthropophagy	0.14	0.80	0.33	1.00	−0.08	0.99
5	Held Captive	0.45	0.81	0.76	0.01	0.54	0.63
6	Victim Disfigured	0.54	0.69	0.33	0.76	−0.22	0.96
7	Dismemberment Postmortem	0.76	0.55	0.39	0.75	−0.19	0.99
8	Sex Organs Assaulted	0.83	−0.41	0.99	0.31	0.95	−0.16
9	Postmortem Sex	0.37	0.89	−0.45	0.96	0.07	0.84
10	Evidence of Object Insert	−0.08	0.85	1.00	−0.31	1.00	−0.54

carried a restraint to the crime scene are plotted in a rectangle on the "X" axis for the middle and last series, and have coefficients of .77 and .70, respectively, as shown in Table 11.5.

Four behaviors in particular — anthropophagy, assaulting the victim's sexual organs, sex postmortem, and evidence of foreign object insertion — give a likely indication that the offender is personally attached to the victim's body. These are instrumental behaviors that require the killer to be physically close and personally involved with the victim whether she is dead or alive. However, within these four behaviors there are various processes that may or may not occur in a serial murder. For example, serial murderers who performed anthropophagy on their victims are more likely to perform post-mortem sex. Figures 11.29 and 11.30 show this apparent pattern. The inter-correlation between serial murderers who commit anthropophagy on their victims for the middle and last offenses have coefficient loadings of 1.00 and .99, respectively, on the "Y" axis as shown in Table 11.5. It is interesting to note that, although the variable anthropophagy has a coefficient of .80 for the first offense, the variable could not be partitioned.

The variable sex postmortem partitioned as an accentuating "L" shape for the middle and last offenses. This suggests that there are serial murderers' profiles that cross the lateral axis and thus show a differentiation between the two crime scene behaviors. This finding is important from an investigative point of view, because it suggests that some serial murderers engage in post-mortem sexual activity and also scatter body parts, preselect their restraints, perform anthropophagy on their victims, and dismember them postmortem. Equally as important are the serial murderers who perform postmortem sexual activity, assault the victim's sex organs, and insert objects but do not perform the remaining behaviors in the CO theme. The finding suggests that

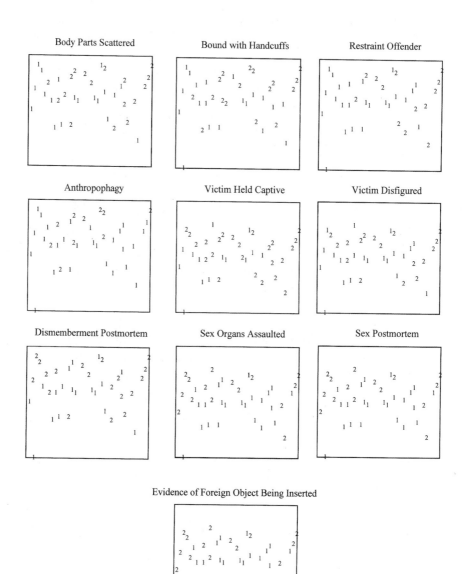

Figure 11.28 Individual POSA Item Plots for Cognitive-Object Thematic Variables: First Murder in the Series

there may be two distinct types of serial murderers in the CO theme with different underlying fetishistic behaviors.

The two remaining personal attachment behaviors are sex organs assaulted and evidence of a foreign object. Serial murderers with these

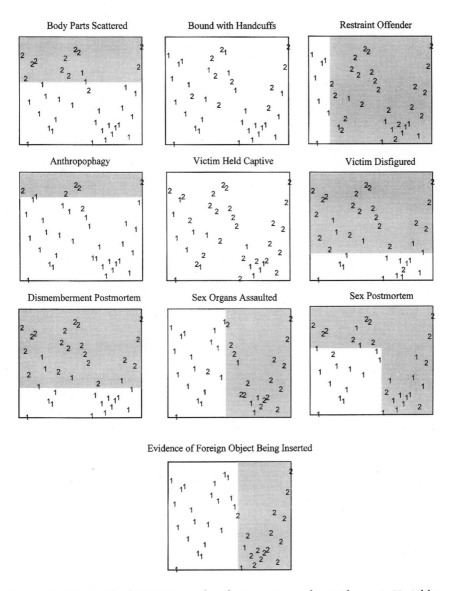

Figure 11.29 Individual POSA Item Plots for Cognitive-Object Thematic Variables: Middle Murder in the Series

attributes in their profiles are plotted in a rectangle in the lower right-hand region of the main item plot. The inter-correction of the variable sex organs assaulted is .99 for the middle offenses and .95 for the last offense, while foreign object has a loading of .99 for the middle and .95 for the last offenses. The coefficients are given in Table 11.5. The relationship between these

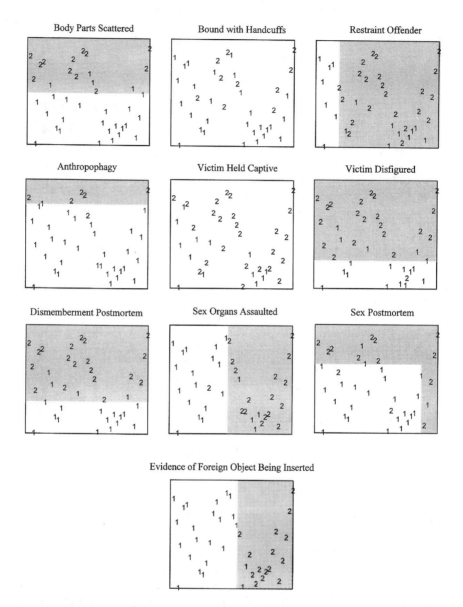

Figure 11.30 Individual POSA Item Plots for Cognitive-Object Thematic Variables: Last Murder in the Series

behaviors supports the study's hypothesis that serial murderers who view their victims as objects are sadistic, as well as high on self-awareness and personal attachment. The position of the profiles in the POSA space in Figures 11.25 and 11.27 show this relationship. As hypothesized, profiles with these two behaviors are distributed in the lower right-hand corner of the POSA space, indicating that those offenders are high on personal attachment.

11.13 Summary

POSA provided a method in which relationships between serial murderers' crime scene actions could be empirically explored. The approach to classifying serial murderers used in the chapter is a major departure from previous attempts where less empirical methods have been used to classify the crime scene actions of serial predators.[2,4,7,17,50,52,57,61,160]

The POSA results support the hypothesis that there are distinctive crime scene behaviors that appear to be more typical of serial murderers. The first example is the affective-vehicle serial murderer. The AV type murderer seems to commit murder during an emotional state and is forensically careless at his crime scene. For example, the POSA configurations for the AV crime scene suggest that the crimes were unplanned due to the offender's use of the victim's clothing as a restraining device and leaving the restraint at the crime scene. The findings for the AV killer seem to suggest disorganization and impersonal attachment. For example, offenders who attempt a sexual assault on their victims and left them fully dressed were more likely to use the victims' clothing as a restraining device.

The next example is the affective-object serial murderer. The POSA results for the AO killer suggest a greater joint spread reflecting greater extremes in relation to the behaviors that define the AO theme. The joint spread of crime scene actions were found for the first, middle, and last murders. The main actions that define the AO serial murderer were blitz and bite marks. For example, the POSA found that offenders who blitz attacked did not bite their victims. However, serial murderers who bludgeoned their victims to death or used a ligature also appeared to be less likely to blitz attack and leave bite marks.

The next crime scene theme is cognitive-vehicle. The CV crime scene suggests more controlling behavior in the first offenses and impersonal attachment in the middle and last offenses. For example, for the first offenses, offenders who drugged their victims were more likely to retain trophies. However, for the middle and last offenses, offenders who used an electrical cord to bind their victims were more likely to perform ritualistic activity at the crime scene, torture their victims, and select male victims. The POSA results for the CV also found that the method of controlling the victim for the middle offenses changed in the last offenses. For example, the method used to control the victim in the middle offenses was a gag, but in the last offenses it was binding with a cord. This change may be due to gaining experience over time.

The final crime scene theme is cognitive-object. CO type serial murderers appear to commit more sadistic acts and have a higher personal attachment to their victims. However, the POSA results found no order in the crime scene actions for the first offenses. This finding suggests that sadistic serial murderers are just as likely to perform all sorts of crime scene actions earlier in their careers. However, for the middle and last offenses, their behaviors become refined, controlling, and more sadistic. For example, offenders were more likely to perform anthropophagy, sexually assault the victims' organs, engage in postmortem sex, and insert foreign objects. These behaviors seem to suggest that the killer had a personal attachment to the victim in later murders compared to the early ones. The POSA results also found that serial murderers who performed anthropophagy were more likely to engage in postmortem sexual activities. Most interesting, though, is that the POSA found two distinct types of CO serial murderers who have different underlying fetishistic behaviors. For example, serial murderers who engaged in postmortem sex, scattered body parts, preselected a restraint, and performed anthopophagy also were likely to dismember their victims postmortem. On the contrary, serial murderers who performed only postmortem sex, assaulted the victims' sexual organs, and inserted objects were more likely not to scatter body parts, preselect a restraint, or perform anthopophagy.

To that end, the POSA results broadly suggest that the crime scene actions of serial murderers remain consistent over their first, middle, and last offenses. However, just how consistent serial murderers are from one crime to the next will be discussed in the next chapter.

Consistency in Serial Murderers and Their Crime Scene Behaviors

12

Much attention in the last decade that has been focused on the offender consistency hypothesis in serial murder seems to be in conflict.[56,163] For instance, there appear to be rather broad opinions as to whether serial murderers are organized at the beginning of their criminal careers, then become disorganized over time. One hypothesis is that crime scene actions in one offense will consistently occur in subsequent offenses. This would imply that serial murderers' crime scene actions are consistent from one offense to the next. However, some researchers argue that serial murderers start their criminal careers as disorganized, and thus become organized over time due to situational learning.[18,50,81] These opinions on the consistency of serial murderers are rather vexing and have been predominately based on deductive work experience and inferences made about an offender's fantasy life or possible Minnesota Multiphasic Personality Inventory (MMPI) scores. As a result, there has been no empirical undertaking to explore how consistent serial murderers are from one crime to the next.

12.1 Consistency in Serial Murderers' Crime Scene Behaviors

Typologies are among the most common methods used to differentiate between serial murderers. However, most typologies of serial murder do not recognize serial murderers along a measurable continuum, but rather draw deductive distinctions according to motivational variations.[13,17] Research by Blackburn points out that research testing the empirical validity of serial murder typologies has failed to determine whether offenders are consistent across their criminal careers.[191]

For example, the FBI does differentiate serial murderers by various elements such as aggression, as discussed in Chapter 2, and through the use of their organized and disorganized types and crime classification manual.[57] However, there is no attempt to isolate which of the variables in each of these sources provide a consistent way to differentiate between offenders. Instead, what is produced is the differentiation of offender consistency by several different criteria over a variety of domains, including motivation, fantasy, and personality constructs. Canter and Heritage cautioned against using fantasy and MMPI scores to determine consistency.[192] Rather, they point out that offender consistency should be defined by offense behavior in terms of *themes* rather than types, as demonstrated in Chapter 10. The first step in testing offender consistency is to determine if the behaviors shown to have a common order by POSA can be used consistently to classify serial murderers' behaviors into the four themes. This is addressed in the next section.

Table 12.1 provides a simplistic way of actually looking at serial murderers and their crime scene behaviors to determine which of the four behavioral themes classifies an offender. A table was constructed for each of the behavioral themes: affective-vehicle, affective-object, cognitive-vehicle, and cognitive-object. For convenience, only an example of the first page of the affective-vehicle table is presented here. The data in Table 12.1 represent 7 of 96 offenders across 288 offenses or cases.

To explain the layout of the table, for example, in the left column is the case or serial murderer as numbered in the original data matrix. In the first row is offender one, below that is offender two, and so forth. The second column is the identification number that the POSA computer program assigned to each offender. For example, in Table 12.1, the affective-vehicle theme, the first offender's POSA identification profile for his first offense is 26, and 41 on his middle offenses and last offenses for the AV theme. If we look at the POSA main item plot for the AV theme in Chapter 11, the number 26 represents offender one in the original data base. After the POSA ID are three columns that represent the crime scene behaviors present across the offender's first, middle, and last murders. Offender one, in his first murder offense, attempted a sexual assault on the victim, left her body openly displayed, and the police recovered the weapon at the crime scene. Similar behaviors were present in his middle and last murders. In all, there were three behaviors in the offender's first offense, two behaviors for the middle offense, and two again in his last offense. In total for his first, middle, and last offenses, serial murderer one performed seven crime scene behaviors, as shown in the far right-hand column in Table 12.1. Tables for each of the four themes were constructed and laid out in the same format as demonstrated in Table 12.1.

Table 12.1 Ninety-Six Serial Murderers' Scores on Crime Scene Behaviors in the Affective-Vehicle Theme Across Their First, Middle, and Last Offenses

Offender	POSA ID	First Actions	Middle Actions	Last Actions	Total Score Across all Offenses
1	26	body openly	sexual assault	sexual assault	
1	41	sexual assault weapon recovered	weapon recovered	weapon recovered	
1	41				
		3	2	2	7
2	13	body openly	body openly	body openly	
2	18	sexual assault hands/feet	sexual assault hands/feet	sexual assault hands/feet	
2	18				
		3	3	3	9
3	8	body openly	body openly	body openly	
3	13 .	restraint victim restraint found	restraint found sexual assault	restraint found sexual assault	
3	13	sexual assault			
		4	3	3	10
4	16	sexual assault	sexual assault	sexual assault	
4	15	hands/feet weapon recovered	hands/feet weapon recovered	hands/feet weapon recovered	
4	15				
		3	3	3	9
5	23	body openly	force/night	force/night	
5	9	fully dressed weapon	body openly fully dressed	body openly fully dressed	
5	9	opportunity	weapon recovered	weapon recovered	
		3	4	4	11
6	37	fully dressed	fully dressed	fully dressed	
6	28	weapon opportunity	weapon opportunity	weapon opportunity	
6	28	2	2	2	6
7	25	fully dressed	fully dressed	fully dressed	
7	22	sexual assault weapon	sexual assault weapon	sexual assault weapon	
7	22	opportunity	opportunity	opportunity	
		3	3	3	9

12.2 Faceted SSA Model of Crime Scene Behaviors

The next step was to explore whether serial murderers' actions could be further classified as belonging to one of the four thematic regions using the 38 variables previously shown to have an order by POSA. It would be expected that if the 38 behaviors are robust, then each facet and facet element should define the "X" and "Y" axes as hypothesized in the Facet Model of serial murder (see Figure 3.1 in Chapter 3). In order to test the hypothesis, a SSA was run on 96 serial murderers over their 288 offenses. In other words, the three individual data matrices used in Chapter 10 were collapsed, forming one matrix consisting of 288 offenses or cases. The data matrix was constructed in a way where the columns represented the crime scene variables and the row cases or offenders. Figure 12.1 shows the SSA results.

Figure 12.1 is a SSA plot showing how the four behavioral themes partitioned on the 38 variables used in the POSA across the offenders' first, middle, and last offenses. The lines in the SSA represent the partition between each theme. It is interesting to note that the radial pattern originally found in the first SSA (Chapter 10) is not evident in Figure 12.1. Rather, two distinct solid lines seem to best divide the SSA plot, one vertically on the "X" and one horizontally on the "Y" axes. This finding has two meanings. First, the facets of behavioral organization and attachment may be orthogonal to each other, which indicates two independent dimensions as hypothesized in Chapter 3. This means that the structure correspondences in one plane are independent of each other. Next, since there was a minimum overlap of variables between themes, this suggests that the "X" axis is defined by the attachment facet, while the "Y" axis is defined by the behavioral facet. In turn, the two orthogonal facets describe the four thematic crime scene regions.

The pattern of space partition shown in Figure 12.1 below is known as a generalized simplex.[88] A facet that gives rise to a generalized simplex is called an axial facet.[147] This type of SSA plot is characterized by a linear ordering of regions, where each region contains items of one facet element that are quantitatively different.

This linear ordering achieved by the SSA lends support to the POSA results in Chapter 11, that the selected 38 crime scene behaviors are densely ordered.[101] Apart from four variables — clothing scattered, victim tortured, trophies, and semen — the SSA retained its original structure. The fact that the SSA retained most of its original structure over the 288 crimes lends further support that the four behavioral modalities are empirically sound for classifying U.S. serial murderers' crime scene actions, as hypothesized by the Facet Model in Chapter 3. Also, the finding agrees with the monotonicity hypothesis; it states that the observations for every two items

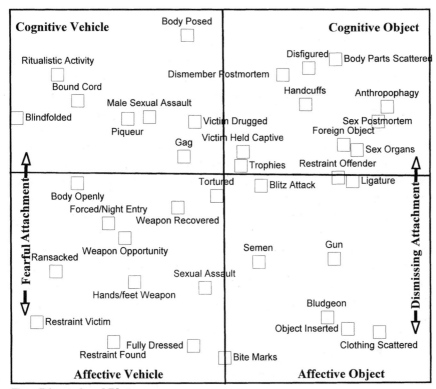

Figure 12.1 A Faceted SSA Model of U.S. Serial Murderers' Crime Scene Behaviors

in a given content universe with a common range are monotonically related.[101] In other words, the behaviors correlated non-negatively among each other. This finding has investigative significance, because it suggests that these variables are robust for developing a computerized model linking system for police investigations.

Although the SSA findings indicated that the crime scene behavior of serial murderers can be classified into four meaningful themes, the SSA did not classify the actual killers themselves. In other words, given a combination of crime scene actions, any one killer may be associated with variables from more than just one of the thematic regions.

12.3 Assigning Serial Murderers to Themes

The first process in developing an empirical classification model of serial murderers involved taking each of the 96 serial murder cases for the first, middle, and last offenses and assigning an unique score that represented the number of crime scene actions present in each theme. So, for example, a theme that has 10 variables possible also has a maximum score of 10. However, in a few cases where the mixture of unequal actions was present in each theme, a proportional method was employed to determine whether the case belonged to a theme or not. This process involved taking the number of actions in a particular case and dividing them by the number of actions that were possible. In other words, a case was classified as belonging to one of the four themes, if the proportional score for that theme is greater than or approximately equal to the score for the other three themes added together. Two themes, cognitive-vehicle and cognitive-object, had a total score of 10 possible actions, while the affective-object theme had 6 possible actions. The affective-vehicle theme had a total score of 12 possible actions. Table 12.2 below shows the number and percentage of serial murderers who were classified in each theme along with any hybrids, meaning that offenders shared behaviors from different themes.

Table 12.2 Frequency of Serial Murderers Assigned to Each Behavioral Theme

Theme	N Offenders	% of Offenders in each theme
Affective Vehicle	16	17
Hybrids AV-AO	10	10
Affective Object	31	32
Hybrids AO-CV	2	2
Cognitive Vehicle	6	6
Hybrids CV-CO	1	1
Cognitive Object	27	28
Hybrids CO-AV	1	1
Hybrids CO-AO	1	1
Hybrids AV-CV	1	1
Total N =	96	99

Each serial murderer was classified using the proportional method on 38 variables previously discussed. In other words, an offender was assigned to a theme if his score in a particular theme over his first, middle, and last offenses was greater than his score in the remaining themes. Each offender's total score across all three offenses formed the backdrop for the results shown in Table 12.2. This step was important for several reasons. First, it allowed a visual inspection of the percentage of offenders assigned to each theme, including any hybrids. Secondly, it provided a way of looking at the consistency of serial murderers by seeing whether offenders in one theme could be classified in the same theme for the middle and last offenses.

Using the proportional method, almost all of the serial murder cases (83%) could be classified as either pure types, while 15% could be classified as hybrids. The most frequent purest type was the affective-object theme (n = 31 or 32%). The next purest type was the most sadistic theme, cognitive-object (n = 27 or 28%). Following that was the affective-vehicle theme (n = 16, or 17%), while the final purest type was cognitive-vehicle (n = 6 or 6%). The most frequent hybrid was between the affective-vehicle and affective-object themes (n = 10 or 10%), while the next three frequent hybrids were between the affective-object and cognitive-vehicle (n = 2 or 2%), cognitive-vehicle and cognitive-object (n = 1 or 1%), cognitive-object and affective-object (n = 1 or 1%), and affective-vehicle and cognitive-vehicle theme (n=1 or 1%).

The finding that the majority of serial murderers classified as belonging to one of the four behavioral themes is due in part to the nature of the SSA structure, that the SSA configuration is produced by groups of consistently co-occurring variables. It is thus worth pointing out that the majority of the hybrids are from contiguous regions.

12.4 Searching for Consistency Between Crime Scene Behaviors Using Cochran's Q Analysis

To test further for consistency between the first, middle, and last offenses, 38 individual data matrices of the 38 crime scene actions were constructed; one matrix for each crime scene action variable. Within each matrix, the columns were the offenders (K = 96) and the rows were the first, middle, and last offenses (N = 3). The data were then analyzed by means of Cochran's Q test. It should be noted here that matching was based on relevant characteristics of the different subjects, not on the basis of the same subjects in different conditions. Thus, each subject was rated according to the presence or absence of the crime-related behavior within each of the three categories: first, middle, and last crimes. The rationale was that if offenders were consistent over their first, middle, and last offense series and different from each other, to the extent to which they committed the actions under consideration, the column means should significantly differ from one another. A high and significant Q score would therefore indicate that serial murderers were consistent in their behavior over the three offenses, and data were not random. The results are shown in Table 12.3 below. Q was significant in every case.

**Table 12.3 Q Analysis of Crime Scene Behavior Across Killers'
First, Middle, and Last Offense Series**

Behavioral Theme	Crime Scene Action	Q Score
Affective Vehicle Theme	Force Entry at Night	285.00
	Ransacked property	285.00
	Body Openly Displayed	281.74
	Restraint Found	285.00
	Fully Dressed	285.00
	Sexual Assault	280.00
	Clothing Scattered	236.98
	Semen Found at Crime Scene	269.21
	Weapon Hands/feet	285.00
	Weapon of Opportunity	279.00
	Weapon Recovered	280.00
Affective Object Theme	Blitz Attack	282.20
	Object Found Inserted	280.58
	Bite Marks	230.00
	Weapon Gun	285.00
	Bludgeon	279.85
	Ligature	285.00
Cognitive Vehicle Theme	Gagged Victim	285.00
	Blindfolded Victim	285.00
	Bound with Electrical Cord	228.77
	Ritualistic Activity	274.25
	Body Posed	285.00
	Piquerism	285.00
	Male Sexual Assault	285.00
	Victim Drugged	282.00
	Tortured Victim	285.00
	Retained Trophies	255.28
Cognitive Object Theme	Body Parts Scattered	241.87
	Bound Handcuffs	279.16
	Restraint Offender	285.00
	Anthropophagy	285.00
	Victim Held Captive	285.00
	Disfigured Victim	285.00
	Dismemberment Postmortem	285.00
	Sex Organs Assaulted	282.00
	Sex Postmortem	285.00
	Evidence of Object Insertion	285.00

K = 96 Offenders
N = 3 Offense Series   Total N = 38
df = 95
Q Significant at $p < 0.01$ level in each

The results are in accord with the hypothesis that both behavioral and attachment facets are stable over time and across situations. It can be noted that several studies have found similar relationships between stability and instrumental or reactive aggression over time.[43,193,194] However, to further develop an empirical classification, we need to know how consistent serial murderers are from one crime to the next. Offender consistency is the focus of the next analysis.

12.5 Consistency of Serial Murderers Across their First, Middle, and Last Offense Series

In order to test offender consistency over the first, middle, and last offense series, it was necessary to construct four data matrices, a matrix for each theme, using the individual scores that offenders received on each variable. For example, looking at Table 12.1 under the first column, we see that offender one performed three behaviors in his first murder, two behaviors in the second murder, and two in his last murder. Each of these three individual scores were entered into a data matrix for each offender for all the four themes, in such a way so the columns represented the 96 offenders and the rows the first, middle, and last offense series.

Kendall's W was thus used to determine the association among offenders on the (N = 38) thematic variables over their (K = 3) offense series. The hypothesis under test was that serial murderers' ranking on their first offense will be similar to their rank on their middle and last offenses. A high or significant value of W may be interpreted as meaning that the offenders are performing essentially the same types of thematic behavior over the three offense series. It should be emphasized, however, that a high or significant value of W does not mean that the offenders scored the same on every variable, only that the overall ordering for all three offenses was similar. The results of Kendall's coefficient of concordance tests are shown in Table 12.4.

Spearman's *rho* was further employed to confirm the results of the Kendall's W^a tests. Between the three offense series for the AV theme, significant correlations were found between the first and middle offenses (rs = .698 p < .01), first and last offenses (rs = .698 p < 0.01), and middle and last offenses (rs = 1.00 p < 0.01). The average of the three r correlations was (rs = .799 p < 0.01), which of course was the same score achieved with the Kendall's W^a test for the AV theme.

Significant correlations between the AO first and middle offenses were found (rs = .788 p < .01), first and last offenses (rs = .549 p < 0.01), and middle and last offenses (rs = .687 p < 0.01). The average of the three r

Table 12.4 Kendall's Coefficients of Concordance Showing Consistency in Rankings Between Serial Murderers Across their First, Middle, and Last Offense Series

Theme	W^a	X^2
Affective Vehicle	0.799	227.72
Affective Object	0.783	223.12
Cognitive Vehicle	0.857	244.13
Cognitive Object	0.857	244.23

N = 96 Offenders

K = 3 Offense Series

Chi-Square Significant at p <0.01 (two-tailed) level df = 95

correlations was (rs = .783 p < 0.01), which again was the same score achieved with the Kendall's W^a for the AO theme as shown in Table 12.4.

For the CV theme, significant correlations were found between the first and middle offenses (rs = .879 p < 0.01), first and last offenses (rs = .813 p < 0.01), and middle and last offenses (rs = .879 p < .01). The average of the three correlations was (rs = .857 p < 0.01) which was the same achieved by the Kendall's W^a test for the CV theme. The final Spearman's *rho* tests on the CO theme found similar significant correlations between the first and middle offenses (rs = .879 p < 0.01), first and last offenses (rs = .813 p < 0.01), and middle and last offenses (rs =.879 p < 0.01). The average of the three correlations was (rs = .857 p < 0.01), which was the same for the Kendall's W^a test for the CV theme.

12.6 Summary

The hypothesis that serial murderers rank consistently over their first, middle, and last offense series is clearly supported by the results reported in this chapter. This finding lends credence to the theory that serial murderers were consistent in their behavior. And, as suggested by the POSA results in Chapter 11, that behavior typically does not change; it only becomes refined over time. These findings agree with Pine's view that individuals who actively repeat old internalized traumatic object relations are most likely to remain consistent in their behavior, and with Freud's idea that the more times an individual repeats the same behavior, the better he or she becomes at it.[62,119]

Modeling Crime Scene Behavior and Background Characteristics

13

Although the media frequently presents what is purported to be the profile of serial murderers, a review of the literature on the background characteristics reveals many dimensions along which offenders differ from one another. A number of serial murder classification schemes rely on descriptive statistics to categorize offenders according to what percentage of offenders had a certain characteristic in their background.[4,50,155] For example, as noted earlier, Ressler and his colleagues found that 81% of their serial murderer sample consumed pornographic materials, while 72% demonstrated fetishistic behavior, such as stealing and wearing or masturbating with women's undergarments.[155]

13.1 The Challenge of Linking Crime Scene Actions to Background Characteristics

In a later publication, Ressler and his colleagues went into more detail about the background history of the 36 murderers who participated in the FBI's serial murder project.[17] Again, as noted previously, the researchers found, for instance, that 70% of the offenders came from alcohol or drug-abusing family environments. Ressler and his co-workers argue that the offenders, as adults, were sexually dysfunctional and unable to sustain consensual adult relationships. Using interviews with convicted murderers, Ressler and his colleagues surmised that there were certain background characteristics that could describe the organized and disorganized serial murderers. For example, the FBI found that organized serial murderers who had an angry frame of mind prior to the murder and carried out the murder only in response to a triggering cue were most likely to work in a skilled occupation, to be married, own a car in good condition, and to follow the crime in the media.[17] In contrast, the FBI found that disorganized serial murderers who committed murders involving mutilation were more likely to have an unstable work history, sexual aversions, be single or divorced, and have a history of mental illness.[17]

In a more in-depth study by Hickey, using Glaser and Strauss's (1967) grounded theory as a methodology, he looked at the background characteristics of 169 male serial murderers.[20] Briefly, grounded theory is a technique used in qualitative research where the researcher makes constant comparisons between the data. Hickey found in his sample of serial murderers that, generally, they were not highly educated, nor did they commonly hold professional or even skilled careers.[20] In a subsample of the 169 serial murderers, Hickey also looked at the criminal history of 58 male serial murderers. He found that 35 (60%) had convictions of sex-related crimes, while 7 (12%) had a conviction for homicide.[20] Additional criminal histories included convictions for such crimes as burglary, 21 (36%); forgery, 5 (.08%); and robbery 24 (41%).[20]

However, the results of classification models such as those discussed above should be viewed with caution. There are ambiguities inherent in the category schemes and most cases are likely to spread across the two categories; the researchers did not compare background characteristics with the murderers' crime scene actions; and the classifications of different offender types are simply presented, then illustrated by the description of particular serial murder cases. Due to these weaknesses, it is therefore not possible to explore the general applicability of these classifications, because no background information or behavior on the samples have been published.

13.2 Point-Biserial Analysis of Crime Scene Behavior and Background Characteristics

In order to proceed with linking crime scene behavior and background characteristics, it was first necessary to determine if there exist any general differences between offenders' characteristics across the four themes.

To carry out the analysis, one data matrix was constructed using the total score on crime scene actions that each serial murderer received across his first, middle, and last offense series. An example of the overall scores can be found in Table 12.1 in Chapter 12 in the far right-hand column. So, for example, if an offender preformed four actions in his first offense, and five apiece in his middle and last offenses, then he would have received a total score of 14. Background characteristics were also included in the data matrix. The categorical data were laid out in such a way where the first four columns in the matrix represented the four themes affective-vehicle (AV), affective-object (AO), cognitive-vehicle (CV), and cognitive-object (CO); and under the four columns, the rows represented the individual scores for 96 serial murderers. The remaining columns represented background characteristics relating to criminal, sexual, and personal history (see Table 13.1), and the rows represented dichotomy scores on each of the background variables.

Pearson's r was employed to analyze the continuous and dichotomous data. When continuous and dichotomous data is analyzed using the *Phi* correlation, this procedure is called a point-biserial correlation.[195] Thus, algebraically, $r_{pb} = r$, where one variable is dichotomous and the other is continuous and more or less normally distributed in arrays.[195]

13.2.1 Results of the Point-Biserial Analysis

Behaviors from each theme were correlated with 15 background characteristics. The overall results found no significant associations between any of the themes and offenders' background characteristics. There was one exception, however, for the CV theme. One background variable, conviction for violent crimes — such as murder, attempted murder, rape, attempted rape, kidnaping, and attempted kidnaping — was found significantly associated with the cognitive-vehicle theme ($r = .262$ $p < 0.05$) two-tailed. The fact that the majority of the crime scene behavior and background characteristics showed no associations suggests that a more detailed examination must be employed to further our understanding of the relationship between serial murderers' crime scene behaviors and their background characteristics.

From the results above, it is clear that developments in the classification of offender characteristics cannot proceed by describing characteristics of one variable at a time. Although it is useful to know if an offender has a criminal history or not, it is essential to understand if he has antecedents for different types of offenses, and if there is a difference between offenders who have combinations of such antecedents. This need to consider the relationships between numbers of variables and characteristics, rather than taking one variable at a time, is part of the multivariate facet process. Employing a multivariate process, the next sections examined the relationship between thematic behavior and background variables in more detail. Accordingly, POSA was used.

13.3 Initial Preparation of the Data

Partial Order Scalogram Analysis (POSA) was explained in detail in Chapter 11. To recap, POSA plots the 96 offenders as points in space according to how similar they are across a number of variables; that is, crime scene behaviors and background characteristics. In some cases, a point may represent one or more offenders if they all had the same scores on all the facets. For example, POSA portrays the order of the offenders according to their scores on variables from each theme and characteristics of criminal history, so that offenders who score high on both facets will be positioned at the top right of the plot; offenders who score low will be positioned at the bottom left of the plot.

The first step in carrying out the POSA was to construct a data matrix where the rows represented the offenders or cases, and the columns the behaviors and characteristics. Due to the inherent large number of profiles that POSA could produce, it was necessary to limit the number of variables to be analyzed by POSA to 20. We know from the SSA in Chapter 12 that variables in each of the four thematic regions, albeit small, were mutually exclusive. Five crime scene behaviors from each of the four thematic SSA regions were selected for the POSA. The criteria for including the final 20 variables were determined by testing which of the 38 variables had the strongest linear relationship. Again, SSA was employed. As a result, the variables that showed the strongest linearity were included in the POSA analysis.

Scores used in creating the P matrix followed a pre-defined content analysis of the offenders' background history (see Appendix B). The background characteristics and the thematic behavior used in the analysis are listed in Tables 13.1 and 13.2.

Table 13.1 List of Offender Background Characteristics

Criminal History	Sexual History	Personal
Juvenile Convictions	Pedophilia	Not Employed
Fraud	Bestiality	Employed
Burglary	Fetishes	Educated
Sex Offenses	Pornography	No Education
Violent Offenses	Voyeurism	Age

Table 13.2 List of Crime Scene Behaviors from Each Theme

Affective Vehicle	Affective Object	Cognitive Vehicle	Cognitive Object
Forced Entry	Blitz	Ritualistic Activity	Body Parts
Ransacked Property	Bludgeon	Body Posed	Anthropophagy
Restraint Found	Ligature	Piqueurism	Disfigured Body
Fully Dressed	Object Inserted	Tortured	Dismember Post
Weapon Recovered	Bite Marks	Trophies	Sex Postmortem

The descriptions of the background characteristics and crime scene behaviors included in the analysis are provided in Appendices A and B. Using the variables listed in Tables 13.1 and 13.2, individual data matrixes were constructed for each of the four themes. In other words, each of the background characteristics was analyzed using behaviors from each theme. In all, 12 POSA tests were carried out on 96 serial murderers or cases.

As previously mentioned, offenders who had past juvenile convictions totaled (n = 53) 55%; fraud (n = 22) 23%; burglary, theft, or robbery (n = 57) 59%; and sex-related offenses (n = 44) 46%, while those who had past convictions of violent crime was (n = 24) 25%. Ten offenders (9.6%) had no past criminal history. The research question is thus whether these different types of background characteristics can be found to be associated with the serial murderer's crime scene behavior.

13.4 Elements of Crime Scene Behavior and Criminal History

13.4.1 Interpreting POSA Main Item Plots for Crime Scene Actions and Criminal History

For purposes of understanding the interpretation of the POSA main item plots in Figure 13.1, it is first necessary to point out that each point or number represents a profile describing a type of serial murderer. How well the profile coordinates in the POSA space reflect the relative order of the empirical profiles is measured by the Correspondence Coefficient (*Correp*). The *Correp* for the AV theme was .88, .84 for the AO theme, .79 for the CV theme, and .79 for the CO theme, respectively.

POSA analyzed the data in a way that maintained the individual data and the actual number of offenders who exhibited the behaviors associated with types of characteristics. The interpretation of the POSA main item plots is best understood by examining how each of the criminal history variables relate to thematic behavior. This is done by examining the subsequent set of plots called individual item plots.

13.5 Affective-Vehicle Theme and Criminal History

13.5.1 POSA Individual Item Plots for the AV Theme and Criminal History

Figures 13.2 to 13.5 are the individual item plots produced by the POSA. Each figure is grouped according to theme as it relates to criminal history. As previous mentioned in Chapter 11, "1's" mean that the offender did not possess that behavior or characteristic and "2's" that the offender did possess that behavior or characteristic. Looking at Figure 13.2, with the exception of one variable (past convictions of violent offenses), the remaining criminal history variables could not be partitioned. This suggests that the four criminal background characteristics — juvenile convictions, fraud, burglary, and sex-related convictions — are not useful for distinguishing or predicting aspects

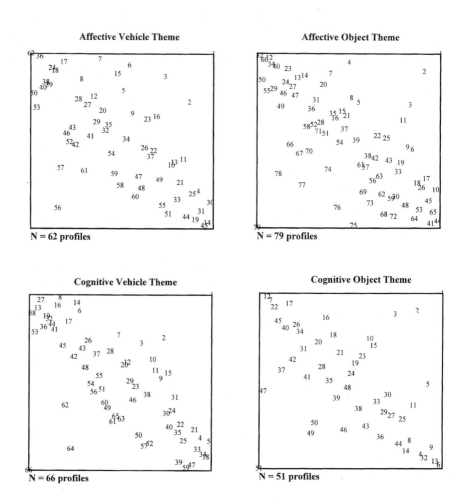

Figure 13.1 POSA Main Item Plots of 96 Serial Murderers for Criminal History and Crime Scene Behavior

of a serial murderers' background. Rather, the POSA results suggest that a variety of offenders are just as likely to possess any of the characteristics as not. Equally as important is the fact that none of the crime scene behaviors partitioned in relation to the four background characteristics, with the exception of violent offenses. Briefly, convictions of violent offenses include crimes such as murder, attempted murder, rape, attempted rape, kidnaping, or attempted kidnaping.

One background characteristic, past convictions of violent offenses, partitioned on the "Y" axis as shown in Figure 13.2. One behavior, ransacked victim's property, partitioned on the "X" axis, while forced entry into the victim's home partitioned as a inverse L shape. The inverse L shape is found

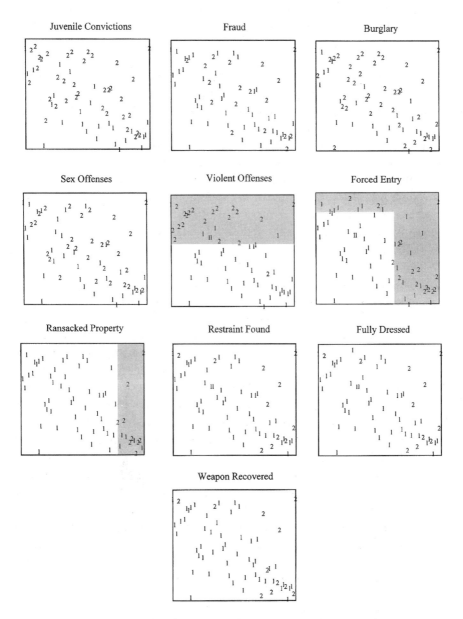

Figure 13.2 POSA Item Plots for Criminal History and Elements of Crime Scene Behavior from the Affective-Vehicle Theme

with items playing a role of polarizers in the scalogram. For the AV theme, this means that serial murderers who gained entry into their victims' home by using force also had past convictions of violent crimes; however, they were less likely to have ransacked the victims' property.

Subsequent tests using Pearson's correlation (r) two-tailed analysis were performed on the same variables used in the previous POSA. Pearson's r measured the strength of the linear association between the background characteristics and crime scene behaviors. It should be noted that the correlation analysis for each scatterplot was first inspected for a linear association. In cases where there was no association between variables, several variables were removed at random to see if the scatterplot was altered. In the original cases where no linear association was found, subsequent tests after the removal of the random variables did not affect the plot. In other words, variables that showed no association in the first instance also showed no association in subsequent analysis when the variables were removed. This procedure was also carried out on variables that showed a linear association. Kruskal and Wish argue that there is probably a real relationship between the two variables, if the shape of the plot is unaltered by the removal of a few random observations.[145]

The Pearson's analysis found no significant r relationships between most of the characteristics and behaviors. A number of variables having significant associations not revealed by the POSA could facilitate our understanding of the AV offender's background. One variable in particular, burglary, had a significant association with past juvenile convictions ($r = .281$ $p < 0.01$) and past violent offenses ($r = .220$ $p < 0.05$). A significant association was found of serial murderers who had a past criminal history of robbery and juvenile convictions ($r = .281$ $p < 0.01$). A relationship was also found between serial murderers who had convictions of sex-related crimes and juvenile records ($r = .205$ $p < 0.05$). Several significant associations between crime scene behaviors were found. For example, serial murderers who used force to gain entry into their victims' homes were found significantly related to those who ransacked their victims' property ($r = .493$ $p < 0.01$), while offenders who left a restraint behind at the crime scene were found to have an association with forced entry ($r = .234$ $p < 0.05$). These findings are in accord with studies cited earlier that suggested that the affective-vehicle serial murderer is emotional and forensically careless during the commission of his crimes. The results also support Meloy's view that affective aggression is disorganized and the offender's reality is often distorted.[98]

13.6 Affective-Object Theme and Criminal History

13.6.1 POSA Individual Item Plots for the AO Theme and Criminal History

Figure 13.3 is the POSA individual item plots for the affective-object thematic behaviors and criminal history. Looking at the individual configurations, we

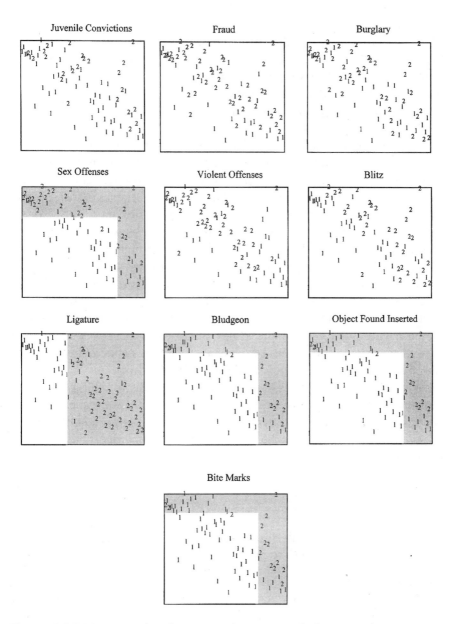

Figure 13.3 POSA Item Plots for Criminal History and Elements of Crime Scene Behavior from the Affective-Object Theme

see that with the exception of one background characteristic and one crime scene behavior, the remaining variables could not be partitioned due to a mixture of "1's" and "2's." This means that in this sample of serial murderers, offenders who left an AO-type crime scene were just as likely to have a criminal history of juvenile convictions, fraud, burglary, and violent offense convictions than not. In other words, it would be difficult to predict with any certainty that serial murderers who performed these sorts of crime scene behaviors would also have a past criminal history. However, there was one exception: serial murderers with past convictions of sex-related offenses were more likely to use a ligature, bludgeon their victims, leave an object inserted, and bite marks.

Serial murderers who used a ligature have their profiles plotted on the "Y" axis. The POSA partition for the variables sex-related offenses, bludgeon, object found inserted, and bite marks is referred to as an accentuating partition.[147] This suggests that offenders who have these variables in their profiles were high on the "J" axis and were associated with profiles plotted low on the "L" axis. In this sample, serial murderers who had low organization and personal attachment to the victim, including foreign objects and bite marks, were more likely to have past convictions of sex-related offenses.

Subsequent analysis employing Pearson's correlation (r) was performed on the AO behaviors and background characteristics. The analysis helped shed some light on the relationship between several important behaviors and characteristics not found by the POSA. Aside from the POSA results that showed sex-related offenses to be associated with crime scene behavior, no new relationships were found between criminal history and crime scene behavior. However, there was one association originally found by the POSA, between the behaviors ligature and bludgeon, that in the subsequent analysis showed a significant association of ($r = .264$ $p < 0.01$). The remaining behaviors that were partitioned by the POSA did not show significant associations in subsequent analysis.

13.7 Cognitive-Vehicle Theme and Criminal History

13.7.1 POSA Individual Item Plots for the CV Theme and Criminal History

Figure 13.4 below is the POSA individual item plots for the cognitive-vehicle (CV) theme and characteristics of criminal history. As found in the previous individual plots, the majority of the variables could not be partitioned due to a mixture of "1's" and "2's" with the exception of two variables: violent offenses and body posed. One background variable, violent offenses, partitioned on the "Y" axis, while one crime scene behavior, body posed, partitioned on the "X" axis. This suggests that serial murderers in this study who had past convictions of murder and rape were not likely to pose their victims' bodies. This finding is important from an investigative

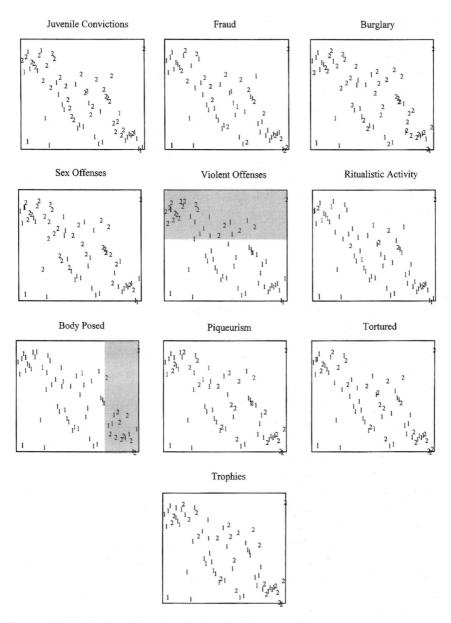

Figure 13.4 POSA Item Plots for Criminal History and Elements of Crime Scene Behavior from the Cognitive-Vehicle Theme

point of view, because traditionally the literature on serial murder argues that offenders who pose their victims are less likely to have past convictions of violent crimes.[17]

As with the previous themes, Pearson's correlation r was employed to test for significant associations between the CV thematic behaviors and criminal history. Overall, the analysis showed no significant associations between the characteristics of criminal history and the CV thematic behaviors. However, in subsequent analysis, one background variable in particular — juvenile convictions — that could not be partitioned by POSA was found to have a significant relationship with violent offenses (r = .220 p < 0.05). Two additional behaviors that could not be partitioned in the POSA, tortured victim and piqueurism, showed a significant association (r = .343 p < 0.01). The relationship between tortured and piqueurism accords with De River's suggestion that individuals who commit piqueurism receive sexual excitement from the action; and that very often they have a fixation (fetish) for some particular part of the body, and they will try to torture the victim in this particular area.[45]

13.8 Cognitive-Object Theme and Criminal History

13.8.1 POSA Individual Item Plots for the CO Theme and Criminal History

Figure 13.5 is the POSA individual item plots for the cognitive-object (CO) theme and characteristics of criminal history. Four background characteristics — juvenile convictions, fraud, burglary, and violent offenses — could not be partitioned due a mixture of "1's" and "2's." One background variable, sex offenses, partitioned on the "Y" axis. Serial murderers with past sex-related convictions are plotted in the upper top region of the POSA space.

Four crime scene variables — body parts scattered, disfigured victim's body, dismembered body postmortem, and sex postmortem — partitioned as an inverse "L" shape. This type of partitioning suggests that serial murderers' profiles that were plotted in the lower right-hand corner for the three crime scene behaviors relate to profiles plotted low on the "L" axis, which are found in the upper left-hand corner for the background variable of sex-related offenses. One crime scene action that could be partitioned is anthropophagy. This variable plotted on the "X" axis as shown in Figure 13.5. The fact that serial murderers whose profiles contained the variable anthropophagy plotted on the "X" axis and sex-related offenses plotted on the "Y" indicates that serial murderers who had these variables in their profiles are quantitatively distinct from one another. However, the results also show that serial murderers who performed anthropophagy were more likely to scatter body parts, disfigure the victim, dismember postmortem, and perform sex postmortem. These findings fit well with previous studies, especially in serial rape cases where the assaults involve a ritualistic quality and fixation on

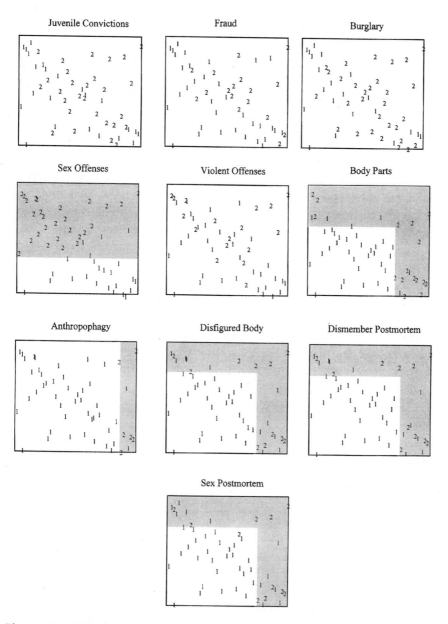

Figure 13.5 POSA Item Plots for Criminal History and Elements of Crime Scene Behavior from the Cognitive-Object Theme

specific areas such as breasts, genitals, and buttocks.[183] Consequently, there is currently no serial murder literature with which the present findings could be compared.

206 Hunting Serial Predators

In a confirmatory analysis, all background characteristics, juvenile convictions, fraud, burglary, sex-related offenses, and violent offenses showed no significant association with any of the behaviors when submitted to the Pearson's correlation test. The POSA found that serial murderers who committed mutilation and sadistic acts had sex-related criminal convictions; therefore, the overall results indicate that the literature on serial murder that suggests organized type killers are most likely not to have a criminal history is definitely open to question.[155,163]

In light of the finding that no significant associations were found between background characteristics and CO thematic behaviors, there were, however, significant associations found between a number of crime scene behaviors that are readily appreciated by looking at the POSA. One variable in particular, body parts scattered, was found to statistically correlate with several other crime scene behaviors, including anthropophagy ($r = .545$ $p < 0.01$), disfigured body ($r = .744$ $p < 0.01$), dismemberment postmortem ($r = .731$ $p < 0.01$), and sexual activity postmortem ($r = .511$ $p < 0.01$). Additional significant associations were found between anthropophagy and dismemberment postmortem ($r = .398$ $p < 0.01$), sex postmortem and dismemberment postmortem ($r = .488$ $p < 0.01$), sex postmortem and disfigured body ($r = .511$ $p < 0.01$), and anthropophagy and sex postmortem ($r = .534$ $p < 0.01$). The fact that similar associations between POSA and regression analysis were found is remarkable. This suggests that using regression approaches to tests the POSA structures is reliable in cases were the data is very clear, precise, and of a strong numerical form.

13.9 Summary

Broadly, there were no obvious clear, consistent relationships between crime scene behavior and the background characteristics studied here. However, some relationships did emerge. For example, both the POSA and subsequent Pearson's correlation results showed an apparent relationship between criminal history in offenders who treated their victims as vehicles. Thus, when a murderer was emotional and disorganized, he was most likely to have a past criminal history of violent crimes such as murder, kidnaping, and rape. This finding agrees with literature cited earlier on individuals who possess a *fearful* attachment style, that these types of people isolate themselves from social relationships and also build up their rage to a point that their crimes involve random attacks where little or no planning is cognitively meditated. Conversely, serial murderers who viewed their victims as objects were found to have a criminal history of sex-related convictions rather than violent convictions. Convictions of this nature included, for example, fondling and crimes against nature. Also, killers with cognitive behaviors were not more likely to have a past criminal history of minor crimes. Although offenders did have convictions for less violent crimes, there were no minor offenses that partitioned in the POSA, meaning that these characteristics are not distinctive for linking to crime scene behavior. This finding is a departure from current serial murder literature that suggests serial murderers who commit lust murders are most likely not to have a criminal record.[155] From an attachment theory perspective, as hypothesized, individuals with *dismissing* styles were most likely to compartmentalize their sadistic behavior and criminal activities, because many of the serial murderers who committed sadistic acts were suspected of committing past violent crimes. Irrespective of this fact, it can be said with some confidence that serial murderers who leave a cognitive-object (CO) or affective-object (AO) crime scene were more likely to have a past history of some sort of sex-related convictions.

13.10 Serial Murderers, Crime Scene Behavior, and Sex

Due to media reports and popular books on serial murder, the public believes that serial murderers possess particularly bizarre and perverted sexual characteristics.[56,163] These types of labels are responsible for serial murderers being portrayed as lust murderers. Classifying individuals who displayed varieties of sadistic behavior in their crimes can be traced back to De River's 1958 book entitled *Crime and the Sexual Psychopath*, where he points out that sadism is the compelling element in lust murder.[45] For example, Arbolita-Florez and Holley found in their research on multiple murderers that most are sexual sadists who derive great satisfaction from publicity surrounding their cases, in addition to the sexual mutilations and deaths they cause.[196]

In a similar vein, FBI researchers argue that the disorganized serial murderer has difficulties with interpersonal relationships and often this is compensated through using the victim as a sex prop.[17,51] As shown by the SSA results in Chapter 10, the focus of sex in serial murder is a salient feature. The studies cited above focus only on one type of serial murderer, lust murderers. As a consequence, there is no empirical research that has specifically looked at crime scene behavior and manifestations of sexual history in individuals who kill a number of people over time.

To reiterate, in the present sample of serial murderers (n = 21) 22% had a history of pedophilia, while (n = 1) 1% had a history of practicing bestiality. Serial murderers who had a fixation or fetishes for specific body parts or inanimate objects, such as dildos and other sex toys, were (n = 57) 59%, while (n = 18) 19% had a history of voyeurism or convictions of peeping tom. Killers who read and/or collected a variety of pornography was (n = 63)

66%. Twenty-two killers (4%) in this study had no history of these sexual predilections. The finding on the use of pornography by serial murderers echoes the FBI's results, where they found that 72% of their serial murder sample consumed pornographic materials.[17]

13.11 Elements of Crime Scene Behavior and Sexual History

13.11.1 Interpreting the POSA Main Item Plots for Crime Scene Behavior and Sexual History

Figure 13.6 is the POSA main item plots for the four themes with facets of sexual history. How well the profile coordinates in the POSA space reflect

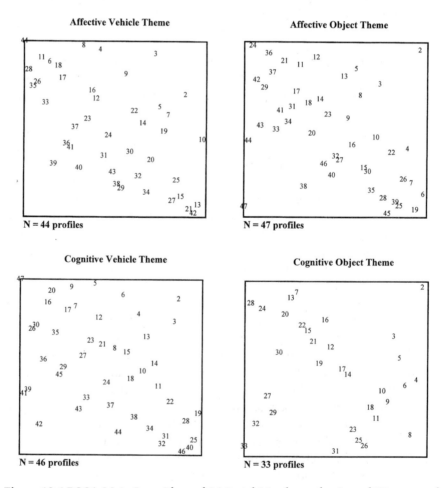

Figure 13.6 POSA Main Item Plots of 96 Serial Murderers for Sexual History and Criminal Behavior

the relative order of the empirical profiles is measured by the Correspondence Coefficient (*Correp*). The *Correp* for the AV theme was .75, .69 for the AO theme, .69 for the CV theme, and .81 for the CO theme, respectively.

POSA produced profiles in all four themes that plotted on both the qualitative "L" axis and quantitatively on the "J" axis. The interpretation of the POSA main item plots is best understood by examining how facets of sexual history relate to thematic behavior. This is done by examining the subsequent set of plots called individual item plots.

13.12 Affective-Vehicle Theme and Sexual History

13.12.1 POSA Individual Item Plots for the AV Theme and Sexual History

Figures 13.7 to 13.10 are the individual item plots produced by the POSA. As previously mentioned, the "1's" represent that the behavior or characteristic was not present in the offender's profile, while the "2's" represent that the behavior or characteristic was present in the offender's profile.

Looking at Figure 13.7, one characteristic — voyeurism— partitioned on the "Y" axis, while one behavior — ransacked victim's property — also partitioned on the"Y" axis. So, in this particular sample of serial murderers, offenders who ransacked their victims' property also had convictions for voyeurism or peeping tom. Subsequent analysis using Pearson's correlation (*r*) found a significant association between these two variables (r = .241 p < 0.05). The finding is also important because it suggests that victims were targeted in their homes and that offenders were conformable in this type of environment. The remaining background characteristics could not be partitioned due to a mixture of "1's" and "2's."

Three variables — restraint found at scene, victim left fully dressed, and weapon recovered at the scene — partitioned on the "X" axis but did not relate to any background characteristics. So, for this sample of serial murderers who had a history of voyeurism or peeping tom and did not ransack their victims' property, they were most likely not to leave a restraint or weapon at the scene or leave their victims fully dressed.

Several behaviors in a subsequent analysis using Pearson's correlation showed an association that was not found by the POSA. Although two background characteristics — pornography and fetishes — could not be partitioned in the POSA configuration, a latter analysis using Pearson's *r* found that the two variables significantly correlated (r = .562 p < 0.01). Additional correlation was found between offenders who left a restraint behind at the scene and pornography (r = .235 p < 0.05). A significant *r* correlation was found to exist between two background characteristics that could not be

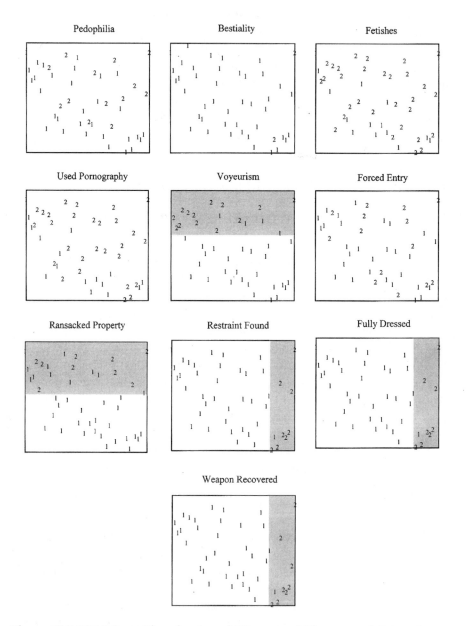

Figure 13.7 POSA Item Plots for Sexual History and Elements of Crime Scene Behavior from the Affective-Vehicle Theme

partitioned by the POSA: a history of pedophilia and fetishes ($r = .335$ $p <$ 0.01). The hypothesis that AV killers leave their crime scenes in disarray appears to be supported by the results; for instance, leaving both a restraint and weapon at the scene and ransacking the victim's property indicates a lack of forensic awareness. The findings also show that for this sample of serial murderers, offenders who enter their victims' homes and leave their crime scenes in disarray are most likely to use pornography and have convictions of peeping tom.

13.13 Affective-Object Theme and Sexual History

13.13.1 POSA Individual Item Plots for the AO Theme and Sexual History

Figure 13.8 has the POSA individual item plots for the affective-object theme and characteristics of sexual history. Looking at the POSA space configurations, we can see that several characteristics could be partitioned. Two background characteristics, fetishes and pornography, are called an inverse "L" or accentuating partitions.[101] Serial murderers who had fetishes for sexual toys and pornography in their profiles are plotted on the "J" axis, with the majority of profiles moving from the middle of the POSA space up towards the right-hand corner of the plots. This suggests that offenders who consumed pornography also engaged in using objects or toys for pleasure.

In regards to crime scene behavior, one behavior, blitz, partitioned on the "Y" axis. Looking at the variable blitz attack, we see that serial murderers who blitz attacked their victims were more likely to possess pornography and display affinity for fetishistic objects. The additional crime scene behaviors — bludgeon, object found inserted, and bite marks — partitioned on the "X" axis. This finding is interesting for several reasons. It shows that some serial murderers who surprised their victims by a blitz attack and did not bludgeon their victims or use a foreign object also did not bite their victims. However, offenders who bludgeoned their victims, used a foreign object, and left bite marks consumed pornography and engaged in the use of fetishistic objects in their personal lives. Three background variables — pedophilia, bestiality, and voyeurism — did not partition, while one crime scene behavior, ligature, also did not partition. However, in subsequent analysis, using Pearson's correlation r, relationships between some variables were found.

Subsequent analysis using Pearson's correlation r confirmed several of the POSA partitions. For example, a significant correlation was found between fetishes and pornography ($r = 562$ $p < 0.01$) and ligature and bludgeon ($r = 264$ $p < 0.01$). However, two variables that did partition and showed an association were fetishes and pedophilia ($r = 335$ $p < 0.01$).

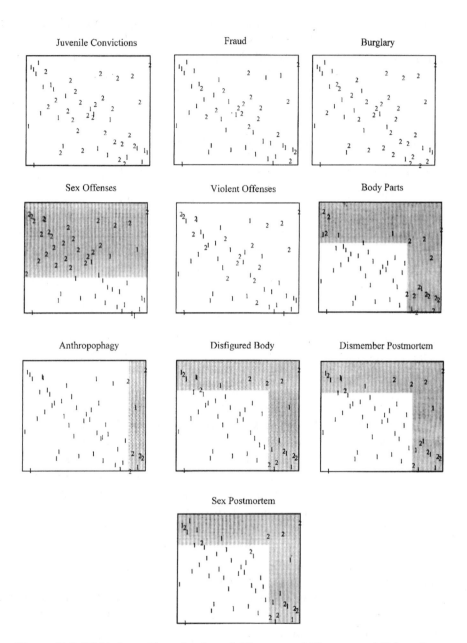

Figure 13.8 POSA Item Plots for Sexual History and Elements of Crime Scene Behavior from the Affective-Object Theme

13.14 Cognitive-Vehicle Theme and Sexual History

13.14.1 POSA Individual Item Plots for the CV Theme and Sexual History

Figure 13.9 is the individual item plots produced by the POSA for the cognitive-vehicle theme and facets of sexual history. Looking at the individual item configurations, we see that the majority of the background and crime scene variables did not partition.

There were three exceptions, however: pornography, fetishes, and body posed. The variable pornography partitioned across the "X" and "Y" axes, indicating that the majority of offenders for the CV theme possessed this background characteristic. The variable fetishes partitioned on the "Y" axis, and offenders with this variable in their profiles are plotted in the upper region of the POSA space. The relative partitions of pornography and fetishes suggest that serial murderers who used pornography also used fetish objects, i.e., sex toys, as a part of their fantasies. One crime scene behavior, offender posed the victim's body, partitioned on the "X" axis. This finding is most interesting because it suggests that serial murderers who posed the victim's body also consumed pornography; however, they did not engage in fantasy play with sex toys.

Several interesting relationships between background characteristics and crime scene behavior not revealed by the POSA were found to exist in subsequent analysis using Pearson's correlation r. A significant correlation was found between pornography and ritualistic activity ($r = .203$ $p < 0.05$), while the variable voyeurism was found to significantly correlate with piquerism ($r = .273$ $p < 0.01$). Several background variables were found to have a correlation: pedophilia and fetishes ($r = .335$ $p < 0.01$) and pornography and fetishes ($r = .562$ $p < 0.01$). The latter association between pornography and fetishes confirmed the POSA partitions.

13.15 Cognitive-Object Theme and Sexual History

13.15.1 POSA Individual Item Plots for the CO Theme and Sexual History

Figure 13.10 shows the POSA individual item plots for the cognitive-object theme and characteristics of sexual history. Looking at the POSA configurations, we see that the majority of background and crime scene behaviors did not partition due to a mixture of "1's" and "2's." What is most interesting, though, are the two variables pedophilia and fetishes. Pedophilia partitioned

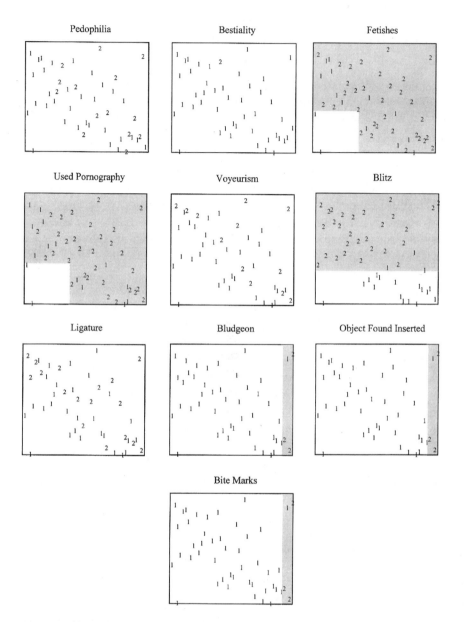

Figure 13.9 POSA Item Plots for Sexual History and Elements of Crime Scene Behavior from the Cognitive-Vehicle Theme

on the "Y" axis and fetishes partitioned across both the "X" and "Y" axes. So, for this sample of serial murderers, those who had a history of pedophilia also used sexual objects to act out their fantasy games; however, they did not

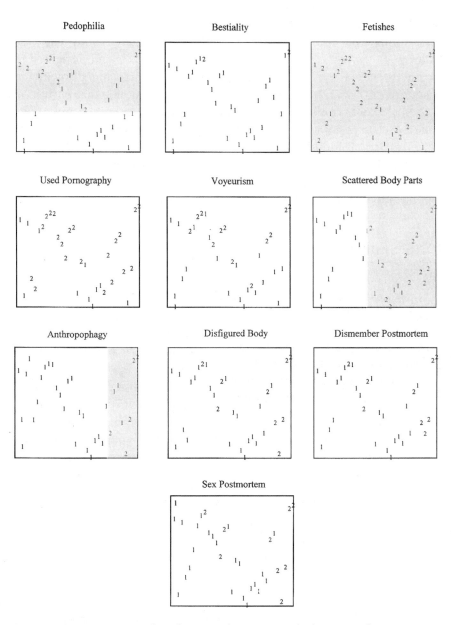

Figure 13.10 POSA Item Plots for Sexual History and Elements of Crime Scene Behavior from the Cognitive-Object Theme

scatter the victim's body parts nor perform anthropophagy. This means that serial murderers who scattered body parts and performed anthropophagy acted out their fantasies by using fetishistic objects when non-offending.

Subsequent analysis using Pearson's correlation found that several variables were related that did not partition in the POSA. For example, significant correlations were found between the variables scattered body parts and anthropophagy ($r = .545$ p < 0.01); scattered body parts and disfigured the victim ($r = .744$ p < 0.01); and scattered body parts and dismembered postmortem ($r = .731$ p < 0.01). One background variable that partitioned in the POSA was confirmed in the subsequent analysis. For example, pedophile correlated significantly with fetishes ($r = .335$ p < 0.01). However, there were associations found in the subsequent analysis that were not revealed by the POSA. For example, a significant correlation was found between voyeurism and fetishes ($r = .289$ p < 0.01), while sex postmortem was found to significantly correlate with fetishes ($r = .213$ p < 0.05).

13.16 Summary

The results of the POSA and Pearson's correlations between characteristics of sexual history and crime scene behavior show that when the offender leaves forensic clues at the scene, he is more likely to have a background history of voyeurism, pornography, and fetishistic behavior. This finding parallels the FBI's position that disorganized serial murderers are most likely to have a history of sexual aberrations in their backgrounds.[17] Serial murderers who were organized in their behavior and sadistic were more likely to have a history of using pornography and fetishistic objects in addition to pedophilic activity, but not voyeurism. This finding matches previous literature on serial murder that suggests an organized-type offender will usually engage in viewing pornographic materials, and act out their fantasies in their personal issues using various sex-related objects.[17,59]

13.17 Elements of Crime Scene Behavior and Personal History

13.17.1 Interpreting the POSA Main Item Plots for Personal History

Figure 13.11 illustrates the POSA item plots for the four themes, with facets of education and employment history. As previously mentioned, how well the profile coordinates in the POSA space reflects the relative order of the empirical profiles is measured by the Correspondence Coefficient (*Correp*).[88] The *Correp* for the AV theme was .89, .85 for the AO theme, .85 for the CV theme, and .92 for the CO theme.

Looking at Figure 13.11, the POSA produced two different types of configurations. In the AV and CV themes, the profiles are plotted on the "L"

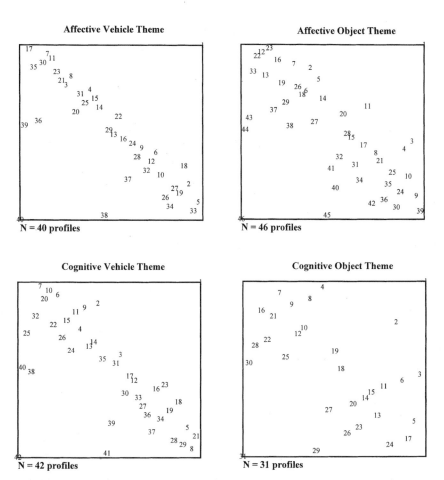

Figure 13.11 POSA Main Item Plots of 96 Serial Murderers for Personal History and Crime Scene Behavior

axes, while in the AO and CO themes, the profiles are plotted more along the "J" axes. This finding suggests that for the AV and CV themes, offenders' profiles are qualitatively different, and the AO and CO profiles are quantitatively different. In order to explore these differences, it is necessary to examine the individual item plots produced by the POSA.

13.18 Affective–Vehicle Theme and Personal History

13.18.1 POSA Individual Item Plots for the AV Theme and Personal History

Figure 13.12 establishes the individual item plots for the affective-vehicle theme and personal history. Looking at the configurations in Figure 13.12

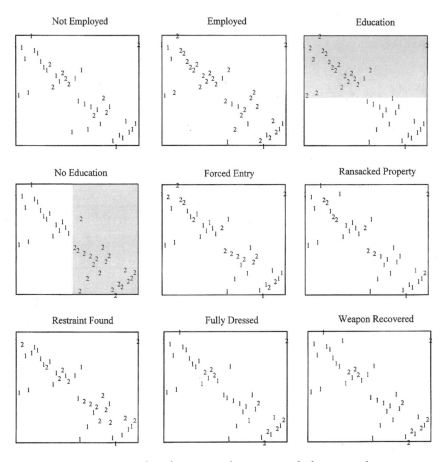

Figure 13.12 POSA Item Plots for Personal History and Elements of Crime Scene Behavior from the Affective-Vehicle Theme

below, we see that the majority of the plots did not partition due to a mixture of "1's" and "2's." There were two exceptions: offenders with a high school educational level or beyond and those who dropped out of high school.

Profiles of offenders who had an education partitioned on the "Y" axis, while those with no education partitioned on the "X" axis. This suggests that the two variables are quantitatively different. It is also interesting that crime scene behavior and employment history could not be partitioned. This finding suggests that serial murderers (at least in this sample) who left disorganized type crime scenes had various employment levels. However, a subsequent analysis using Pearson's correlation r found significant correlations between education and being employed ($r = .340$ $p < 0.01$), and education and not employed ($r = .225$ $p < 0.05$). In other words, serial murderers who left their crime scenes in disarray were just as likely to have had an education and a job as not.

13.19 Affective–Object Theme and Personal History

13.19.1 POSA Individual Item Plots for the AO Theme and Personal History

Figure 13.13 is the POSA individual item plots for the affective-object theme and personal history. Several interesting relationships were revealed in Figure 13.13 As in the previous section, the variables education and no education plotted on the "Y" and "X" axes, respectively. However, there were three crime scene variables — ligature, object found inserted, and left bite marks — that were found to relate to education and no education. The three crime scene behaviors partitioned as an inverse "L." The indication given by the POSA results show that serial murderers who used a ligature, left an object inserted, and left bite marks on the victim were just as likely to be educated as not.

A subsequent test, using Pearson's correlation r, found no significant correlations between the background characteristics and crime scene behaviors highlighted by the POSA. However, significant correlations were found between ligature and bludgeon ($r = .264$ $p < 0.01$), and education and employed ($r = .340$ $p < 0.01$). These findings underscore the FBI's suggestion that disorganized serial murderers are less educated and likely to be unemployed.[17] In other words, disorganization at the crime scene is not a good predictor of a serial murderer's education or if he or she is employed.

13.20 Cognitive–Vehicle Theme and Personal History

13.20.1 POSA Individual Item Plots for the CV Theme and Personal History

Figure 13.14 presents the POSA item plots for the cognitive-vehicle theme and personal history. Similar to the individual configurations in the AV and AO themes, we see that education and no education partitioned on the "X" and "Y" axes. One background characteristic, employed, partitioned on both the "X" and "Y" axes. This finding indicates that serial murderers who were employed had a variety of educational levels. The remaining background variables and behaviors did not partition due to a mixture of "1's" and "2's."

Subsequent analysis employing Pearson's correlation r found some interesting correlations between the CV thematic behaviors, employment, and educational levels that did not partition by the POSA. For example, a significant correlation was found between offenders who had no education and posing the victim's body ($r = .238$ $p < 0.05$). In addition, significant correlations were found between employed and ritualistic activity ($r = .305$ $p < 0.01$) and not employed and ritualistic activity ($r = .305$ $p < 0.01$). One

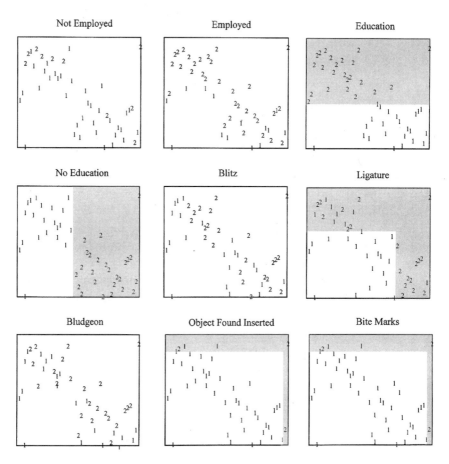

Figure 13.13 POSA Item Plots for Personal History and Elements of Crime Scene Behavior from the Affective-Object Theme

significant correlation absent from the POSA was found between the variables tortured victim and piqueurism ($r = .343$ $p < 0.01$). No correlations were found for the remaining background characteristics and behaviors. Broadly, the results show that serial murderers in the CV theme have a variety of educational levels; however, they are more likely to have a job.

13.21 Cognitive–Object Theme and Personal History

13.21.1 POSA Individual Item Plots for the CO Theme and Personal History

Figure 13.15 shows the individual item plots for the cognitive-object theme and personal history. Looking at the POSA plots, we see that the variables

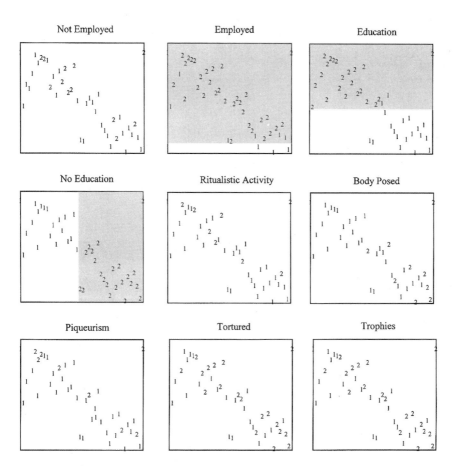

Figure 13.14 POSA Item Plots for Personal History and Elements of Crime Scene Behavior from the Cognitive-Vehicle Theme

education, no education, and employed partitioned similarly to the CV theme. Employed and educated partitioned on the "Y" axis, while no education partitioned on the "X" axis.

However, several interesting relationships for the CO theme were revealed. Three behaviors — disfigured victim's body, dismemberment postmortem, and sex postmortem — partitioned as an inverse "L." This finding suggests that in this sample of serial murderers, offenders who performed these three behaviors were employed, but came from different educational backgrounds. The remaining background variables and behaviors could not be partitioned.

Further analysis using Pearson's correlation r found no additional correlations between the CO behaviors and background characteristics. Several significant correlations found between crime scene behaviors that did not

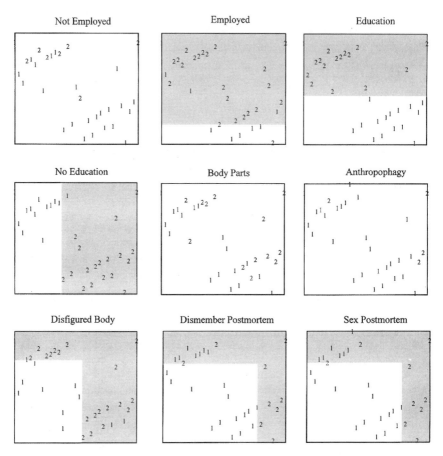

Figure 13.15 POSA Item Plots for Personal History and Elements of Crime Scene Behavior from the Cognitive-Object Theme

partition are: body parts scattered and dismemberment postmortem (r = .731 p < 0.01); body parts scattered and victim disfigured (r = .744 p < 0.01); and body parts scattered and anthropophagy (r = 545 p < 0.01). The general finding for the cognitive-object theme, is that serial murderers who disfigured, dismembered postmortem, and performed sexual acts postmortem, had a job; however, they had various educational backgrounds. This finding is a departure from previous studies that argue that serial murderers who commit lust murders are likely to be unemployed and have no education.[2,17]

13.22 Elements of Crime Scene Behavior and Age

The age of the perpetrator in current serial murder literature is rarely discussed. For example, the FBI researchers briefly mention that their sample of 36 offenders had birth years ranging from 1904 to 1958.[61] However, in subsequent FBI studies there is no information provided on the offenders' ages and whether they were likely to have committed certain sorts of crime scene behaviors or possess particular background characteristics. More traditional literature on single homicide suggests that offenders who commit spontaneous acts of violence tend to be young. A more recent study that looked at individuals who murdered children found that, in 621 cases, the average age of the perpetrator was 27 years.[156] In research by Goetting, she found that her sample of the offenders' mean age was 26 years.[197] In Hickey's study of male serial murderers, he found that the average age of the offenders when they started their killing was approximately 28 years.[20] In a subsequent study, Hickey divided his sample of serial murderers into a subgroup of offenders that included 32 cases, comprising 76 offenders. Hickey found that the average age of his male serial murderer sample was 30.[20]

From the general discussion above we see that age varies according to what type of crime is studied. However, none of these studies empirically linked age to crime scene behavior or to background characteristics that could be meaningful for developing a heuristic classification model of serial murder.

13.23 Age and Thematic Classifications

In Chapter 12, serial murderers, including those offenders labelled as hybrids, were assigned to one of the four thematic classifications. This step was important because it allowed us to easily classify each offender's age according to the theme to which he belongs. The age ranges of serial murderers classified in each of the themes are presented in Table 13.3.

Table 13.3 Age Range of Serial Murderers Classified in Each Theme

Theme	N	Age Range	Mean Age	SD
Affective Vehicle	16	22–42	30	5.00
Affective Object	31	24–48	31	6.70
Cognitive Vehicle	6	20–37	28	4.60
Cognitive Object	27	23–45	31	5.00
Hybrids	16	21–40	29	4.90

13.24 Difference Between Offenders' Ages Across the Four Themes

The next step in the study was to examine whether there were any differences between offenders' ages across the entire sample. To look at this across the four themes, a one-way analysis of variance ANOVA was used. To carry out

ANOVA, one data matrix was constructed with each serial murderers' raw age from all four themes in one column, and the grouping variable in the next column. Groups were scored according to different years of age: (1 = 18 to 25), (2 = 26 to 31), (3 = 32 to 36), (4 = 37 to 42), and (5 = over 42).

13.24.1 ANOVA Results

The ANOVA results found no significant differences between serial murderers' ages across the four themes. The results are shown in Table 13.4.

Table 13.4 One-Way Analysis of Variance of Serial Murderers' Ages Across the Four Themes

Source	Sum of Squares	DF	Mean Square	F-ratio	F-probability
Between Groups (Combined)	26.647	4	6.662	0.155	0.96
Linear Term (Unweighted)	2.476	1	2.476	0.058	0.811
Weighted	3.871	1	3.871	0.09	0.765
Deviation	22.776	3	7.592	0.177	0.912
Within Groups	3913.26	101	43.003		
Total	3939.906	106			

13.25 Elements of Crime Scene Behavior, Personal History, and Age

In order to present a clear picture of a serial murderer, it is necessary to test which crime scene behaviors and background characteristics relate to age. Therefore, in the final stage of the analysis, a series of Pearson's correlation r tests were carried out using 38 crime scene behaviors, 15 background characteristics, and the variable age.

13.25.1 Results of the Point-Biserial Correlation Between Age, Crime Scene Behavior, and Background Characteristics

The Pearson's correlation tests found no significant relationships between any of the background variables and age. With the exception of the variable past convictions of sex-related crimes ($r = .339$ $p < 0.01$), no other significant associations were found between crime scene behavior and age.

13.26 Summary

Regarding crime scene behavior and personal history, a number of interesting relationships emerged. In particular, serial murderers who did not plan their crimes and showed little forensic awareness were just as likely to be educated as serial murderers who cognitively planned their murders and destroyed evidence. Also interesting is the fact that serial murderers who left an affective-type crime scene were more likely to have a job than offenders who showed control over their crime scene behavior. However, for crimes that involved the victim being viewed as a vehicle, crime scene behavior was not very reliable for predicting with any confidence the offender's educational level or if he had a job. In contrast, though, for murderers who viewed their victims as objects, several crime scene variables proved fruitful for predicting whether the offender had a job, but not an education. Six behaviors — ligature, object found inserted, bite marks, disfigured body, dismembered postmortem, and sex postmortem — were found to be robust for predicting that an offender was more likely to be employed. However, the variables were less useful for predicting whether the offender was educated.

The variable age was less useful for predicting aspects of the killer's crime scene behavior or their other background characteristics. This fits with James' view that in a serial murder investigation, there is a chance equal to the flip of a coin that the person who has committed a certain type of crime is in a particular age bracket.[154]

Applications To Police Investigations

14

The thrust of this research was to develop an empirical model of the crime scene actions of U.S. serial murderers based on information available to a police inquiry. On the whole, the data supports the hypothesized two-facet, four-element model proposed in Chapter 3. Also, a limited number of background characteristics were found to be related to aspects of this model and crime scene behavior. However, if the present analysis has any validity, it should be possible to apply these conclusions to a number of illustrative real-life serial murder cases. To this end, and by way of summary, four representative cases — including an actual serial murder case that the author profiled — are considered in this final chapter.

14.1 Case Study Research

A case study is an empirical inquiry that investigates a contemporary phenomenon within its real-life context, especially when the boundaries between phenomenon and context are not clearly evident.[198] Case studies have traditionally been stereotyped as weak. For example, one question often asked about the use of case studies is, "How can you generalize from a single case?" Yin provided an elegant answer by asking another question: "How can you generalize from a single experiment?" Yin goes on to point out that scientific facts are rarely based on single experiments; they are usually based on a multiple set of experiments, which have replicated the same phenomena under different conditions.[198] Irrespective of these shortcomings, case studies continue to be used extensively in social sciences, including the traditional disciplines of psychology, sociology, political science, anthropology, and history.[198]

Yin suggests that case studies should be selected just like a laboratory investigator selects the topic of a new experiment. Yin calls this approach analytic generalization, in which a previously developed theory is used as a template with which to compare the empirical results of the case study.[198] In this regard, the multivariate procedures that were used in developing the Facet Model of serial murder in this book satisfy this criterion.

Five archival sources were used to obtain information for the following cases:

- Police Records
- Psychiatric Reports·
- Geographical Maps
- Court Transcripts
- Miscellaneous Published Sources (nonfiction books)

The first four of the archival sources listed above were the primary sources used to retrieve the case data from. In most of the cases, court transcripts were used to corroborate the police records and psychiatric reports. A fifth source, miscellaneous, was used in rare instances to corroborate the police records. Briefly, as previously mentioned, the term organized and disorganized does not have the same meaning as defined by the FBI. Rather, the two words were chosen simply because they best describe the differences between a crime scene that reveals little clues versus one that is sloppy. The two terms as used here do not imply certain personality characteristics.

14.1.1 Presentation of Case Studies

Four cases, one for each theme, showing the crime scene behavior and background characteristics are presented below. Variables in each classification theme were derived from the multivariate facet analysis carried out in this thesis. The main crime scene thematic behaviors were chosen from Chapters 12 and 13 as most representative, and are considered as the offenders' signature behaviors. The alternate thematic behaviors were taken from the original SSA analysis in Chapter 10. The alternate behaviors could occur in any combination with any signature theme.

It is worthwhile to emphasize, however, that as with all classifications, these in a sense are oversimplifications; not all offenders fit neatly into one type or another. Furthermore, there is evidence that one type of serial murderer can, while in prison, develop the practices of other types.[50] This is another important reason why this book examined the crime scene behavior of serial murderers rather than rely on information garnered from interviews.

CLASSIFICATION OF THE
AFFECTIVE VEHICLE SERIAL MURDERER

PROPOSED
MODEL
CHARACTERISTICS

Disorganized
Low Self-Awareness
Impersonal Attachment
Rage

SIGNATURE
THEMATIC
BEHAVIORS

Forced Entry into Home
Ransacked Property
Victim Fully Dressed
Restraint Found
Weapon Recovered

ALTERNATE
THEMATIC
BEHAVIORS

Weapon Hands/feet
Weapon of opportunity
Attempted sexual assault
Semen found at scene
Victim's vehicle stolen
Restraint victim's clothing
Entry made at night

BACKGROUND
HISTORY

Race - White or African-American
Average Age 30
Juvenile Convictions
Violent Offenses (Murder, Rape, Kidnap)
Burglary
Robbery
Sex Related Crimes
Voyeurism
Consume Pornography
Sexual Fetishes
Pedophilia
Employment Varies
Educational level Varies

Figure 14.1

14.2 Inner Themes — Outer Behaviors of an Affective-Vehicle (AV) Serial Murderer

The affective-vehicle (AV) theme is distinguishable by the disarray in the offender's crime scene. Out of the all the facet themes, the AV is the most unstructured. The AV theme represents a subset of serial murderers who target, murder, and leave their victim's body in the same location, such as the victim's residence. For example, in preparation for the crime, the offender will stake out a particular house. He will then break and enter the home to canvass for photos, names of children, and get a feel for the general layout of the scene. Returning later to the victim's home, the killer will then use force to enter the house, usually during the night. The thrill of breaking into a person's home is a form of impersonal attachment; the victims are violated, but at a distance. Research by Rubenstein on the escalation of criminal careers found that in some cases the burglar, on breaking into the victim's house or stealing the victim's vehicle, is aware of the sexual arousal.[199] These actions could suggest preplanning, but the offender's actions during and after the murders are completely disorganized. The disorganization is demonstrated, for example, by the offender's use of a weapon of opportunity that is recovered at the crime scene.

In the AV theme, victims are often attacked while they sleep and usually left fully dressed. This suggests the crime is an emotional one where the actual murder of the victim is the most important thing. Two variables in the AV theme, attempted sexual assault and victim's clothing as a restraint, are actions that indicate low self-awareness and show lack of planning. Often in crimes of this type, the offender's original intent is rape. However, during the attack the victim may block the offender's advances; he therefore may react by killing the victim. Due to the emotional component, the preferred weapon is the offender's hands and feet. Other opportunistic behaviors in the AV theme are ransacking the victim's property and stealing the victim's vehicle.

All these behaviors point to disorganization because the actions could link the offender to the murder. Figure 14.1 summarizes the empirical- and theoretical-derived Facet Model of the AV serial murderer. As a possible example of the affective-vehicle serial murderer, let us consider the serial killer Gary A. Walker.

The following homicides were committed by Gary Walker between 1984 to 1985.

14.2.1 Walker's Victims

On May 7, 1984, a male victim, age 63, was found dead at his home in Broken Arrow, Oklahoma, a suburb of Tulsa. His van was missing when the body was discovered. The victim was bludgeoned to death with a brick, and an electric cord from a vacuum cleaner was found wrapped around his neck. Later that same evening, 36-year-old Margaret Bell vanished, with her car, from a Porteau, Oklahoma, tavern. She was reported missing on May 8, but police had no reason at that time to connect the crimes.

On May 14, Jayne Hilburn, 35, was strangled in her home at Vinita, 45 miles northeast of Tulsa; her classic black Camaro was reported stolen from the scene. Six days later, in Skiatook, another Tulsa suburb, Walker abducted a 17-year-old girl, raping her at knifepoint before she scrambled free of his Camaro. The car was found abandoned on May 22, indicating that the killer rapist may have been searching for another set of wheels. The next day, in Van Buren, Arkansas, Gary Walker invaded a home and abducted two girls, taking them on a wild 22 minute ride in their own car. The girls later escaped.

On the morning of June 2, Walker barged into another Van Buren home, threatening the female tenants with a pistol and escaping in their car. However, by noon on June 2, the two girls who had previously escaped identified Walker's photograph to the police, and new alerts were issued in the Tulsa area. On the evening of June 2, Walker was apprehended. Over the next six days, Walker directed police to the bodies of missing victims Janet Jewell (near Beggs, Oklahoma), Valerie Shaw-Hartzell (near Claremore, east of Tulsa), and Margaret Bell (in an old barn near Princeton, Kentucky). In 1985, Walker was convicted on five counts of murder and sentenced to die (*Author's personal files, 1996*).

14.2.2 Walker's Background History

Prior to embarking on a spree of rape and murder, Walker managed to compile a record of convictions spanning 15 years, with charges that included auto theft, burglary, narcotics abuse, and firearms violations. He also had convictions of burglary while a juvenile. He was unemployed at the time of the murders. Walker had been confined to mental institutions on numerous occasions. While confined in the Oklahoma State Prison between 1977 and 1980, Walker was sent to the state hospital at Vinita on three occasions (*Author's personal files, 1996*). He was divorced, and was a high school dropout. Listed below are the crime scene behaviors exhibited by serial murderer Walker, in addition to his background characteristics. As can be seen, a majority fall within the affective-vehicle thematic model in Figure 14.1.

Crime Scene Dynamics of Gary Walker
- Forced entry
- Night and day entry
- Victims were strangers
- Bludgeoned victims
- Murders committed in victims' homes
- Some victims' bodies left openly displayed
- Victims' vehicles stolen
- Weapons of opportunity
- Some victims found fully clothed

- Vaginal penetration
- Attempted sexual assaults
- Weapon hands and feet
- Used a knife to control victim
- Used victim's clothing as a weapon (Restraint victim)

Background Characteristics
- White
- Divorced
- High school dropout
- Age 30
- Past convictions of burglary
- Unemployed
- Juvenile convictions
- Drug convictions
- Previous history of mental problems

14.2.3 Summary of Walker

The serial murder case of Gary A. Walker is notable in the sense that he targeted his victims primarily in their homes, at night.

Although Walker would most likely fit the FBI's disorganized offender type, their serial murder typology does not identify serial murderers who primarily carry out their crimes indoors. Rather, they look only at the crime scene actions and often neglect the fact that the location of an attack can play an important role in the manifestation of the offender's behavioral makeup. Several additional factors enter the picture in the Walker case that are rarely discussed in the serial murder literature. Here is a series of murders where the offender did not complete his sexual act, left some victims fully clothed, and stole many of the victims' vehicles. Arguably, in the serial murder literature, nowhere is there any discussion of a classification framework that would accommodate the aspects of Walker's crimes.

14.3 Inner Themes — Outer Behaviors of an Affective-Object (AO) Serial Murderer

Figure 14.2 represents the affective-object (AO) serial murderer. The affective-object serial murderer's crime scene is more organized than that of the AV murderer. The affective component in the AO theme manifests itself, for example, by the victim being blitz attacked and receiving bite marks.

The AO theme reflects a crime scene where the offender seems to exert power over his victims. For example, the offender may feel a sense of failure

```
┌─────────────────────────────────────────────┐
│           CLASSIFICATION OF THE               │
│      AFFECTIVE OBJECT SERIAL MURDERER         │
└─────────────────────────────────────────────┘
```

```
          ┌─────────────────────┐
          │      PROPOSED        │
          │       MODEL          │
          │   CHARACTERISTICS    │
          └─────────────────────┘
```

Disorganized
Low Self-Awareness
Personal Attachment
Rage

```
┌──────────────────┐        ┌──────────────────┐
│    SIGNATURE      │        │   BACKGROUND      │
│    THEMATIC       │        │    HISTORY        │
│    BEHAVIORS      │        │                   │
└──────────────────┘        └──────────────────┘
```

Blitz Attack   Race White
Ligature   Average Age 31
Object Found Inserted   Sex Related Crimes
Bite Marks   Consume Pornography
Bludgeon   Sexual Fetishes
                             Pedophilia
                             Employment Varies
```                          Educational level Varies
┌──────────────────┐
│    ALTERNATE      │
│    THEMATIC       │
│    BEHAVIORS      │
└──────────────────┘
```

Weapon Gun

Figure 14.2

and his emotional rage may thrust him into a murderous assault. The control
the offender initially has often leads to the crime scene appearing organized
in the initial encounter, but as the crime proceeds, the offender's actions
become unstructured. Hence, the offender's actions are ultimately affective.
The AO theme reveals a killer whose desire is expressive rage, but one that
has a personal attachment; that is, a sadistic focus toward the victim. Also,
the fact that the killer bites and bludgeons his victims to death suggests that
the crime is one of rage.

Victims in the AO theme are more likely to be strangers, among them
prostitutes or hitchhikers, who are invested with a symbolic importance by

the AO killer. The killer may see in others distorted representations of their earlier traumatic relations; for example, the offender may have a low opinion of women who work the streets. The offender therefore abducts and kills his victims for wrongs he believes women have done to him, and takes out his rage and anger in the form of excessive blunt trauma to the victim's body. As a possible example of the affective-object serial murderer, let us consider the serial murderer David J. Carpenter.

The following rapes and murders were committed by David Carpenter, during the late 1970s and early 1980s.

14.3.1 Carpenter's Victims

14.3.1.1 Rapes

Soon after being paroled, Carpenter embarked on a string of rapes throughout the San Francisco area. Carpenter used the ruse of a car wreck to lure his first victim. As the victim got out of her car to inspect the damage done to her vehicle, Carpenter attacked her using a knife. He told her that he was going to rape her and proceeded to attack the victim. During the course of the attack, the victim managed to break loose from Carpenter; however, he slashed her on the arm with a knife. The first victim of Carpenter's crime spree managed to survive his attack without being raped. Following the attack, Carpenter chose to leave his car behind, hiding it not too far from where he originally attacked the victim. He then hitchhiked back to his apartment on Sutter Street to change his bloody clothes. After changing into clean clothes, Carpenter left his apartment on Sutter Street and decided to hitchhike towards the city of Santa Cruz, California. He knew that the police would soon find his abandoned car near the location where he had attacked the last victim.

Carpenter, armed with a crime kit that included a knife, handcuffs, garrotes, and a change of clothing, proceeded to rape at least twelve women during a seven-month period. His methods of targeting the victims ranged from entering their homes to stalking and attacking them while they walked on trails in the Redwood Forest in California. During many of these rapes, Carpenter made the children of his victims watch as he brutalized their mothers.

On October 29, 1979, Carpenter pleaded guilty to kidnaping and burglary charges and was sentenced from one to twenty-five years to run consecutively in Folsom Prison. However, he was not convicted on any sexually related charges, which is important when serving time in prison. Sex offenders are treated differently in prison and Carpenter knew this. During Carpenter's imprisonment, he took college-level courses in finance, mathematics, accounting, and philosophy and received top grades.[200]

On May 21, 1979, Carpenter was released on parole under conditions to Reality House, a San Francisco halfway house for federal prisoners. Carpenter was under certain restrictions about times that he could be out of the house. However, in August 1979, soon after he was paroled, Carpenter eventually ended up taking the lives of at least 12 innocent people. The victims were mostly females, but several of the ladies' boyfriends were also victims.[200]

14.3.2 Carpenter's Murders

The first murder Carpenter committed after being paroled took place in August 1979, in the mountainous Sleepy Lady, Mill Valley vicinity on the outskirts of San Francisco's, Tamalpais area.[200] The victim was a women in her mid-60s who went for an early morning hike along the mountaintop trails. The victim was later found by park rangers. She was in a kneeling position, lying face down, and had been shot in the back of the head with a .44 caliber handgun. The victim was completely nude, except for one sock. Her personal items had been stolen, including credit cards and ten dollars (*Author's personal files, 1996*). There was no forensic evidence that she had been sexually assaulted. Carpenter struck again on October 21, this time in Lincoln Park near Land's End in San Francisco. The victim, age 23, was attacked while she jogged in the park. She was stabbed over 25 times and buried in a shallow grave near where she had been murdered.[200]

Carpenter waited for several months to pass before he killed his next victim. On March 28, 1980, he killed again. The victim, also age 23, started out on a hike along with her dog in the slopes of the Sleepy Lady mountain.[200] Several other hikers noticed the victim as she made her way down the mountain trail. Soon after the two other hikers disappeared down the trail, the victim was accosted by her attacker, who proceeded to stab her in the neck and breast area. However, unbeknown to Carpenter, his attack had been witnessed by the two hikers who had previously seen the victim. The two witnesses contacted the police immediately, and the police arrived on the scene shortly after being contacted. However, the suspect had already escaped into the woods. The police did find a pair of eyeglasses that appeared to have fallen off the suspect during the struggle with the victim.[200]

Immediately following the murder, Carpenter drove himself to the hospital emergency room to receive treatment from a knife wound to his hand. He informed the doctors that the wound had occurred during a struggle with a robber at a local 7-11 store. The police were notified and later questioned Carpenter; they did not link him to the recent murder near the Golden Gate Bridge.

Carpenter's next victim was a 26-year-old research scientist who had decided to go hiking on the trails in Mount Tamalpais, near Sleeping Lady.[200] The victim was found lying in a dirt path next to the Green Amphitheater, near Rock Spring Trail. Like the first murder victim, she too was shot, but in the right side of her head instead of the back. However, none of the victim's jewelry had been taken. The victim's body was found face up, propped against a rock. She was still clothed. The victim had been sexually assaulted, confirmed by the presence of semen stains.[200]

To confuse the police, as many serial killers attempt to do, David Carpenter decided to move his killing location to Point Reyes, a 70,000-acre National Seashore area a short drive North from San Francisco.[200] On November 28, 1980, the killer struck again — but this time, Carpenter took a longer time to stalk his victims. The November 28th incident involved three college students who set out for a hike along the wilderness trails in Bear Valley.[200] Using a gun, Carpenter forced the two women to strip, while he folded each article of their clothing carefully in front of them. Then Carpenter placed the clothes on top of their knapsacks. He then made the women kneel, as he had done to previous victims, and he shot both women in the back of the head.[200] The victims were later found by two park rangers, laying face down, side by side. The women were nude. The coroner's report determined that the women had been strangled by thin wire similar to a piano wire. A pair of panties was found stuffed into one victim's mouth. During their search for these two victims, the police found the decomposed remains of two other individuals located one half mile from the current murder scene. The victims were fully clothed. However, the police could not tell the sex of the victims due to decomposition. The victims were found laying face down.

Carpenter often changed his M.O. as evidenced by his last few murders. However, his signature behavior practically remained intact throughout his murder career. The remaining two known murders committed by Carpenter were carried out in similar fashion as the previous ones. The two victims included two women, and one male, who survived the ordeal, who were stalked and murdered while walking along mountain trails near Henry Cowell Redwood State Park, Santa Cruz.[200] All the victims were shot and the women raped.

14.3.3 Carpenter's Background History

David Joseph Carpenter was born May 6, 1930.[200] He was the elder of two siblings. Carpenter's pathological history started around the age of seven years, when he first started stammering. His parents, brother, sister, and extended family members were not fond of him at all, being somewhat ashamed of his speech impediment.

Carpenter's criminal career can be traced back to the age of 12. At age 14, Carpenter was committed to Napa State Hospital for sex offenses. He escaped many times from the institution and committed burglaries in the surrounding neighbors, so many that the neighbors in the Boulder Creek area near Santa Cruz requested they be notified the next time Carpenter left his home. Carpenter's juvenile records show an embittered, incorrigible teenager with five arrests on sex charges, and a history of one escape from juvenile hall. Carpenter was an high school dropout, but he completed his high school education while serving time at McNeil Island Prison. Carpenter was divorced, but later remarried in 1979. He had two children from his first marriage.[200]

Dr. Allison, a Forensic psychiatrist who examined Carpenter, wrote in his report, "During moments of extreme stress, sexual urges often reached such a point they became an overwhelming impulse." [200] Dr. Allison further pointed out that Carpenter had poor impulse control, and diagnosed him a mentally disordered sex offender. Carpenter was convicted of seven murders in the State of California and sentenced to die in February 1989. Listed below are the crime scene behaviors exhibited by the serial murderer David Carpenter; again, the majority seem to fall within the affective-object classification model in Figure 14.2 above.

Crime Scene Dynamics of David Carpenter
- Blitz attacked victims
- Weapon gun
- Forensic evidence found at crime scenes
- Ligature
- Victims bound
- Vaginal penetration
- Insertion of foreign object found in victim on discovery
- Victims' clothing scattered or completely removed
- Some victims found nude

Background Characteristics
- White
- Divorced
- High school dropout
- Age 57 (in 1987)
- Past convictions of burglary
- Past convictions of sex offenses
- Employed (part-time)
- Juvenile convictions
- Previous history of mental problems and treatment

14.3.1.4 Summary of Carpenter

The serial murder case of David J. Carpenter is distinct because he mainly targeted his victims in mountain areas of Santa Cruz. Carpenter would probably be classified by the FBI as a disorganized serial murderer due to his randomness and the opportunistic nature of his attacks. Carpenter's victims were surprise attacked while hiking, bound, and immediately shot or strangled to death. Also, although some victims were not penetrated, there were a few victims who were violated by the insertion of foreign objects, which suggest a personal attachment to the victim in the form of an object. Thus, Carpenter was a killer who showed affective behavior in his crimes, but with a personal attachment to his victims. Hence, he treated his victims as objects for his anger.

In murders such as those of Carpenter, the assaults are characterized by physical brutality. Far more force was actually used in the commission of the murders than would be necessary if the intent were simply to overcome the victim. It seems that as a result of his anger and hostility, sex became Carpenter's weapon, and the sexual violations constituted the ultimate expression of his anger. Also, a fetishistic focus in Carpenter's murders was his locations of attack. Although Carpenter changed the geographical location of his attacks, the type of the location remained consistent throughout his crimes. For example, the salient feature of Carpenter's murders was his pattern of attacking and murdering his victims in secluded and woody areas.

14.4 Inner Themes — Outer Behaviors of a Cognitive-Vehicle (CV) Serial Murderer

In the cognitive-vehicle (CV) theme the focus is impersonal. So, for instance, the murderer may retain trophies, indicating a reflection of the murder and victim at a distance. Also, the victim may be gagged or blindfolded, which could again suggest that the killer may have difficulty facing the victim in a personal way.[201]

The CV theme also has an organized feature. The CV theme suggests an offender who mainly preplans and organizes his crimes throughout. Variables such as the victim being blindfolded, body posed, and retaining trophies are also organized actions.

One important feature of the CV theme is the fact that these are serial murderers who target males. This fact is recognized by the presence of the variable, male sexual assault, plotted in CV thematic region (see Figure 10.4 Chapter 10). As a possible example of the cognitive-vehicle serial murderer,

**CLASSIFICATION OF THE
COGNITIVE VEHICLE SERIAL MURDERER**

**PROPOSED
MODEL
CHARACTERISTICS**

Organized
High Self-Awareness
Impersonal Attachment
Sadistic

**SIGNATURE
THEMATIC
BEHAVIORS**

**BACKGROUND
HISTORY**

Ritualistic Activity
Victim's Body Posed
Piqueurism
Victim Tortured
Offender Retains Trophies

Race - White
Average Age 28
Juvenile Convictions
Violent Offenses (Murder, Rape, Kidnap)
Consume Pornography
Sexual Fetishes
Voyeurism
Employed
Educational level Varies

**ALTERNATE
THEMATIC
BEHAVIORS**

Victim Gagged
Male Sexual Assault
Victim Blindfolded
Victim Drugged
Victim Bound with Electrical Cord

Figure 14.3

let us consider the killer, Randolph Steven (Randy) Kraft. The following murders committed by the serial murderer Kraft during the 1970s and 1980s illustrate an offender who fits the cognitive-vehicle theme. Kraft combined a successful business career in computers in Southern California with more a sinister life as a serial murderer. He was convicted of 16 murders, while 35 murders were eventually cleared; however, he was believed to have murdered 67 persons between 1972 and 1983.[202]

14.4.1 Kraft's Victims

The first established victim of Kraft's murder series was a marine, 20 years old, whose body was found in the Seal Beach area of California in December 1972 (*Author's personal files, 1996*). The victim had been sexually assaulted and strangled, with traces of drugs found in his body. Between 1973 and 1975, six more young men were found dead of similar circumstances in the Wilmington, Huntington Beach, and Long Beach, California areas.

On December 29, 1973, hikers found a 23-year-old Long Beach State University art student at the bottom of a ravine in the San Bernardino Mountains.[202] The victim was fully clothed, except for his shoes and one sock found forced inside his rectum. The killer had shaved his face and head postmortem, according to the medical examiner's report. Both of the victim's hands were cut off, and the stubs were wrapped in a plastic sandwich bag; the hands were never found. Later, it was learned that the victim was homosexual and frequently visited gay bars in the local area.

On June 2, 1974, the nude body of a 20-year-old male was found propped up against a mesquite tree along Highway 86, just west of the Salton Sea area in California.[202] The victim's legs were found spread wide and his genitals were missing. A tree branch had been forced six inches into his rectum.

Twenty days later, on June 22, 1974, the nude body of an 18-year-old U.S. Marine was found, located at a dead-end street in Laguna Beach, California.[202] The killer had bit and chewed his penis and left nipple; the victim had been sodomized and strangled to death. The autopsy revealed a modest amount of alcohol, but the forensic report also found a considerable amount of the drug diazepam, the generic name for Valium.

The predator struck again on August 3, 1974, in Long Beach, near a harbor oilfield.[202] The victim was 25 years old and worked as a waiter in a nearby restaurant. He died due to manual strangulation. On August 12, 1974, the body of a 23-year-old male was found down an embankment near Cabot Road and Oso Parkway near Cordova, California.[202] The cause of death was acute intoxication due to the ingestion of alcohol and diazepam.

The predator's next killing occured on November 29, 1974 in Irvine, California. The victim was a 19-year-old male, and his body was found near the San Diego Freeway.[202] Except for a white T-shirt, the victim was completely nude. The victim was found with his legs spread wide apart, and a four-foot-long tree branch three inches in diameter was found inserted into his rectum.[202] The victim, it was later discovered, was homosexual and was last seen in a gay bar in Belmont Shore, California.

The similarities among the murder victims were: all were male; Caucasian's between the ages of 17 and 25 years; and all had similar physical characteristics. According to the case files, all except three were homosexuals.

With the exception of one victim, all of the victims' bodies were placed in a location where they could have easily been found by the police or passing motorists. Four of the victims had stockings inserted into their anus, while in two of the victims white tissue was found to have been used to plug their noses.

At the end of 1978 and the beginning of 1979, Kraft's aggression and sadistic behavior escalated. During this period, more bodies of males were found dumped along roads in southern California. For example, one of Kraft's most sadistic murders involved a 21-year-old Long Beach truck driver who was found lying near the Seventh Street off ramp, at the intersection of the San Diego and 605 Freeways.[202] The victim's eyelids and hand had been branded with a cigarette lighter and he had been emasculated. The body had been dumped only 20 feet from where the Seal Beach Police had found one of the very first victims back in 1972.

Kraft's criminal career continued and on June 16, 1979, a witness saw a slow-moving vehicle dump a body on the northbound onramp of the 405 Freeway at Irvine Center Drive, not far from Silverado Canyon, CA.[202] However, none of the witnesses could identify the suspect's car because it was too dark. The victim, age 20, was a Marine originally from Arkansas. The victim was clad only in his boxer shorts; had red rope marks around his neck and one on his wrists; and his left nipple was burnt from an automobile cigarette lighter. He had died from drugs and alcohol, mixed to a lethal level, according to the pathologist's report. However, the main cause of death was the alcohol combined with toxic doses of Tylenol, antihistamine, decongestant, stimulant, and appetite suppressant.

Over the next two and a half years, a dozen more bodies with similar crime scene characteristics were found along the southern California roadsides. The State Police of California called in the FBI profilers from the Behavioral Sciences Unit located in Quantico, Virginia. FBI Agent Teton, commenting on the unsolved series of murders, said, "The killer exhibits complete indifference to the interests and welfare of society and displays an irresponsible and self-centered attitude; the killer is fully cognizant of the criminality of his acts and its impact on society, and it is for this reason that he commits his acts." [202]

14.4.2 Kraft's Background History

Randall Steven (Randy) Kraft was born March 19, 1945. He was the only boy in the family of three older sisters. Kraft's parents had migrated from Wyoming to California at the outbreak of World War II.[202] Kraft's family eventually ended up living in the Long Beach area of Beach Boulevard. There was no indication or records to suggest that Kraft had ever been abused as a child.

Kraft excelled in school. He was intelligent, and played saxophone for the school band. In 1963, Kraft graduated from high school. During this time, the uprise of the youth revolution was emerging. Kraft began visiting gay bars, and developed the name Crafty Randy.[202] However, Kraft later stated that he knew that he was gay since early childhood. After high school graduation, Kraft enrolled at Claremont College. In 1965, while in his second year at Claremont, he declared his homosexuality. Two years later, Kraft rejected the Vietnam War. By his third year at Claremont, he wore his hair longer and grew a mustache. Commenting later about his relationship with Kraft, one of his former college friends said that the one thing weird about Kraft was that he would disappear for days and even weeks without anyone knowing where he was.[202]

The first confirmable record of Kraft getting into trouble with the law was in 1966, when he offered to have sex with a man near the Huntington Beach pier during that summer.[202] Kraft did not graduate for Claremont on time in June 1967, due to his absenteeism from his econometrics classes. However, Kraft finally earned his Bachelor of Arts degree in economics in February 1968.[202]

Records show that in June 1968, Kraft joined the United States Air Force, having scored very high on all the Air Force aptitude tests. Kraft was stationed at Edwards Air Force Base in Southern California. On July 26th, 1969, the Air Force discharged Kraft for medical reasons, although the speculation is that they found out that he was gay.[202]

Kraft's murderous career came to a halt on 14 May 1983, when two California Highway Patrol officers chased a car being driven erratically and ordered it to pull off the freeway. Once the vehicle was stopped, the driver identified himself as Randolph Kraft, and his job as a computer programmer. Sitting next to Kraft was the dead body of another marine, who had died from an overdose of a stupefying drug that Kraft had earlier slipped into his beer. The victim had been strangled with some type of belt, and Kraft was booked on suspicion of murder, held in lieu of $250,000 bail. The search of Kraft's impounded vehicle turned up 47 color photographs depicting several young men; some of them naked, some apparently unconscious. A briefcase in the trunk of Kraft's car contained a notebook filled with more than 60 cryptic messages in some personal code.[202] A search of Kraft's home uncovered additional evidence, enough to convince the detectives that they had a sadistic serial murderer on their hands. For example, Kraft's photographs depicted three young men whose deaths were still unsolved in Southern California. One of the pictured victims, a teenage Marine, had been found dead in September 1980; now, police examined snapshots of his naked body, lying on a couch recovered from Kraft's home. Another picture depicted a male victim, age 20, who was last seen alive while hitchhiking with a friend on February 12.

Further evidence found in Kraft's home included fibers from a rug in his garage, which matched those recovered from the corpse of the teenage Marine, discarded beside the Riverside Freeway in April 1978. Detectives found personal items in Kraft's home, including property stolen from three other murder victims in Oregon, plus two items belonging to a man found dead near Grand Rapids, Michigan, in December 1982. Investigators learned that Kraft had worked for a Santa Monica-based aerospace firm between June 1980 and January 1983, visiting company offices in Oregon and Michigan at the times of the unsolved murders in both states. As names were added to the list of Kraft's victims, prosecutors cracked the code in his notebook.

Kraft was tried in Orange County, California, on sixteen charges of murder, nine of sexual mutilation, and three of sodomy. Kraft was convicted on all counts in November 1989, and sentenced to die at San Quentin. However, as of this writing, Kraft has never confessed to murder. Listed below are the crime scene behaviors and background characteristics exhibited by the serial murderer Kraft. If we look at his crime scene actions and characteristics, we see that the majority fall within the cognitive-vehicle thematic model in Figure 14.3.

Crime Scene Dynamics of Randy Kraft

- Victim drugged
- Victim bound
- Victim tortured
- Victim sodomized
- Photographed his victims postmortem
- Piqueurism
- Mutilation
- Upper stab wounds
- Lower stab wounds
- Retained trophies
- Male victims

Background Characteristics

- White
- Single
- Age 38 (in 1983)
- Gay
- Minor convictions as an adult
- Consumed pornography
- Sexual fetishes
- Employed
- College educated

14.4.3 Summary of Kraft

The serial murder case of Randy Kraft is distinct for several reasons. The first is that he murdered only males, both straight and gay. Kraft foraged for many of his victims at gay bars after he and his male lover had fallen out in an argument. As a result, it could be possible that Kraft's rage at his victims was a derivative of the abandoning boyfriend, and the targeted victim was conceptualized on a more impersonal level. A sadistic serial murderer, Kraft's crime scene actions were predominantly organized. For example, it was determined later by the police investigations, that Kraft brought some of his victims back to his apartment, drugged them, and proceeded to torture them until they passed out and died. Kraft seem to find the intentional treatment of his victims as vehicles intensely gratifying, and he took pleasure in their torment, anguish, distress, helplessness, and suffering. Kraft's assaults on his male victims involved bondage, torture, and ritualistic acts. Research by Groth and his colleagues points out that sexual areas of the victim's body, i.e., genitals and buttocks, become a specific focus of injury and abuse.[183] Kraft tortured many of his victims by inserting small, slim objects into their urethrae; since Kraft did not interact with his victims' bodies for a great deal of time, his actions were primarily impersonal. Kraft's obsession with fetishistic toys, such as dildos, was also clear. In fact, when the police searched Kraft's apartment, they found in a bedside cabinet a can of cooking oil along with assorted dildos that varied in widths and lengths.[202]

14.5 Inner Themes — Outer Behavior of a Cognitive-Object (CO) Serial Murderer

In the cognitive-object (CO) theme, there is assumed to be an implicit mastery of the victim in the form an object. For instance, Dietz and his colleagues argue that the killer's wish to inflict pain on his victims is not the essence of sadism.[80] Rather, it is to have complete mastery over another person, to make him or her a helpless symbolic object of his will, to do with him or her as one pleases.[80]

The CO killer's crime scenes reflect organized behavior and a personal attachment to his victims; thus the killer may spend time interacting with the victim's body, by such acts as mutilation and by performing postmortem sex acts. Other actions may include using a con or ploy to lure victims, using a crime kit, and burying the victim's body. As an example of the cognitive-object serial murderer, let us consider the killer Robert A. Berdella.

**CLASSIFICATION OF THE
COGNITIVE OBJECT SERIAL MURDERER**

**PROPOSED
MODEL
CHARACTERISTICS**

Organized
High Self-Awareness
Personal Attachment
Sadistic

**SIGNATURE
THEMATIC
BEHAVIORS**

**BACKGROUND
HISTORY**

Body Parts Scattered
Body Disfigured
Sexual Acts Postmortem
Dismemberment Postmortem
Anthropophagy

Race - White
Average Age 31
Consume Pornography
Sexual Fetishes
Sex-Related Convictions (not rape)
Pedophilia History
Employed
Educational level Varies

**ALTERNATE
THEMATIC
BEHAVIORS**

Ploy or Con Approach
Victim Held Captive
Crime Kit
Body Buried
Forensic Evidence Destroyed

Figure 14.4

The following murders were committed by the serial murderer Robert
Berdell between 1984 and 1988. Berdella, a former college art student and
self-employed curio shop owner in Kansas City, Missouri was responsible for
the murder of six young men (Jackman and Cole, 1992).[203] Berdella lured
his victims to their deaths by renting boarding rooms to them in his three-
story home at 4315 Charlotte Street in Kansas City.

14.5.1 Berdella's Victims

Attention was brought to Berdella's crimes on April 2, 1988, when a neighbor saw a naked man crouching on Berdella's porch outside his house. The victim, a male, age 22, wore nothing but a dog collar, buckled around his neck. The victim, while still alive, shouted to the neighbor to phone the police. When the police arrived on the scene, the victim told a story that he had been held captive in Berdella's home for the past five days, subjected to repeated sexual assaults before he finally clambered through a second-story window and escaped.[203] Following their interview with the victim, detectives picked Berdella up and searched his home for evidence. In doing so, they found a vast amount of physical evidence linking him to several missing men.

Police discovered some 200 photographs of naked men, depicted as being bound and clearly suffering from cruel abuse.[203] Detectives also found hardcore gay pornographic magazines and a file folder of news clippings on serial murderers. Torture devices were also seized in the raid, along with a pair of human skulls, occult literature, and a satanic ritual robe. Detectives also unearthed bone fragments and a human head in Berdella's yard.

Berdella's M.O. was to sedate his victims with animal anaesthetics and tranquilizers he had obtained from a local veterinary supply house.[116] In order to gain complete control over his victims, he placed drugs into their food or gave them potent sedatives in place of vitamins. Once the victims passed out, Berdella restrained them with ropes, gags, or a dog collar around their necks. Following hours and sometime days of assaults on his victims, Berdella would progressively dehumanize his victims, depriving them of all sensations except those of his tortures. He blinded his victims with chemicals, probed his finger down into their eyes, and poured drain cleaner down their throats.[203] Other forms of torture included use of an electrical transformer and metal spatulas to apply electric shocks to their bodies and genitals. Berdella sodomized his victims with sex toys, his arm, and a variety of vegetables. For example, two victims eventually died of suffocation, while the others died from medical complications arising out of drug overdoses, infections, and head injuries.[203] Berdella dismembered each corpse and placed it in plastic bags, although none of the victims' bodies were ever recovered. However, police did discover two human heads — one in Berdella's closet, and the other buried in his backyard.

14.5.2 Berdella's Background History

Robert Berdella was born in Cuyahoga Falls, Ohio.[203] There is no record of Berdella having any disciplinary problems outside the home, and he was an excellent student throughout his years in school. However, Berdella's home life was totally different. His scholastic and artistic achievements apparently were not good enough for his parents, who Berdella later claimed abused him physically and verbally. Dr. Reid Meloy points out that Berdella's relationship with his father, before and during the murders, was regressive.[203] Meloy further states that initially, Berdella saw himself as the father figure, attempting to nurture and assist the young men who lived with him; then he shifted and became the predator. For Berdella, the victim shifted and became the child he could dominate. Meloy suggests that Berdella was carrying out projections about himself.[203] Other research carried out on serial murderers has found similar relationships between offenders and their fathers. For example, in their interviews with serial murderers, the FBI found that most offenders said they did not have a satisfactory relationship with their fathers, and their relationships with their mothers were highly ambivalent in emotional quality. Sixteen of the men reported cold or uncaring relationships with their mothers, and 26 reported such relationships with their fathers.[17]

Berdella acknowledged while in prison that he was aware of his homosexuality during adolescence. In an interview with a psychiatrist, Berdella could not explain why he had murdered, and was unwilling to face what he had done. Berdella seems to be a classic example of an individual with a *dismissing* attachment style. It appears that during the time of the murders and after his arrest, he was able to compartmentalize his sadistic actions into tasteless chunks so he could deal with them on a conscience level, as was previously discussed in Chapter 3.

A highly gifted artist, some of Berdella's paintings, entered in various scholastic competitions, won several awards.[203] When he was not in school, he performed volunteer work at the Cuyahoga Falls City's Civic Art Centre and with the parks department. Berdella also earned spending money by working in local restaurants. In 1967, Berdella enrolled in college, majoring in painting. However, it only took a year for Berdella to become heavily disillusioned with the academic world. In 1968, Berdella moved out of his college dormitory to a house at 4106 McGee Street.[203]

Berdella increasingly became sarcastic and anti-authoritarian during this period of his life. In January of his sophomore year, Berdella was arrested after selling amphetamines to a federal undercover agent.[203] He eventually pleaded guilty, and was given a five-year suspended sentence. However, one month later, he was arrested again, this time in Johnson County, Kansas for possession of marijuana and LSD.[203] The charges were later dropped.

In 1969, Berdella dropped out of college and purchased a house at 4315 Charlotte Street, Kansas City. Berdella began working full time as a cook. In the early 1970s he began collecting and trading arcane artifacts and eventually opened up his own business calling it Bob's Bazaar Bizarre. Berdella made contact with some of his victims through his business. Berdella advertised apartments for rent, and very carefully selected his future male tenants.[203]

On April 4, 1988, Berdella was arraigned on seven counts of sodomy, one count of felonious restraint, and one count of first-degree assault.[203] While excavation continued on Berdella's property and prosecutors contemplated murder charges, homicide investigators started checking out their list of missing persons dating back to 1984. Berdella entered a guilty plea on one count of murder and was sentenced to prison for life, but authorities suspected him of at least seven other deaths. On December 19, 1988, Berdella pleaded guilty to first-degree murder in the deaths of two victims, and to four counts of second-degree murder involving additional male victims. He was sentenced to a term of life imprisonment, during which he died due to natural causes.[203] The death penalty was not imposed due to a technical fault on part of the prosecution.[203]

Listed below are the crime scene behaviors exhibited by the serial murderer Berdella. Comparing Berdella's crime scene actions and background characteristics to those in Figure 14.4, it appears that a majority fall within the cognitive-object theme.

Crime Scene Dynamics of Robert Berdella
- Ploy
- Victims gagged
- Victims' faces covered
- Bound with rope
- Bound with handcuffs
- Victims tortured
- Evidence of foreign objects being inserted
- Crime kit
- Sexual organs assaulted
- Destroyed evidence
- Dismembered victims
- Body parts scattered
- Body parts buried
- Male victims

Background Characteristics
- White
- Single
- Age 36 (in 1988)
- Educated (some college)
- Drug Convictions
- Employed
- Sexual Fetishes
- Consumed pornography

14.5.3 Summary of Berdella

The case of Robert A. Berdella demonstrates a sadistic serial murderer. In FBI terms, Berdella would most likely be classified as a lust murderer who killed to act out his fantasies. The crime scene dynamics of Berdella show that his behavior was sadistic and organized. For example, Berdella used the ploy of renting rooms to potential male victims. Also, he committed his crimes indoors, thereby reducing the chance of being seen. He went to great lengths to destroy forensic evidence; for example, he dismembered all his victims and buried some of their body parts. Some of the victims were dismembered postmortem, and their remains wrapped in trash binds and left for the trash truck to pick-up. Additionally, Berdella was employed, which is a characteristic most likely to be associated with a cognitive-object killer.

Berdella's crimes were fully cognized and personal; he maintained considerable self-awareness of his sexual sadistic actions and devoted significant energy to self-scrutiny, and his attachment to his victims was personal. For example, one dominant signature behavior in Berdella's murders was his continual use of foreign objects. As mentioned earlier, these ranged from various sizes of dildos to large vegetables. Another dominant signature of Berdella's was that he photographed all his victims in various positions before and after death. This is in accord with Dietz and his colleagues' study on sexually sadistic offenders, where he found that 53% retained records of their crimes, including writings, photographs, and electronic recordings.[80] All these behaviors reflect time spent with the victim.

In sum, therefore, it could be argued that the Facet Model of serial murder described in this book does a reasonable job of classifying some notorious serial murder cases. While it was important to show how the Facet Model applies to solved serial murder cases, as was demonstrated above, its application to unsolved murders is imperative. The heuristic value of the Facet Model in profiling a series of murders is the focus of the next section.

14.6 The Representation of Crime Information

There are many potential methods of crime representation, which carry assumptions about the role of the investigator. These approaches to aid a criminal investigation range from the purely graphical to the statistical. The more statistical the decision-making tool chosen is, the more processed the information becomes. This results in a more predetermined decision. Conversely, the more graphical the approach, the less processing is carried out on the crime information, and the less predetermined the decision.

There are currently several new computerized, professional visualization and analysis tools on the market which aid investigators in making their decisions. One of the most popular is called the *Analyst's Notebook*. This computerized program advertises that it assists investigators by uncovering, interpreting, and displaying complex information in easily-understood chart form. The program claims that it can automatically analyze data sets; navigate through large networks in order to unravel complex relationships; and quickly discover key information and relationships. Another computerized program that is widely used by police forces is called *Watson*, manufactured by Harlequin Group, Inc. *Watson* is a high-level relational database integration that is for modeling data and representing information. A similar product that is used by police forces is *SIUSS*, a criminal intelligence analysis software program that stores, correlates, and analyzes crime information in order to identify and compare offenders' M.O.s for serial correlation in chart form. The implications of these approaches, including the most popular linking software used today in law enforcement, are based on what is referred to as ANACAPA. ANACAPA is purely graphical, rather than assessing the co-occurrence of behaviors in a given series of crimes. Assessing the cooccurrence of behaviors in a crime is purely statistical; for example, Smallest Spatial Analysis, which was defined in Chapter 10.

A system of information structuring, originally developed in America after the assassination of President John F. Kennedy in 1963, ANACAPA is named after an island off the west coast of the U.S. that is perpetually shrouded in mist. When the mist rises, all becomes clear. Hence, ANACAPA means "the parting of the mist."

Originally, the technique started off as a paper-based system of information analysis; however, since computers have become more powerful and cheaper, programs have been developed to perform similiar functions. For example, in the paper-based ANACAPA approach, if one has information about a number of people who know each other or have met each other, this relationship can be drawn using circles and lines connecting them. The circles would represent the people and the lines some kind of relationship or link. Text is usually written along the circles or links to identify the people or describe the relationship, such as friends or business associates. The link lines can be solid or dotted to indicate the strength or reliability of the information about that link. However, in its computer form, ANACAPA is a tabulation process whereby all information considered relevant to an enquiry can be collated in chart form. From this visual display of relationships between variables, investigators may attempt to define the relationships between information concerning, for instance, a series of murders or rapes. This technique, and less organized forms of it, is the most frequently used method of structuring crime data in police forces today.

The ANACAPA approach to analyzing and linking crime patterns is thus viewed as a content-orientated approach that records all available information with no attempt to process the details. As a result, the investigator is asked to establish links, using all the available information before him or her. The limitations of information processing abilities ensures that this form of information systemization and linking crimes is extremely prone to bias by individual experience during the assimilation and interpretation phase. Drawing deductive inferences using past experiences of a similar type of crime is extremely difficult to avoid with this type of crime information representation. This method of accessing crime information and recognizing behavioral patterns maintains the most reliance on the investigator's personal and subjective judgement.

14.7 Profiling a Serial Murderer and his Offenses: Linking Crimes Using the Facet Model

Beginning in 1996 through March of 1997, the City of Raleigh, North Carolina, located in the eastern part of the state, was faced with a series of unsolved murders of six African-American females. The six women were slain inside the Beltline, a major thoroughfare within the city limits of Raleigh. Initially, the Raleigh Police Department assured the public that a serial murderer had not murdered the six women.[204] The police stated that beyond the fact that the victims suffered sheer brutality, the cases were not linked in any way.[204] The police views were confirmed later by North Carolina Chief Medical Examiner John Butts, who acknowledged the circumstances and causes of the deaths were similar, but the crimes lacked a "signature that would point to a serial murderer." [205]

Throughout 1996, police investigators discounted the possibility of a serial murderer; however, by the end of 1996, with the murders still unsolved, police acknowledged they were looking for one suspect. Later, Raleigh detectives determined that one of the six homicides was not related to the others, and a suspect was arrested and charged on January 17th, 1997. On February 4th, 1997, Raleigh Police arrested John Williams, Jr., 36, an African-American male, who was a drifter from Augusta, Georgia. He was charged with two of the five murders. The remaining three murders have not yet officially been linked to Williams, and the three remaining cases are still open. Williams had a lengthy record of sexual assault, as he was trying to rape a women when he was apprehended by the police. Williams worked at a fast-food restaurant and drifted between homeless shelters within the City of Raleigh.

What follows is a general discussion of the five murders which occurred in Raleigh, North Carolina, two of which Williams was arrested, charged, and sentenced to death for committing. DNA tests linked Williams to two of the murders. Included are details about each victim and the crime scene evidence. The following crime information was obtained from the police, the medical examiner's office, and published newspaper accounts of the murders. Presented below is the original case analysis and subsequent psychological and geographical profiles, which were constructed by this author prior to the murders being solved. The profiles presented below formed the backdrop for several newspaper articles about this author.[206]

14.8 The Victims

Victim One

The body of victim one, a Black female, 33, was found the afternoon of January 7th, 1996 behind a business in the 1500-block of South Blount Street, Raleigh, North Carolina. She had been strangled and beaten to death by the offender's hands. She also had been sexually assaulted, vaginally. The presence of semen was found. The victim was found nude, lying back on a bench, her legs sprawled, and the only article of clothing that remained was her socks.[204] Scratches and abrasions were found on the victim's shoulders, mid back, and left buttock. One of the victim's shoes was found under a table and the other nearby in the snow. The victim worked as a prostitute and was a known drug user. John Williams, Jr. was charged for victim one's murder.

Victim Two

The second victim's body, a Black female, 38, was found at 916 Oakwood Avenue in Raleigh, North Carolina. The victim was found in Oakwood Cemetery by groundskeepers. The victim was found wearing only a bra, which was in disarray, and an ankle bracelet. According to the Medical Examiner's report, several upper teeth were missing, which was concluded to be the result of the homicide. There were multiple abrasions and contusions to the victim's face, head, and neck areas. Smaller abrasions and contusions were found on the victim's hands, forearms, lower legs and back. There were no skull fractures. The presence of blood was found in the victim's mouth. There was no evidence of external genitalia injury; however, semen was found in the anal area. The cause of death was manual or possible ligature strangulation with an article of clothing from the victim, including a contributing factor of multiple blunt trauma to the face and head. The victim worked as a prostitute and was a drug user. No arrests have been made in this case.

Victim Three

The third victim, a Black female, 30, was found close to a homeless camp near some railroad tracks under Morgan Street bridge in Raleigh, North Carolina. The victim was found nude except for a pair of high-top trainer shoes and white socks. Vaginal penetration had taken place, and a condom was found within the vagina. The cause of death was due to acute aortic rupture of the main vessel to the heart. This was caused by blunt chest trauma. Evidence of head and neck trauma was found, which was consistent with strangulation. Near the body, police investigators found the possible murder weapon, a brick. There was also a footprint impression visible on the victim's left head and side. The victim was a known drug user. No arrest has been made in this case.

Victim Four

The fourth victim, a Black female, 32, was found at the Martin Luther King Boulevard extension project near Dawson Street in Raleigh, North Carolina. She was found in a South side Raleigh construction site. Her body was found laying on its back, partly skelontonized. She had been strangled, and one hand was missing. Her clothing was found scattered nearby. The victim had an extensive record of drug, theft, and prostitution arrests. No arrest has been made in this case.

Victim Five

The fifth victim's body, a Black female, 35, was found nude in an empty building that was being renovated at the intersection of North and West streets in Raleigh, North Carolina. The victim's body showed signs of trauma, and she had been beaten to death. Her clothes were found scattered nearby. There were no forensic reports on whether a sexual assault occurred or not. The victim had no prior criminal record, however, she was a known drug user. John Williams, Jr. was charged with this victim's murder.

14.9 Linking Behaviors Using Jaccard's Coefficients

14.9.1 Co-occurrence of Behaviors Across a Series of Murders

A review of the case files for the five unsolved Raleigh murders produced a list of variables appropriate for analysis. For example, the nine crime scene actions shown below were just a few chosen for analysis using the Smallest Space Analysis (SSA-I) program. Briefly, SSA-I was discussed in Chapter 10; however, a short description is provided here on how SSA can be used to link offenses.

Ligature
Semen found at crime scene
Bludgeon
Restraint victim
Weapon hands/feet
Anal penetration
Vaginal penetration
Clothing scattered
Victims nude

As an empirical alternative to purely graphical methods of establishing links between offenses, for example *Analyst's Notebook* and *Watson*, there is Smallest Space Analysis (SSA). Briefly, SSA uses the Jaccard's coefficient to measure the association between variables. The results are mapped under the monotone mapping condition.[147] Monotonic relationship states that the greater the similarity, such as correlations, between two behavior items, the greater the proximity; that is, the smaller the distance between their geometric image points.[88] So in a series of murders, if a killer performed similar actions in his first two murders, but not in his third and fourth, then it would be expected under the conditions of a monotonic relationship that the behaviors from the first two crimes will have higher Jaccard's coefficients. Jaccard's coefficients are represented by "0.00," meaning that two variables do not share any similar behaviors to "1.00," a perfect correlation. The Jaccard's coefficient represents the percentage of co-occurrence between two variables; for example, crime scene behaviors. The use of the Jaccard's coefficient has the luxury of each incident to be compared with every other incident.

14.9.2 Preparing the Data for SSA-I Analysis

Using a list of crime scene variables gleaned from the unsolved case files, chosen after careful inspection of the offenses, a SSA was carried out to test whether particular actions in the Raleigh murders could be linked. To carry out this procedure, 15 serial murder cases were chosen for the overall analysis, 10 of which came from a larger database owned by this author, which originally formed the backdrop for the research carried out in this book and discussed thoroughly in Chapter 5. The 10 solved serial murder offenses occurred in various parts of the U.S. The additional five serial murder offenses represented the unsolved murders in Raleigh. John Williams, Jr. was convicted for two of the murders. A research assistant from the University of Liverpool combined the crime scene actions from the Raleigh series with serial murder offenses unrelated to the Raleigh crimes. The data matrix was then given to the author for analysis. Consequently, prior to the analysis, the author had no knowledge of which offenses or offenders the columns or rows of data belonged to. It was only after the analysis that comparisons and links were made to the actual offenses.

In constructing the data matrix, the cases or offenses represented the columns, while the rows represented the crime scene actions. Presenting the data in this form allowed the SSA program to look at the co-occurrence of how each killer scored across each crime scene action. It should be noted, however, that this process does not classify offenders, but rather looks at whether there are similarities (co-occurrences) between crime scene actions in the same series. This was an important step in the analysis, because it provided an empirical backdrop to test whether the SSA could link the offenses and if there would be an interpretable pattern to the SSA matrix.

Using the Investigative Process Management (IPM) approach discussed throughout this book, the author applied an inductive methodology to link the five unsolved murders in Raleigh. The results of the analysis are discussed in the next section.

14.10 SSA Results of Raleigh Murders

As discussed throughout this book, it is imperative that police investigators recognize early on that a series of murders are linked or not. In regard to the murders of five Black females in Raleigh, the authorities continually denied that the murders were not the work of one person. A similar scenario was played out between 1992 and 1994 in Charlotte, North Carolina, where a series of 10 murders were not linked to the now-convicted Henry Louis Wallace.

Shown in Table 14.1 is the Jaccard's coefficient matrix that was derived from the SSA analysis. As previously mentioned, each of the decimal numbers in the matrix are Jaccard's coefficients, which represents the percentage of co-occurrence between any two variables. The shaded squares in the data matrix shows the Jaccard's coefficients of co-occurrence between offenses carried out by the same offenders. The empty squares indicate zero co-

Table 14.1 Jaccard Coefficients for 15 Murder Offenses According to Aspects of Crime Scene Behavior

Offenses		A1	A2	A3	B1	B2	B3	C1	C2	C3	C4	D1	D2	D3	D4	D5
Three Separate Killers	A1															
	A2	0.04														
	A3	0.13	0.04													
Same Killer	B1	0.09	0.12	0.26												
	B2	0.03	0.20	0.15	0.23											
	B3		0.20	0.04	0.32*	0.26										
Same Killer	C1	0.04	0.30*	0.08	0.35*	0.24	0.50									
	C2		0.08	0.07	0.12	0.28	0.25	0.29								
	C3	0.03	0.28	0.10	0.22	0.45*	0.25	0.19	0.06							
	C4	0.07	0.20	0.11	0.12	0.08	0.14	0.60*	0.32*	0.04						
Raleigh Killer	D1		0.20	0.04	0.25	0.26	0.47*	0.12	0.12	0.11	0.07					
	D2		0.23	0.10	0.22	0.35*	0.30*	0.39*	0.50*	0.12	0.20	0.43*				
	D3		0.23	0.10	0.22	0.35*	0.30*	0.39*	0.50*	0.12	0.20	0.43*	1.00*			
	D4		0.23	0.10	0.22	0.35*	0.30*	0.39*	0.50*	0.12	0.20	0.43*	1.00,*	1.00*		
	D5		0.23	0.10	0.22	0.35*	0.30*	0.39*	0.50*	0.12	0.20	0.43*	1.00*	1.00*	1.00*	

N = 6 Serial murderers - N = 15 Offenses - N = 9 Crime scene variables * = Co-efficient above 0.30

occurrence. The squares that are not shaded represent the co-occurrence between offenses not related to the same offender. For example, a loading of 0.30 means that there exist a 30% of crime scene actions occurring between two offenses. All coefficients with a loading of 0.30 or higher are highlighted by an asterisk and shaded. The Jaccard's coefficient does not tell the investigator or researcher which actions are co-occurring. In order to determine this, one must revert back to the original data matrix for comparisons.

Looking at the matrix in Table 14.1, both vertical and horizontally, the letters A through D represent 15 offenses. Let us look at the first three offenses, A1, A2, and A3; these murders were carried out by three separate serial murderers, taken from the author's original database of serial murder offenses. For the first three offenses, we see that the coefficients are rather low — 0.04, 0.13, and 0.04 — indicating that these offenses have few actions in common. Therefore, it could be concluded that the three offenses or murders are unrelated.

The next series of murders, B1 through B3, were committed by the same serial murderer. Looking at the shaded areas between B1, B2, and B3, we see that the co-occurrence between offense three and offense one has a coefficient of 0.32, indicting that the crimes have similar crime scene actions in common. As for the link between the two remaining offenses, B1 to B2 and B2 to B3, while their coefficients of 0.23 and 0.26, respectively, are less than 0.30, the coefficients nonetheless are approaching the 0.30 level. Considering the overall coefficient levels in this series, it could be concluded that the same offender committed these three murders.

In the next offense series, there are four murders carried out by the same serial murderer. These offenses are represented by labels C1 through C4. Looking at the four rows in the middle of the matrix, we see the shaded squares that represent these four murders. Two offenses show a link, C1 to C4 and C2 and C4, having coefficients of 0.60 and 0.32, respectively. The coefficient of 0.29, between offenses C1 and C2, although lower than 0.30, suggests that these offenses are probably linked. The remaining coefficients, 0.04, 0.06, and 0.19 suggest that the actions performed in these three murders differ considerably, although they were committed by the same killer.

The final five offenses shown in Table 14.1, D1 through D5, represent the murders of the five Black females in Raleigh, North Carolina. John Williams, Jr. was convicted for two of the murders, labelled D4 and D5. Briefly, label D4 corresponds to victim one, while label D5 corresponds to victim five. As for the remaining three murders, no individual has been charged with these crimes, although the police suspect Williams. On inspection, the coefficients for the five unsolved homicides suggests that the murders may be linked. For example, beginning with the link between offense D1 and offense D2, the coefficient reached a level of 0.43, indicting that 43% of the crime scene actions that occurred in the first offense also occurred in the second offense. The exact same co-occurrences were achieved between offense D1 and offenses D3, D4, and D5; the coefficient between these offenses was 0.43. This finding suggests that the murders were most likely committed by the same individual. However, a remarkable finding was found between the remaining offenses.

It was mentioned above that Williams was convicted of committing offenses D4 and D5, but that the police could not link the other three murders to Williams. The finding of this analysis clearly indicates that Williams was probably the same killer in all five murders. To support this hypothesis, let us first examine the coefficients between offenses D4 and D5, the crimes for which Williams was linked through DNA and subsequently convicted. The coefficients are given in the very last squares located in the right bottom of the data matrix in Table 14.1. Briefly, as previously mentioned, the coefficient loading of 1.00 indicates a perfect co-occurrence of crime scene actions in these murders. This means that 100% of the crime scene behaviors from offense four were also present in offense five, suggesting that Williams most likely committed the fifth murder. The SSA findings thus support the DNA results that Williams did commit these two murders.

Now, let us examine the remaining coefficients for the Raleigh murders that have not been linked to Williams by traditional investigative methods or by the North Carolina HITS system. Looking at offenses D2 and D3, in relation to the offenses that Williams was convicted of, D4 and D5, we find a remarkable similarly in the crime scene actions. The coefficients between offenses D2, D3, D4, and D5 achieved a perfect score of 1.00, meaning that 100% of the crime scene behaviors in offenses D2 and D3 were also present in offenses D4 and D5. This finding suggests that it can be said with some confidence that Williams was most likely responsible for the three remaining unsolved murders.

The relatively high co-occurrences of crime scene behaviors in the murders of five Black females in Raleigh, North Carolina are far more than just by chance. The present findings clearly show that behaviors from the murders that Williams was convicted of were strikingly similar to crime scene actions in the three remaining unsolved murders.

The remaining unshaded squares in Table 14.1 are the coefficients between offenses that are not related. Looking at Table 14.1, the majority coefficients show no high co-occurrence, which would be expected since the behaviors in the offenses differ and the crimes were committed by different serial murderers. However, there were a few offenses not associated with the same offender that showed co-occurrences. For example, the co-occurrences between offense C2 and offenses D2 to D5 was 0.50. Although these crimes are not related, the high coefficients suggest that some crime scene actions performed in offense C2 are similar to actions in offenses D2 to D5. This may appear to be a problem in using SSA to link offenses; however, considering the high coefficients achieved specifically between the Raleigh offenses, all other coefficients between the other offenses can be disregarded as being committed by Williams.

The previous discussion provided an empirical framework for linking the five Raleigh murders to the killer Williams. However, the linking process did not provide a classification of Williams. It was necessary to develop a psychological profile of the offender so investigators could understand his behavior and background characteristics. To classify the crime scene actions of the Raleigh serial murderer (unknown at the time the profile was constructed), the crime scene actions were compared with the Facet Model described in Chapter 3 and then a final determination on the profile was made, based on the SSA and POSA results outlined in Chapters 10, 11, and 12.

14.11 Original Psychological Profile Offered in the Five Unsolved Murders in Raleigh, North Carolina

The purpose of this profile is to outline the behavioral characteristics of an offender who would commit such murders. This is not a profile of a particular individual.

Offender Profile

Sex — Male
Age — 28 to 35
Ethnicity — Black
Employment — Unskilled (e.g., construction worker or cook)
Education — High School Dropout
Marriage Status — Single or Divorced
Military Service — If he does have a military history, then it will consist of a dishonorable discharge.
Arrest Record — Past convictions of burglary, DWI convictions, reckless driving, and petty crimes. However, this does not reflect the actual crimes that the offender has committed. He will most likely have committed a series of rapes within the same geographical area of where the murders took place. This offender has killed in the past and will continue to kill — until caught.
The offender has an explosive personality, one who is impulsive, quick-tempered, and self-centered. He is not reclusive, but he may have some trouble fitting into the crowd. Generally speaking, however, his social

relationships are superficial and limited to drinking buddies and visiting prostitutes. Conflicted over his relationships with women, he often feels dependent and aggressively resistant to them. While he is contested by women, he uses various forms of aggression to get even and degrade them. Historically, if ever married, his marriage has been ill fated and he is usually in some phase of estrangement. In the marriage, there would have been some history of spousal abuse.

The offender will most likely live alone, or among his peers of the same age (e.g., in a hostel). Sexually, he is frustrated and may feel impotent. He links anger with sexual competence.

He may use soft pornography, but not hardcore pornographic materials for stimulation.

Due to the offender's unpredictable behaviors and aggression, he may have a record of being referred to a mental health worker. He has difficulty with authority figures.

The offender's crimes will be committed in a stylized violent burst of attack for the purposes of retaliation, or getting even and revenge on women. The victim is used as a vehicle to be exploited. The crimes are unplanned.

The attack on the victims will likely be blitz with heavy trauma to the face. The mildest reaction from the victim can lead to the murder. The crime is an emotional one due to the anger and often results in non-completed sexual acts. The offender will leave evidence scattered about and will show no signs of being forensically aware.

Blunt force trauma on the victim will be present. The offender often is influenced by the weapon of opportunity such as hands and rocks. Any restraints used will not be brought to the crime scene, but will be of opportunity. If strangulating is indicated, it is likely to be manual strangulation. The murder weapon and restraint will likely be found not too far from the crime scene. Victims of this type of offender are usually strangers, but can be acquaintances from the offender's own peer group.

The offender will be relevantly new to the area (less than a year). He will live less than $1^1/_2$ miles from some of the murders. If there is a series of unsolved rapes in the same vicinity of the murders, then he will mostly have committed the rapes and live in that area. The offender will drive an older (six years older or more) vehicle, but most of his traveling is by foot or public transportation.

The offender's place of residency will be closer to where he first encountered his victims, rather than where their bodies were eventually discovered. He will most likely live in the southern part of Raleigh. The home area will most likely be located (going from east to west direction) between the body dump sites of Cynthia Louise Brown and

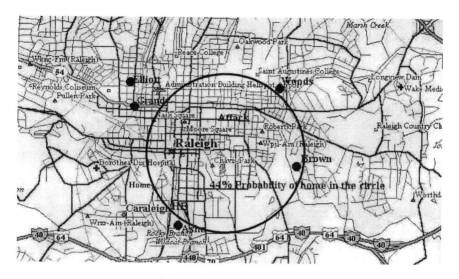

Figure 14.5

Patricia Anne Ashe (going from northwest down toward a southerly direction). A geographical map showing the predicted home base area is presented in Figure 14.5.

14.12 Discussion of Offender Profile

The profile of the unsolved series of murders in Raleigh presented above was accurate on most of the key points. For example, the profile said the killer would be a Black man between the age of 28 and 35 years old; would have an unskilled job, such as being a cook; would be single or divorced; and probably live alone or in a hostel or similar place with his peers of the same age. The convicted killer, Williams, turned 36 soon after his arrest; he was a cook at a Wendy's restaurant. Williams was unmarried, and he was a transient who was relatively new to the city of Raleigh. He lived in South Raleigh in a homeless shelter less than one half mile from where the victims were attacked and murdered, as the geographical and psychological profiles suggested. Furthermore, Williams is a suspect in several rapes in the same vicinity of where the murders occurred, as predicated. Similarly, Williams had an extensive criminal record of sexual assaults.

Figure 14.5 is the geographical map showing the victims' surnames and locations of where their bodies were discovered. The geographical program used to profile the Raleigh murders is called Predator®*. Predator developed

---

* Registered Trademark of Grover Maurice Godwin, Raleigh, North Carolina.

from research carried out by this author while a doctorate student at the University of Liverpool, England. Looking at the map, the circle indicates the highest probable area of where the offender was likely to live. This circular area is roughly one mile in diameter. The analysis predicated that there was a 44% probability that the killer would live within the circle, as shown. In the lower left-hand corner of the circle near the victim Ashe, we see the letters HB, which represents the offender's predicted home base. This is the location within the probability circle where the author predicated the killer would likely live. Immediately to the left and up from the predicted home base area is the word "home." This represents the actual home base where John Williams, Jr. was living during the murders. Remarkably, although where Williams was actually living was located just outside of the probability circle, it was less than one block from the predicated home base area.

14.13 Summary

This chapter outlined the value of using Jaccard's coefficients as a decision support system. The one important finding provided in this chapter and throughout the book is, regardless of the effect of the representational system chosen to link offenses, the accuracy of the decision-maker is inevitably influenced by the appropriateness of the information chosen in the selection phase of the task of discriminating between offenders. For example, the crime scene actions of the killer John Williams, Jr. were juxtaposed between the affective-object (AO) and affective-vehicle (AV) themes. This finding reminds us it is important to remember that the actions that may be characteristic of one offender across a series of offenses may be quite different from those actions that help to discriminate him from other offenders. Equally important was the finding that the representation of crime information can only be useful provided the information used in it is a valid measure. Also, the results support the notion that to correctly link crimes, behaviors selected must be valid indices of offender consistency, as discussed earlier in Chapter 12. Hence, the use of an empirical method such as Facet Theory to classified crime scene behavior. By using behaviors that have been tested and found to be empirically consistent over different offenses, a framework was provided for linking crimes and modeling the actions of a series of unsolved murders.

Two methods of intermediate representation outlined illustrated that the actual decisions made by the investigator are determined by the nature of the representational system. As previously mentioned, in the case of ANA-CAPA, information processing remains entirely in the control of the investigator or police officer, with the ANACAPA chart merely recording all the available information and displaying it graphically. Recognizing crime patterns using this approach has been successful with aggregated crime data; however, it has proven less productive when considering a series of crimes carried out by one offender.

The use of Jaccard's coefficients contrast with ANACAPA in that it processes all the crime information and provides a predetermined decision. The results can then be used, as was demonstrated by this author's profile in the Raleigh murders, as a decision-making process along with other evidence which may be pertinent. The use of Jaccard's coefficients in linking offenses can reduce ampliative blindness, which is the failure of police to go beyond the information in hand and recognize patterns in offending behavior that may be linked to one individual. For example, if the Raleigh Police Department had had a linking system in place, based on the principles outlined in this book, it would have helped investigators recognize similar behavioral patterns in the five murders. Consequently, the crimes could have been linked earlier, resulting in less money being spent, reduction in man hours, and most importantly, lives could have been saved.

General Discussion and Conclusions

15

It is possible, therefore, that this type of Facet Classification Model of serial murder may provide researchers and police alike with a more heuristic and robust framework for classifying serial murderers. The model presented in this book also provides useful information for linking crime scene behavior and background characteristics that might assist profilers in drawing up more accurate offender profiles. The Investigative Process Management (IPM) afforded to the police by this empirical Facet Model could therefore assist in portraying accurately the actions of the most dangerous and highly elusive predator, the serial murderer.

However, in order for any classification system to be really effective, its development must be directly related to the possible utilization of the model by detectives. Awareness of this requirement was central to the research carried out in this book. How well it will enable police investigators to seek out suspects remains to be seen. Although the model is fairly robust and consistent, it is obviously subject to a number of criticisms.

Most important is the fact that the interpretation of the main analysis — multidimensional scaling procedures — is somewhat subjective; therefore, what has been described here may present a different picture to others. It is important, therefore, that other researchers should conduct similar analyses to see if equivalent interpretations are made.

Another problem is that the analysis in the book refers to predominant statistical trends. Although groups of individuals may be consistent in their actions over time, this does not mean that one can necessarily predict the behavior of a particular individual over time. A third related problem arose from the three SSAs and individual case studies: although most of the crime scene behavior examined here can be construed in terms of the model, the "fit" is not always perfect. In other words, individuals can be sometimes inconsistent in their actions in ways that do not fit the model. For example, in Figure 12.1 (see Chapter 12), the variable torture, which in terms of the Facet Model is supposed to represent the CV theme, fell into another category over time. Again, how serious these problems are in predicting future cases awaits further empirical investigation.

Reflecting on what Lester has suggested, in order to develop a robust model of serial murder, a large data set must be analyzed.[52] It is to the future that such analyses as those employed in this book must now look, to develop larger and more comprehensive databases and expand the classification types. In so doing, the thematic approach used in this book may give way to concise categorization of many crime scene variables in which observed intensity and scale may be derived that will benefit law enforcement's fight against the serial predator.

Nevertheless, the exploratory techniques used in the book do offer empirical support for classifying serial murderers and their crime scene behavior. The results indicate that the Facet Model analysis to offender profiling when combined with an (IPM) approach may be a viable tool for investigating serial murder and other violent crimes. It is hoped that the benefits of what this book has achieved will be of assistance to police investigators, researchers, and all others who follow.

Appendix A: Crime Scene Variables

Variables Numbered 1-65 Correspond to SSA Model in Chapter 10

Variable 1
blitz
Blitz Attack   0 = No   1 = Yes
The sudden and immediate use of violence, whether preceded by a confidence or ploy approach or not, which incapacitates the victim. Typically, the victim succumbs to the power and control of the offender.

Variable 2
con
Con Approach   0 = No   1 = Yes
The offender initiated contact with the victim prior to attack by use of a con or deception. This would include any verbal contact, questions asked, pseudo introductions, or story told.   This would include any pseudo names or businesses used to gain entry into victims' homes.

Variable 3
ploy
Ploy Approach   0 = No   1 = Yes
The offender initiated contact with the victim prior to the attack by the use of a ploy or subterfuge. This also would include any role taken, such as having a fake broken leg or arm.

Variable 4
gag
Gagging   0 = No   1 = Yes
The use at any time during the attack of any physical article placed in or around the victim's mouth. This does not include manual gagging. The gag may be used to prevent noise, or associated with sexual role playing or bondage.

Variable 5
blindfol
Blindfold   0 = No   1 = Yes
The use at any time during the attack of any physical interference with the
victim's ability to see. This included only the use of articles and not verbal
threats or the temporary use of the offender's hands.

Variable 6
facecov
Facecover   0 = No   1 = Yes
The use at any time during the attack of any physical article which is used
to cover the victim's entire head.

Variable 7
forced
Forced Entry   0 = No   1 = Yes
Entry into the victim's home was by force. This included prying windows
and doors, plus breaking locks and windows. This does not include physical
force upon the victim.

Variable 8
night
Night Entry   0 = No   1 = Yes
Entry into the victim's home was during the night. This included any entry
made between sunset and sunrise.

Variable 9
destevid
Destroyed Evidence   0 = No   1 = Yes
A forensic awareness variable. The offender destroyed or attempted to destroy
physical evidence at the crime scene. The focus of this category is to characterize those offenders who have performed some act which can be interpreted as interference with the possible forensic examination of the crime
scene or victim. This would not simply include wearing gloves, which is a
common practice among most criminals. This involves activities such as
wiping and washing the victim, as well as removal from the scene of incriminating articles or other evidence.

Variable 10
ransacke
Ransacked Property   0 = No   1 = Yes
This variable focuses on the condition of the victim's property at the crime scene. This would include property at a crime scene whether indoors or outdoors. This would include personal belongings of the victim found torn apart as if the offender were looking for something specific. The position or placement of the victim's clothing is not included in these four property variables. The condition of the victim's clothing would be included.

Variable 11
undistur
Undisturbed (Property)   0 = No   1 = Yes
The victim's property at the crime scene was found in its original form prior to the crime. The property was left undisturbed.

Variable 12
bdopenly
Victim (Body Openly Displayed)   0 = No   1 = Yes
The victim's body when discovered was found openly displayed. The body could be viewed with ease and was not obstructed by any trees or other barriers.

Variable 13
bdhidden
Victim (Body Hidden)   0 = No   1 = Yes
The victim's body when discovered was found hidden. The body could not be viewed with ease and visibility was obstructed by trees or other barriers. This variable did not include bodies that were buried.

Variable 14
bodymove
Victim (Body Moved)   0 = No   1 = Yes
The victim's body was moved from the assault or murder site to the disposal site. This would include either moving the body by foot or transport.

Variable 15
bdburied
Victim (Body Buried)   0 = No   1 = Yes
The victim's body was found completely buried in the ground. No part of the body was exposed or could be visually seen. This does not include the body being completely covered up by some article.

Variable 16
bodparts
Body Parts   0 = No   1 = Yes
Victim's body parts were found scattered away from the area where the body was lying; also under this category would be any body part found any distance away from the crime scene.

Variable 17
house
Victim (Found in House)   0 = No   1 = Yes
The category covers victims whose bodies were discovered in a house.

Variable 18
bounrope
Victim Bound (Rope)   0 = No   1 = Yes
The category covers victims who were found bound by rope, string, or twine or who showed evidence of being restrained by same.

Variable 19
bountape
Victim Bound (Tape)   0 = No   1 = Yes
The category covers victims who were found bound by tape or who showed evidence of being restrained by tape. This variable would not include those victims who were gagged with tape.

Variable 20
bouncord
Victim Bound (Cord)   0 = No   1 = Yes
The category covers victims who were found bound by an electrical cord or who showed evidence of being restrained by same.

Variable 21
bouncuff
Victim Bound (Handcuffs)   0 = No   1 = Yes
The category covers victims who were found bound by handcuffs or who showed evidence of being restrained by same.

Variable 22
restroff
Restraint Offender   0 = No   1 = Yes
The category covers any offender who brought the restraining device(s) to the crime scene.

Variable 23
restvict
Restraint Victim   0 = No   1 = Yes
The category covers any victim who brought the restraining device(s) to the crime scene. This does not imply that the victim purposely or intentionally carried a restraining device to the crime scene, but rather property owned by the victim was used to restrain or bind them.

Variable 24
restrfound
Restraint Found   0 = No   1 = Yes
The category covers any offense where the offender left the restraining device at the crime scene.

Variable 25
Anthropophagy
Cannibalism/Drinking Blood   0 = No   1 = Yes
The category covers any offender who engaged in cannibalism and/or drinking the victim's blood.

Variable 26
heldcapt
Victim (Held Captive)   0 = No   1 = Yes
The category covers any offender who held a victim captive for more than eight hours prior to the murder.

Variable 27
revisit
Revisited Crime Scene   0 = No   1 = Yes
The category covers any offender who after the murder revisited the crime
scene. This would include any trips made back to the actual murder site if
different from the victim's body dump site.

Variable 28
ritualsc
Ritualistic Activity   0 = No   1 = Yes
The category described any evidence found at the crime scene that suggests
the offender performed ritualistic acts on, with, or near the victim's body.
This would include, for example, evidence of candle burning, stacking of
rocks, or dead animals found at the crime scene.

Variable 29
bodposed
Victim Body Posed   0 = No   1 = Yes
The category described the position of the victim's body when found. This
would include the intentional posing of the victim's body for shock value
when discovered. This does not include staging the body.

Variable 30
piqueur
Piqueurism   0 = No   1 = Yes
The category described acts performed on the victim's body with a knife
or other sharp instruments that indicates excessive stabbing, cutting, or
ripping of the flesh. These wounds are usually inflicted near the genital or
breast areas.

Variable 31
fullydrs
Victim (Full-dress)   0 = No   1 = Yes
One of four variables that described how the victim was dressed when discovered. This does not include the position of the victim's shoes.

Variable 32
nude
Victim Nude   0 = No   1 = Yes
As above, this variable described how the victim was dressed when discovered. The variable described the victim as being completely nude; no clothes

were found on the victim's body. This would include whether the victim's shoes were intact or not.

Variable 33
riptorn
Victim Clothes Ripped   0 = No   1 = Yes
As above, this variable described how the victim's clothes were removed. This would also include the tearing of the victim's clothing.

Variable 34
scatterd
Clothing Scattered   0 = No   1 = Yes
A variable that describes the placement of the victim's clothing (not on the body) found at the crime scene.

Variable 35
hidden
Clothing Hidden   0 = No   1 = Yes
This variable describes an offender who intentionally hides the victim's clothing to avoid detection. This would include any burning of the victim's clothing.

Variable 36
stolen
Personal Items Stolen   0 = No   1 = Yes
The taking of small personal items (other than clothing) from the victim. These items may or may not be valuable, (e.g., photos, drivers license, real or costume jewelry, etc.).

Variable 37
disfigur
Victim's Body Disfigured   0 = No   1 = Yes
This category described elements of torture or unusual assaults on the victim's body. This would include any removal of body parts, burns, mutilation of body cavities.

Variable 38
hacked
Victim's Body Hacked   0 = No   1 = Yes
This variable described a method of dismemberment by hacking or chopping off body parts.

Variable 39
sexorgan
Sex Organs Assaulted   0 = No   1 = Yes
This variable describes any evidence that suggests the offender explored the victim's body cavities or assaulted his or her sexual organs. This includes any attempts and insertion of fingers or foreign objects into the victim.

Variable 40
sexassau
Attempted Sexual Assault   0 = No   1 = Yes
This variable described any evidence that suggests the offender attempted a sexual assault on the victim. This would also include any evidence of masturbation on the victim's body.

Variable 41
Dismember postmortem   0 = No   1 = Yes
This variable described a method of dismemberment by hacking or chopping off body parts postmortem.

Variable 42
vaginal
Vaginal Penetration   0 = No   1 = Yes
This variable described intercourse with the victim. This would not include penetration by a foreign object or fingers.

Variable 43
analsex
Anal Penetration   0 = No   1 = Yes
This variable described anal intercourse with the victim. This would not include any penetration by a foreign object or fingers.

Variable 44
maleanal
Male Sexual Assault   0 = No   1 = Yes
This variable described the act of anal assault carried out only on male victims by the use of any foreign object or penis.

Variable 45
sexpost
Sexual Assault (postmortem)   0 = No   1 = Yes
This variable described necrophilic acts performed on the victim's body.

Variable 46
semen
Semen Evidence   0 = No   1 = Yes
The offender's semen was found on and/or in or around the victim's body.

Variable 47
foreobj
Foreign Object(s)   0 = No   1 = Yes
This variable described any foreign object(s) found inside the victim's body
on discovery.

Variable 48
insert
Foreign Objects Inserted   0 = No   1 = Yes
This variable described any evidence that a foreign object(s) had been
inserted into the victim's body cavity.

Variable 49
bitemark
Bitemarks   0 = No   1 = Yes
This variable described any evidence of bite mark(s) on the victim's body.
This would include any evidence of chewing on a particular body part.

Variable 50
firearm
Weapon Type (Firearm)   0 = No   1 = Yes
One of five variables that describes the type of weapon that caused the death
of the victim. This particular variable would include any type of gun (e.g.,
shotgun, rifle, or handgun).

Variable 51
knife
Weapon a Knife/Cutting   0 = No   1 = Yes
This particular variable would include any cutting or sharp instrument, such
as a knife, sword, or machete.

Variable 52
bludgeon
Bludgeon   0 = No   1 = Yes
This particular variable would include any blunt instrument, such as a club
or tire iron.

Variable 53
ligature
Ligature   0 = No   1 = Yes
This particular variable would include any article used to strangle the victim.
This would not include the offender's hands, legs, or feet.

Variable 54
handfeet
Weapon Hands/Feet   0 = No   1 = Yes
This particular variable would include any use of the offender's hands, feet,
legs, or arms to strangle or beat the victim.

Variable 55
weaponop
Weapon of Opportunity   0 = No   1 = Yes
One of two variables that describe where the weapon(s) used in the murders
came from. This particular variable would include any weapon that was
found at the crime scene or brought to the scene by the victim.

Variable 56
weapoff
Weapon Offender   0 = No   1 = Yes
This variable described an offender who preselected a weapon and carried it
to the crime scene.

Variable 57
weaponre
Weapon Recovered   0 = No   1 = Yes
The weapon used to commit the murder was found at the crime scene.

Variable 58
crimekit
Crime Kit   0 = No   1 = Yes
The variable described an offender who possessed a crime-kit for torturing
the victims. This would include any electrical devices, cutters, pliers, etc. for
use in submitting the victim to sadistic torture. It would also include items
used to bind the victim, such as duct tape and rope.

Variable 59
tortured
Victim Tortured   0 = No   1 = Yes
This variable described an offender who performed sadistic acts upon the victim's body while he/she was alive. This would include sadistic acts such as electric shock, cutting, or flagellation. Also included would be any mental torture such as forcing the victim to write a letter to loved ones prior to death. If the victim suffered ten or more stab wounds, then it was coded in this category.

Variable 60
victdrug
Victim Drug   0 = No   1 = Yes
The victim was neutralized by chemical soporifics.

Variable 61
upbody
Stabbed/Upper Body   0 = No   1 = Yes
This is one of two variables that described the location of the stab wounds on the victim's body. This would include any stabbing or cutting above the waist.

Variable 62
lowbody
Stabbed/Lower Body   0 = No   1 = Yes
As above, this variable described the location of the stab wounds on the victim's body. This would include any stabbing or cutting wounds below the waist.

Variable 63
trophies
Trophies   0 = No   1 = Yes
This variable described any offender who retained personal items or body parts of the victim.

Variable 64   0 = No   1 = Yes
vehstole
Vehicle Stolen
The victim's vehicle was stolen by the offender.

Variable 65   0 = No   1 = Yes
vicresid
Crime at Victim's Residence
The abduction, death, and body disposal site was the victim's home.

Additional variables used in the descriptive chapters only

Variable 66
Hitchhiker   0 = No   1 = Yes
At the time of the offender-victim encounter, the victim was hitchhiking.

Variable 67
Prostitute   0 = No   1 = Yes
At the time of the offender-victim encounter, the victim was working as
a prostitute.

Variable 68
Victim-Offender Relationship Stranger   0 = No   1 = Yes
One of four variables dealing with the victim-offender relationship prior to
the fatal encounter. At the time of the offender-victim encounter, the victim-
offender relationship was stranger to stranger. The victim and offender were
completely unknown to each other prior to the crime.

Variable 69
Victim-Offender Relationship Casual   0 = No   1 = Yes
At the time of the offender-victim encounter, the victim-offender relationship
was a casual sort. This was based on if the offender and victim saw each
other, say, once a year.

Variable 70
Victim-Offender Relationship Friend   0 = No   1 = Yes
At the time of the offender-victim encounter, the victim-offender were
friends. This was judged based on if the offender and victim socialized and
saw each other on a regular basis.

Variable 71
Victim-Offender Relationship Family   0 = No   1 = Yes
At the time of the offender-victim encounter, the victim-offender were blood
related. This included any extended family relationships.

Variable 72
Soliciting Sex   0 = No   1 = Yes
Initial contact with the victim was made through soliciting for sex. This would include any forms of prostitution or two persons meeting at a hetero-sexual or homosexual nightclub or bar.

Variable 73
Photos   0 = No   1 = Yes
This variable described an offender who took photos and/or videos of the victim prior to or after death.

Variable 74
Diary   0 = No   1 = Yes
This variable described an offender who maintained a written or taped account of the murders. This would include any newspaper clippings of stories about the murders.

Variable 75
Victim Stalked   0 = No   1 = Yes
This variable described an offender who stalked a victim for one day (24 hours) or longer prior to committing the murder. This would include any break-ins to the victim's home while the victim was not home prior to the murder, if the burglary occurred at least 24 hours prior to the murder.

Variable 76
Offender Interjected in Investigation   0 = No   1 = Yes
This variable described an offender who interjected himself into the murder investigation. This would include any phone calls made to the investigating department or assistance in looking for victims.

Appendix B: Victim and Offender Background Characteristics

Victim Data

Variable 1
Victim is a male   0 = No   1 = Yes
Victim is a female   0 = No   2 = Yes

Variable 2
Victim's race   1 = White
                                                     2 = Black
                                                     3 = Hispanic
                                                     4 = Asian

Variable 3
Victim under age of 10   0 = No   1 = Yes
The under age 10 victim is, typically, a child who has not reached sexual maturity, and remains immature in nearly all respects and situationally vulnerable.

Variable 4
Victim ages 11 to 17   0 = No   1 = Yes
The victim age between 11 to 18 years is a person who is typically more sexually developed or developing. Most, but not all, are still living with their parents. There are, however, a few individuals who are married or living with a partner. The person is usually more financially independent if employed, which allows them to be mobile, thereby placing them in more vulnerable situations.

Variable 5
Victim ages 18 to 50   0 = No   1 = Yes
The 18 years or older person will have a greater independence, reveal more maturity, and are usually married or living separately from their parents. This greater independence allows the individual to engage in the consumption of alcohol and drugs, thereby placing them in vulnerable situations.

Victim age over 50   0 = No   1 = Yes
The over the age 50 person will usually, but not always, be retired. In many instances, this category includes elderly individuals who are often prone to vulnerable situations.

Offender Data

Variable 6
Offender's Age   1 = 18–25
                                                     2 = 26–31
                                                     3 = 32–36
                                                     4 = 37–42
                                                     5 = over 42

Variable 7
Offender's sex   1 = Male
                                                  2 = Female

Variable 8
Offender's Race   1 = White
                                                  2 = Black
                                                  3 = Hispanic
                                                  4 = Asian

Variable 9
Heterosexual   0 = No   1 = Yes
Offender engages in sexual relations only with adult females.

Variable 10
Homosexual   0 = No   1 = Yes
Offender engages in sexual relations with persons of the same sex and both
individuals are over the age of 18.

Variable 11
Pedophilia   0 = No   1 = Yes
Offender engages in sexual relations with either a male or female child who
is under the age of sixteen.

Variable 12
Bisexual   0 = No   1 = Yes
Offender engages in sexual relations with both adult females and males, who
are over the age of 18.

Variable 13
Transvestite   0 = No   1 = Yes
Offender is a male who engages in cross-dressing in female clothing.

Variable 14
Bestiality   0 = No   1 = Yes
Offender engages in sexual relations with animals.

Variable 15
Fetishes   0 = No   1 = Yes
Offender gains sexual pleasure by interacting with specific body parts and/or
the use of objects (e.g., dildos and other sexual toys).

Variable 16
Pornography   0 = No   1 = Yes
The offender read and/or collected a variety of pornographic materials.
These would include books and videotapes.

Variable 17
Voyeurism   0 = No   1 = Yes
Offender engages in voyeurism. Information based on prior convictions and/or
psychiatric reports. This includes any charges or reports of peeping tom.

Variable 18
Psychiatric History   0 = No   1 = Yes
Offender as a juvenile or adult displayed symptoms of/or was treated for
mental health problems. This variable includes any reports which recommended or showed that the offender had been treated by a psychologist or
psychiatrist for mental health problems other than alcohol or drugs.

Variable 19
Chemical Dependence   0 = No   1 = Yes
Offender as a juvenile or adult was treated for alcohol or drug dependency.
This variable includes any reports which showed that the offender was com-
mitted to and/or visited on an outpatient basis any treatment program for
alcohol or drug dependency.

Variable 20
Juvenile Record   0 = No   1 = Yes
Any criminal charges, whether convicted or dismissed, that occurred under
the age of 18.

Variable 21
Domestic Disturbances   0 = No   1 = Yes
Any police calls or criminal charges and/or convictions related to a history
of domestic disturbances.

Variable 22
Fraud and Forgery Criminal History   0 = No   1 = Yes
Any charges whether or not they were later dropped, including any convic-
tions for fraud or forgery.

Variable 23
Criminal History of Burglary   0 = No   1 = Yes
Any charges whether or not they were later dropped, including any convic-
tions for burglary, theft, or robbery.

Variable 24
Criminal Sexual History   0 = No   1 = Yes
Any sexual-related charges whether or not they were later dropped, including
any convictions. Rape is not included in this variable. This category included
crimes against nature, such as cunnilingus and fellatio. Also included are
peeping tom, voyeurism, exposing oneself, and fondling.

Variable 25
Violent Criminal History   0 = No   1 = Yes
Any charges whether or not they were later dropped, including any convictions
for violent crimes. Violent crime includes acts such as murder, attempted
murder, rape, attempted rape, kidnaping, and attempted kidnaping.

Variable 26
Drug Convictions   0 = No   1 = Yes
Any drug-related charges whether or not they were later dropped, including
any convictions.

Variable 27
Self-Employed   0 = No   1 = Yes
At the time of arrest, the offender was self-employed. He ran his own
business.

Variable 28
Employed   0 = No   1 = Yes
At the time of arrest, the offender was employed. He worked for some
business other than his own.

Variable 29
Unemployed   0 = No   1 = Yes
At the time of arrest, the offender was unemployed. The offender was not
working at a legally held job.

Variable 30
Armed Services   0 = No   1 = Yes
The offender was at some time in the military service. This was recorded whether the offender received a honorable or dishonorable discharge. No particular branch of service is specified.

Variable 31
Parole Status   0 = No   1 = Yes
At the time of arrest, the offender was either on probation or parole.

Variable 32
High School   0 = No   1 = Yes
At the time of arrest, the offender was a high school graduate or had completed a similar high school diploma course (e.g., GED).

Variable 33
High School Dropout   0 = No   1 = Yes
At the time of arrest, the offender was a high school dropout.

Variable 34
Some College   0 = No   1 = Yes
At the time of arrest, the offender had attended college, but did not graduate. This includes any courses taken at the college level.

Variable 35
Bachelor's Degree   0 = No   1 = Yes
At the time of arrest, the offender had a Bachelor's degree.

Variable 36
Post-Graduate   0 = No   1 = Yes
At the time of arrest, the offender had attended or graduated with a post-graduate degree. This would include any degree or course work taken beyond a Bachelor's degree.

Variable 37
Single   0 = No   1 = Yes
At the time of arrest, the offender's marital status was single.

Variable 38
Married   0 = No   1 = Yes
At the time of arrest, the offender's marital status was married.

Variable 39
Divorced   0 = No   1 = Yes
At the time of arrest, the offender's marital status was divorced.

Variable 40
Aliases   0 = No   1 = Yes
During the crime series, the offender used names other than his legal name. This includes any nicknames or slang names. Also included are any forged names, social security numbers, and drivers license numbers.

Variable 41
Alcohol/Drug   0 = No   1 = Yes
Prior to committing murder, the offender ingested alcohol and/or used drugs. The report of alcohol and drug use was taken from the offender's account, in most instances based on interviews with the police and court transcripts. Other instances of alcohol use were based on the testimony of surviving victims' accounts from court transcripts and/or police records (i.e., that she could smell liquor/beer on the offender's breath, or that the offender consumed alcohol in her presence).

Variable 42
Law-Enforcement Related Work   0 = No   1 = Yes
Any direct or auxiliary-related work by the offender within the law enforcement area.

Variable 43
Suicide/Attempted Suicide   0 = No   1 = Yes
Any police, medical, or mental health reports that suggests the offender committed suicide or attempted to commit suicide.

Variable 44
Emotional Setback   0 = No   1 = Yes
Any mental health records that revealed an emotional life experience which caused mental stress on the offender prior to the murders. Examples of these emotional life experiences include such setbacks as breaking up or an argument with a girlfriend or boyfriend. This includes a temporary or permanent separation from a spouse or deaths within the immediate family.

References

1. Storr, A., *Human Destructiveness*, New York: Basic Books, 1971.
2. Egger, S., *The Killers Among Us: An Examination of Serial Murder and its Investigation*, New Jersey: Prentice Hall, 1997.
3. Ellis, A. and Gullo, J., *Murder and Assassination*, New York: Lyle Stuart Inc., 1971.
4. Hickey, E., *Serial Murderers and Their Victims*, 2nd ed., Belmont, CA: Wadsworth, 1997.
5. Leyton, E., *Hunting Humans: Inside the Minds of Mass Murderers*, New York: Pocket Books, 1986.
6. Caputi, J., *The Age of Sex Crime*, London: The Women's Press Ltd., 1987.
7. Leyton, E., *Compulsive Killers: The Story of Modern Multiple Murder*, New York: New York Press, 1986.
8. Bailey, K. G., *Human Paleopsychology*, New Jersey: Erlbaum, 1986.
9. MacLean, P. D., The triune brain, emotion, and scientific bias, in *The Neurosciences: Second Study Program*, Schmitt, F. O., Ed., New York: Rockfeller University Press, 336–349, 1970.
10. DeHart, D. D. and Mahoney, J. M., The serial murderer's motivations: An interdisciplinary review, *Omega*, 29, 29–45, 1987.
11. Restak, R., *Murder by Number*, interview/videotape, Atlanta, GA: CNN, 1993.
12. Griffiths, R., *Murder by Number*, producer and director/videotape, Atlanta, GA: CNN, 1993.
13. Liebert, J. Contributions of psychiatric consultation in the investigation of serial murder, *International Journal of Offender Therapy and Comparative Criminology*, 29, 187–200, 1985.
14. Meissner, W. W., *The Paranoid Process*, New York: Jason Aronson, 1978.
15. Bandura, A., *Aggression*, Englewood Cliffs, NJ: Prentice Hall, 1973.
16. Cleckley, H., *The Mask of Sanity*, St. Louis: The C. V. Mosby Company, 1964.
17. Ressler, R., Burgess, A. W., and Douglas, J., *Sexual Homicide: Patterns and Motivations*, Lexington, MA: Lexington Books, 1988.

18. Burgess, A. W., Hartman, C. R., Ressler, R. K., Douglas, J. E., and McCormack, A., Sexual homicide: A motivational model, *Journal of Interpersonal Violence,* 1, 251–272, 1986.

19. Cleckley, H., *The Mask of Sanity,* 6th ed., St. Louis: The C.V. Mosby Company, 1976.

20. Hickey, E., *Serial Murderers and Their Victims,* Pacific Grove, CA: Brooks and Cole, 1991.

21. Jesse, F. T., *Murder and Its Motive,* New York: Alfred A. Knopf, 1924.

22. Willie, W. S., *Citizens Who Commit Murder: A Psychiatric Study,* St. Louis, MO: Warren H. Green, 1975.

23. Prentky, R. A., Burgess, A. W., and Seghorn, T. K., Development of a rational taxonomy for the classification of sexual offenders: Rapists, *Bulletin of the American Academy of Psychiatry and the Law,* 13, 39–70, 1985.

24. Wolfgang, M. E., *Patterns in Criminal Homicide,* Philadelphia: University of Pennsylvania Press, 1958.

25. Wolfgang, M. E. and Ferracuti, F., *The Subculture of Violence: Towards an Intergrated Theory in Criminology,* London: Tavistock, 1967.

26. Wolfgang, M. E., Figlio, R. M., and Sellin, T., *Delinquency in a Birth Cohort,* Chicago: University of Chicago Press, 1972.

27. Megargee, E. I., Under-controlled and over-controlled personality types in extreme antisocial aggression, *Psychological Monographs,* 80, 611, 1966.

28. Toch, H., *Violent Men: An Inquiry Into the Psychology of Violence,* Chicago: Aldine, 1969.

29. Monahan, J., *Predicting Violent Behaviour: An Assessment of Clinical Techniques,* Beverly Hills, CA: Sage, 1981.

30. Athens, L., *Violent Criminal Acts and Actors,* Chicago: University of Illinois Press, 1997.

31. Megargee, E. I., Assault with intent to kill, *Transaction,* 2, 27–31, 1965.

32. Megargee, E. I., Recent research on under-controlled and over-controlled personality patterns among violent offenders, *Sociological Symposium,* 9, 37–50, 1973.

33. Megargee, E. I., Psychological determinants and correlates of criminal violence, in *Criminal Violence,* Wolfgang, M. and Weiner, N., Eds., Beverly Hills, CA: Sage, 81–170, 1982.

34. Athens, L., The self and the violent criminal act, *Urban Life and Culture,* 3, 98–112, 1974.

35. Bartol, C. R., *Criminal Behaviour: A Psychosocial Approach,* 3rd ed., Toronto: Prentice-Hall, 1995.

36. Felson, R. B., Aggression as impression management, *Social Psychology,* 41, 205–213, 1978.

37. Berkowitz, L., Frustration-aggression hypothesis: Examination and reformulation, *Psychological Bulletin*, 106, 59–73, 1989.

38. Hartup, W. W., Aggression in childhood: Development perspectives, *American Psychologist*, 29, 336–341, 1974.

39. Baron, R. A., *Human Aggression*, New York: Plenum, 1977.

40. Buss, A. H., *The Psychology of Aggression*, New York: Wiley, 1961.

41. Feshbach, S., The function of aggression and the regulation of aggressive drive. *Psychological Review*, 71, 257–272, 1964.

42. Zillmann, D., *Hostility and Aggression*, Hillsdale, N.J.: Erlbaum, 1979.

43. Cornell, D. G., Warren, J., Hawk, G., Stafford, E., Oram, G., and Pine, D., Psychopathy in instrumental and reactive violent offenders, *Journal of Consulting and Clinical Psychology*, 64, 783–790, 1996.

44. Guttmacher, M., *The Mind of the Murderer*, New York, Grove Press, 1973.

45. De River, J. P., *Crime and the Sexual Psychopath*, Springfield, IL: Charles C. Thomas, 1958.

46. Nettler, G., *Killing One Another: Criminal Careers*, Vol. 2, Cincinnati, OH: Anderson, 1982.

47. Revitch, E. and Schlesinger, L. B., Murder, evaluation, classification, and prediction, in *Violent Perspectives on Murder and Aggression*, Kutash, S. B., Schlesinger, L. B., and Associates, Eds., San Francisco: Jasey, 138–164, 1978.

48. Hare, R. D., *Without Conscience*, New York: Pocket Books, 1991.

49. Banay, R. S., Psychology of mass murderer, *Journal of Forensic Science*, 1, 1–7, 1956.

50. Holmes, R. M. and Holmes, S., *Profiling Violent Crimes: An Investigative Tool*, 2nd ed., Newbury Park, CA: Sage, 1996.

51. Geberth, V. J. and Turco, R. N., Antisocial personality disorder, and sexual sadism, malignant, narcissism, and serial murder, *Journal of Forensic Science*, 42, 49–60, 1997.

52. Lester, D., *Serial Killers: The Insatiable Passion*, Philadelphia, PA: The Charles Press, 1995.

53. Drukteinis, A., Serial murder: The heart of darkness, *Psychiatric Annals*, 22, 532, 1992.

54. Jackson, J. L. and Bekerian, D. A., *Offender Profiling: Theory, Research, and Practice*, West Sussex, England: Wiley, 1998.

55. Ault, R. L. and Reese, J. T., Psychological assessment of criminal profiling, in committee on the judiciary hearing before the subcommittee on juvenile justice of the committee on the judiciary United States Senate ninety-eight congress first session on patterns of murders committed by one person in large numbers with no apparent rhyme, reason, or motivation, July 12, 1983, Serial No. j-98-52, Washington D.C.: U.S. Government Printing Office, Reprinted from *FBI Law Enforcement Bulletin*, September, 1–4, 1980.

56. Douglas, J. and Olshaker, M., *Mindhunter*, New York: Scribner, 1995.

57. Ressler, R., Douglas, J., Burgess, A. W., and Burgess, A. G., Crime classification manual, London: Simon and Schuster, 1992.

58. Brown, J. S., The psychopathology of serial sexual homicide. *American Journal of Forensic Psychiatry*, 12, 11–24, 1991.

59. Douglas, J. and Burgess, A., Criminal profiling: A viable investigative tool against violent crime, *FBI Law Enforcement Bulletin*, 55, 9–13, 1986.

60. Meloy, J. R., *Violent Attachments*, New Jersey: Aronson, 1997.

61. FBI Law Enforcement Bulletin, *Classifying Sexual Homicide Crime Scenes: Inter-rater Reliability*, Quantico, VA, 1985.

62. Freud, S., Beyond the pleasure principle, in *The Complete Psychological Works of Sigmund Freud*, J. Strachey, Ed., London: Hogarth Press, Vol. 18, 1920/1962.

63. Dietz, P. E., Sex offender profiling by the FBI: A preliminary conceptual model, in *Criminal Criminology: The Assessment and Treatment of Criminal Behavior*, Ben-Aron, M. H., Hucker, S. J., and Webster, C. D., Eds., Pittsburgh, PA: American Academy of Psychiatry and Law, 1985.

64. Fox, J. and Levin, J., Serial Killers: How Statistics Mislead Us, *Boston Herald*, 45, December, 1985.

65. Lewis, D. O., Pincus, J. H., Bard, B., Richardson, E., Prichep, L. S., Feldman, M., and Yeager, C., Neuropsychiatric, psycho-educational, and family characteristics of 14 juveniles condemned to death in the United States, *American Journal of Psychiatry*, 145, 584–589, 1985.

66. Shapiro, D., *Autonomy and Rigid Character*, New York: Basic Books, 1981.

67. Crepault, C. and Couture, M., Men's erotic fantasies, *Archives of Sexual Behavior*, 9, 565–81, 1980.

68. Terr, L., Forbidden games: Post-traumatic child's play, *J. Am. Acad. Child and Adolescent Psychiatry*, 20, 741–760, 1981.

69. Lion, J., Pitfalls in the assessment and measurement of violence, *Journal of Neuropsychiatry and Clinical Neurosciences*, 3, 540–543, 1991.

70. Ressler, R., Burgess, A., and Douglas, J., Rape and rape-murder: One offender and twelve victims, *American Journal of Psychiatry*, 140, 36–40, 1983.

71. Ressler, R., Burgess, A., D'Agostino, R., and Douglas, J., Serial murder: A new phenomenon of homicide, *Paper presented at the tenth triennial meeting of the International Association of Forensic Sciences*, Oxford, England, 1984.

72. Busch, K. A. and Cavanaugh, J. L., The study of multiple murder: Preliminary examination of the interface between epistemology and methodology, *Journal of Interpersonal Violence*, 1, 5–23, 1986.

73. Canter, D., *Criminal Shadows: Inside the Mind of the Serial Killer*, London: Harper Collins, 1994.

74. Prentky, R. A., Burgess, A. W., Rokous, F., Lee, A., Hartman, C., Renler, R., and Douglas, J., The presumptive role of fantasy in serial sexual homicide, *American Journal of Psychiatry*, 146, 887–891, 1989.

75. Katz, J., *Seductions of Crime*, New York: Basic Books, 1988.

76. Stephenson, G. M., *The Psychology of Criminal Justice*, Oxford: Blackwell, 1992.

77. Wilson, P., Lincoln, R., and Kocsis, R., Validity, utility and ethics of profiling for serial violent and sexual offenders, *Journal of Psychiatry, Psychology and Law*, 4, 1–12, 1997.

78. Hilgard, E. R., *Divided Consciousness: Multiple Controls in Human Thought and Action*, New York: Wiley, 1977.

79. Sewell, J. D., An application of Megargee's algebra of aggression to the case of Theodore Bundy, *Journal of Police and Criminal Psychology*, 1, 14–24, 1985.

80. Dietz, P. E., Hazelwood, R., and Warren, J., The sexually sadistic criminal and his offenses, *Bulletin American Academy of Psychiatry and Law*, 18, 163–178, 1990.

81. Holmes, R. M. and DeBurger, J. E., *Serial Murder*, Newbury Park, CA: Sage, 1988.

82. Gresswell, D. M. and Hollin, C. R., Multiple murder: A review, *The British Journal of Criminology*, 34, 1, 1–13, 1994.

83. Hazelwood, R. R. and Warren, J., Serial rapists, *FBI Law Enforcement Bulletin*, 18–25, January, 1989.

84. Peirce, C. S., Ampliative reasoning, in *Induction: An Essay on the Justification of Inductive Reasoning*, Rescher, N., Ed., Oxford: Blackwell, 1980.

85. Newman, J. H., *Apologia Pro Vita Sua: Being A History of His Religious Opinions*, London: Oxford University Press, 1870.

86. Godwin, M., A multivariate facet model of U.S. serial killers' crime scene actions, *Journal of Contemporary Criminal Justice*, in press, 1999.

87. Godwin, M. and Canter, D., Encounter and death: The spatial behavior of U.S. serial killers, *Policing: An International Journal of Police Management and Strategies*, 20, 24–38, 1997.

88. Shye, S., *Theory Construction and Data Analysis in the Behavioral Sciences*, San Francisco: Jossey Bass, 1978.

89. Brown, J., An introduction to the uses of facet theory, in *Facet Theory Approaches to Social Research*, Canter, D., Ed., New York: Springer-Verlag, 17–57, 1985.

90. Canter, D., *Facet Theory: Approaches to Social Research*, New York: Springer-Verlag, 1985.

91. Donald, I., Facet theory: Defining research domains, in *Researching Methods in Psychology*, Breakwell, G. M., Hammond, S., and Fife-Schaw, C., Eds., London: Sage, 1995.

92. Borg, I., Some basic concepts of facet theory, in *Geometric Representations of Relational Data*, 2nd ed., Lingoes, J. C., Roskam, E. E., and Borg, I., Eds., Ann Arbor, MI: Mathesis Press, 90–110, 1979.

93. Sullivan, H. S., *The Interpersonal Theory of Psychiatry*, New York: Norton, 1953.

94. Greenberg, J. R. and Mitchell, S. A., *Object Relations in Psychoanalytic Theory*, Cambridge, MA: Harvard University Press, 1983.

95. McAdams, D. P., *Power, Intimacy, and the Life Story: Personological Inquires Into Identity*, New York: Guilford Press, 1988.

96. Canter, D., Heritage, R., and Johannessen, K. K., *Offender Profiling*, Second interim report to the Home Office, Review of pilot studies, University of Surrey, November 1989.

97. Bartol, C. R. and Bartol, A. M., *Criminal Behavior: A Psychosocial Approach*, New Jersey: Prentice Hall, 1986.

98. Meloy, J. R., Violent and homicidal behavior in primitive mental states, *Journal of the American Academy of Psychoanalysis*, 16, 381–394, 1988.

99. Cormier, B. M., Angliker, C. C., Boyer, R., and Mersereau, G., The psychodynamics of homicide committed in a semi-specific relationship, *Canadian Journal of Criminology and Corrections*, 14, 335–44, 1972.

100. Holsti, O., *Content Analysis for the Social Sciences and Humanities*, Massachusetts: Addison Wesley, 1969.

101. Borg, I. and Shye, S., *Facet Theory: Form and Content*, Newbury Park, CA: Sage, 1995.

102. Rosenberg, M., *Occupations and Values*, Glencoe, IL: Free Press, 1960.

103. Levy, S., Lawful roles of facets in social theories, in *Facet Theory: Approaches to Social Research*, Canter, D., Ed., New York: Springer, 1985.

104. Feshbach, S., The function of aggression and the regulation of aggressive drive, *Psychological Review*, 71, 257–272, 1965.

105. Levy, S. and Guttman, L., Cultural analysis of some core social values, in *Facet Theory: Approaches to Social Research*, Canter, D., Ed., New York: Springer, 205–221, 1985.

106. Moyer, K. E., Kinds of aggression in their physiological basis, *Communication, Behavior and Biology*, Part A, 2, 65–86, 1968.

107. Meloy, J. R., A psychotic (sexual) psychopath: I just had a violent thought, *Journal of Personality Assessment*, 58, 480–493, 1992.

108. Weiss, J., Lamberti, J., and Blackman, N., The sudden murderer: A comparative analysis, *Archives of General Psychiatry*, 2, 669–678, 1960.

109. Ruotolo, A., Dynamics of sudden murder, *American Journal of Psychoanalysis*, 28, 162–176, 1968.

110. Goldstein, P. J., Drugs and violent crime, in *Pathways to Criminal Violence*, N. A. Weiner and M. E., Wolfgang, Eds., Newbury Park, CA: Sage, 1986.

111. Buss, A. H., *The Psychology of Aggression*, New York: Wiley, 1961.

112. Kopp, S., The character of sex offenders, *American Journal of Psychotherapy*, 16, 64–70, 1962.

113. Williams, A. H., *A Psychoanalytic Approach to the Treatment of Murderer*, London: Oxford, 1960.

114. Dietz, P. E., Patterns in human violence, in *American Psychiatric Association Annual Review*, R. Hales and A. Frances, Eds., 6, 465–490, Washington, D.C.: American Psychiatric Press, 1987.

115. Keppel, R. and Birnes, W., *The Riverman: Ted Bundy and I Hunt for the Green River Killer*, New York: Pocket Books, 1995.

116. Fox, J. and Levin, J., *Overkill: Mass Murder and Serial Killing Exposed*, New York: Plenum Press, 1994.

117. Parens, H., Rage toward self and others in early childhood, in *Criminology*, Glick, R., Ed., Boston: Allyn and Bacon, 1995.

118. McDevitt, J. B., The emergence of hostile aggression and its defensive and adaptive modifications during the separation-individuation process, *Journal of American Psychoanalysis Association*, 31, 273–300, 1983.

119. Pine, F. The four psychologies of psychoanalysis and their place in clinical work, *Journal of the American Psychoanalytic Association*, 36, 571–596, 1985.

120. Bowlby, J., Childhood mourning and its implication for psychiatry, *The American Journal of Psychiatry*, 118, 481–498, 1962.

121. Bowlby, J., *Attachment and Loss: Loss, Sadness, and Depression*, Vol. 3, New York: Basic Books, 1980.

122. Bartholomew, K., Avoidance of intimacy: An attachment perspective, *Journal of Social and Personal Relationships*, 7, 147–178, 1990.

123. Suttie, H., Analyzing childhood trauma, 1935, in *The Development of Aggression in Early Childhood*, H. Parens, Ed., New York: Aronson, 1979.

124. Klein, M., On criminality, 1934, in *Love, Guilt, and Reparation and Other Works 1921-1945*, Klein, M., New York: Free Press, 258–261, 1975.

125. Swann, W. B., Self-verification: Bringing social reality into harmony with the self, in *Psychological Perspectives on the Self*, Suls, J. and Greenwald, A. G., Eds., Hillsdale, NJ: Lawrence Erlbaum, 2, 1983.

126. Sullivan, H. S., *The Interpersonal Theory of Psychiatry*, New York: Norton, 1953.

127. Chomsky, N., *Syntactic Structures*, The Hague: Mouton, 1957.

128. Shapiro, D., *Autonomy and Rigid Character*, New York: Basic Books, 1981.

129. Gifford, R. and O'Connor, B., The interpersonal circumplex as a behavior map, *Journal of Personality and Social Psychology*, 52, 1019–1026, 1987.

130. Kagan, J., *The Second Year: The Emergence of Self-Awareness*, Cambridge, MA: Harvard University Press, 1989.

131. Miller, R. S., Humiliation and shame: Comparison of two affective states as indications of narcissistic stressors, *Bulletin of Menninger Clinic*, 52, 40–51, 1983.

132. Birtchnell, J., Attachment-Detachment, directiveness-receptiveness: A system for classifying interpersonal attitudes and behavior, *British Journal of Medical Psychology*, 60, 17–27, 1987.

133. Laing, R. D., *The Divided Self*, Penguin Books: London, 1965.

134. Gacono, C. and Meloy, R., A Rorschach investigation of attachment and anxiety in antisocial personality disorder, *Journal of Nervous and Mental Disease*, 179, 546–552, 1991.

135. Webb, E. and Weick, K. E., Unobtrusive measures in organizational theory: A reminder, *Administrative Science Quarterly*, 24, 650–659, 1979.

136. Weiss, J., Lamberti, J., and Blackman, N., The sudden murderer: A comparative analysis. *Archives of General Psychiatry*, 2, 669–678, 1960.

137. Keppel, R. and Weis, J., HITS: Catching criminals in the Northwest, *FBI Law Enforcement Bulletin*, 14–19, April, 1993.

138. Keppel, R., *An Analysis of the Effect of Time and Distance Relationships in Murder Investigations*, Unpublished doctorate dissertation, University of Washington, 1992.

139. Janis, I. L. and Mann, L., *Decision Making: A Psychological Analysis of Conflict, Choice and Commitment*, New York: Free Press, 1977.

140. Krippendorf, K., *Content Analysis: An Introduction to its Methodology*, Beverly Hills: Sage, 1980.

141. Guttman, L, What is not what in theory construction, in *Multidimensional Data Representations: When and Why*, Borg, I., Ed., Ann Arbor, MI: Mathesis Press, 1979.

142. Levy, S., Use of the mapping sentence for coordinating theory and research: A cross cultural example, *Quality and Quantity*, 10, 117–125, 1976.

143. Guttman, L. and Guttman, R., The theory of generality and specificity during mild stress, *Behavioral Sciences*, 21, 469–477, 1976.

144. Foa, U. G., New developments in facet design and analysis, *Psychological Review*, 72, 262–274, 1965.

145. Kruskal, J. B. and Wish, M., *Multidimensional Scaling*, Beverly Hills: Sage, 1978.

146. Coxon, A. P. M., *The User's Guide to Multidimensional Scaling*, London: Heinemann, 1982.

147. Shye, S., Elizur, D., and Hoffman, M., *Introduction to Facet Theory: Content Design and Intrinsic in the Behavioral Research*, Applied Social Research Methods Series, CA: Sage, 1994.

148. Coombs, C. H., *A Theory of Data*, New York: Wiley, 1964.

149. Silverman, R. A. and Mukherjee, S. K., Intimate homicide: An analysis of violent social relationships, *Behavioral Sciences and the Law*, 5, 37–47, 1987.

150. Cheatwood, D., Notes on the theoretical, empirical and police significance of multiple-offender homicides, in *Homicide: The Victim-offender Connection*, Wilson, A. V., Ed., Cincinnati, OH: Anderson Publishing, 1993.

151. Godwin, M., Victim target networks as solvability factors in serial murder, *Social Behavior and Personality: An International Journal*, 26, 75–84, 1998.

152. Jenkins, P., Chance or choice? The selection of serial murder victims, in *Homicide: The Victim-offender Connection*, Wilson, A. V., Ed. Cincinnati, OH: Anderson Publishing, 1993.

153. Pokorny, A. D., Human violence: A comparison of homicide, aggravated assault and attempted suicide, *Journal of Criminal Law, Criminology and Police Science*, 56, 488–497, 1965.

154. James, E., *Catching Serial Killers: Learning From Past Serial Murder Investigations*, Lansing, MI: International Forensic Service, Inc., 1991.

155. Ressler, R., Burgess, A. W., and Douglas, J., Sexual killers and their victims: Identifying patterns through crime scene analysis, *Journal of Interpersonal Violence*, 1, 288–308, 1986.

156. Hanfland, K. A., Keppel, R. D., and Weis, J. G., *Case Management for Missing Children: Homicide Investigation*, U.S. Department of Justice, Attorney General Office, Washington, D.C., Grant # 93, 1997.

157. Zahn, M. A. and Sagi, P. C., Stranger homicides in nine American cities, *Journal of Criminal Law and Criminology*, 78, 377–397, 1987.

158. Jenkins, P., African-Americans and serial homicide, *American Journal of Criminal Justice*, 2, 47–60, 1993.

159. Lunde, D. T., *Murder and Madness*, San Francisco: San Francisco Books, 1976.

160. Sears, D., *To Kill Again*, Wilmington, DE: Scholarly Resources, 1991.

161. Dickson, G., *Murder by Numbers*, London: Robert Hale, 1958.

162. Giannangelo, S., *The Psychopathology of Serial Murder*, Westport, Connecticut: Praeger, 1996.

163. Ressler, R and Shachtman, T., *Whoever Fights Monsters*, New York: Simon and Schuster, 1992.

164. McDougal, D., *Angel of Darkness*, New York: Warner Books, 1993.

165. Rappaport, R. G., The serial and mass murderer, *American Journal of Forensic Psychiatry*, 9, 39–48, 1988.

166. Walter, R., *Personal Communications*, Michigan Department of Corrections, Lansing, Michigan, September 1998.

167. Hazelwood, R. R., Dietz, P. E., and Warren, J., The criminal sexual sadist, *FBI Law Enforcement Bulletin*, 61, 1–10, 1992.

168. Gallagher, B. J. III., *The Sociology of Mental Illness*, 2nd ed., Englewood Cliffs, NJ: Prentice Hall, 1987.

169. Gee, D. J., A pathologist's view of multiple murder, *Forensic Science International*, 38, 53–65, 1988.

170. Keppel, R. and Birnes, W., *Signature Killers*, New York: Pocket Books, 1997.

171. Blennerhassett, R., The serial killer in film, *Irish Journal of Psychological Medicine*, 10, 101–104, 1993.

172. Hazelwood, R. R. and Douglas, J., The lust murderer, *FBI Law Enforcement Bulletin*, 18–22, April, 1980.

173. Harrington, J. and Burger, R., *Eye of Evil*, New York: St. Martin's Press, 1993.

174. Canter, D., Offender profiling, *The Psychologist*, 2, 12–16, 1989.

175. Lingoes, J. C., The multivariate analysis of qualitative data, *Multivariate Behavioral Research*, 3, 61–94, 1973.

176. Canter, D., Heritage, R., and Kovackik, M., *A Facet Approach to Offender Profiling*, Final Report to the Home Office, University of Surry, Psychology Department, Vol. 1 and 2, 1991.

177. Donald, I. and Canter, D., Temporal and trait facets of personnel assessment, *Applied Psychology: An International Review*, 39, 413–429, 1990.

178. Breakwell, G. M., Hammond, S., and Fife-Schaw, C., Eds., *Research Methods in Psychology*, London: Sage, 1995.

179. Levy, S., Lawful roles of facets in social theories, in *Multidimensional Data Representation: When and Why*, Borg, I., Ed., Ann Arbor, MI: Mathesis Press, 1981.

180. Dancer, L. S., Introduction to facet theory and its application, *Applied Psychology: An International Review*, 39, 365–377, 1990.

181. Terr, L., Childhood traumas: An outline and overview, *American Journal of Psychiatry*, 148, 10–20, 1991.

182. Cronbach, L. J., *Essentials of Psychological Testing*, New York: Harper and Row, 1960.

183. Groth, A., Burgess, A., and Holmstrom, L., Rape, power, anger, and sexuality, *American Journal of Psychiatry*, 134, 1239–1243, 1977.

184. Carlisle, A. L., The divided self: Toward an understanding of the dark side of the serial killer, *American Journal of Criminal Justice*, 27, 23–26, 1993.

185. Cartel, M. D., *Disguise of Sanity: Serial Mass Murder*, Toluca Lake, CA: Pepperbox Books, 1985.

186. Balint, M., *The Basic Fault: Therapeutic Aspects of Regression*, London: Tavistock, 1967.

187. Chassequet-Smirgel, J., *Creativity and Perversion*, New York: W. W. Norton, 1985.

188. Donald, I., *Personal Communications*, Department of Psychology, The University of Liverpool, England, November, 1997.

189. Shye, S. Partial order scalogram analysis, in *Theory Construction and Data Analysis in the Behavioral Sciences*, S. Shye, Ed., San Francisco: Jossey Bass, 60–70, 1985.

190. Horowitz, L., Horowitz, S., Rosenburg, E., and Bartholomew, K., Interpersonal problems, attachment styles, and outcome in brief dynamic psychotherapy, *Journal of Consulting and Clinical Psychology*, 61, 549–560, 1993.

191. Blackburn, R., The *Psychology of Criminal Conduct: Theory, Research and Practice*, Chichester, England: Wiley, 1993.

192. Canter, D. and Heritage, R., A multivariate model of sexual offense behavior: Developments in offender profiling, *Journal of Forensic Psychiatry*, 1, 185–212, 1990.

193. Pulkinnen, L., The role of impulsive control in the development of antisocial and prosocial behavior, in *Development of Antisocial and Prosocial Behavior: Research, Theories, and Issues*, D. Olweus, J. Block, and M. Radke-Yarrow, Eds., New York: Academic Press, 56–60, 1986.

194. Huesmann, L. R. and Eron, L. D., Cognitive processes and the persistence of aggressive behavior, *Aggressive Behavior*, 10, 234–251, 1984.

195. Howell, D. C., *Statistical Methods for Psychology*, Belmont, CA: Duxbury Press, 1997.

196. Arbolita-Florez, J. and Holley, H., What is mass murder? in *Psychiatry: The State of the Art*, T. Pichat and P. Berner, R. Wolf, and U. Thaw, Eds., New York: Plenum Press, 6, 1985.

197. Goetting, A., Female victims of homicide: A portrait of their killers and the circumstances of their deaths, *Violence and Victims*, 6, 159–168, 1991.

198. Yin, R. K., *Case Study Research: Design and Methods*, 2nd ed., Thousand Oaks, CA: Sage, 1994.

199. Rubenstein, H., *The Link Between Crime and the Built Environment: The Current State of Knowledge*, Vol. 1, Washington, D.C., National Institute of Justice, 1980.

200. Graysmith, R., *The Sleeping Lady: The Trailside Murders Above the Golden Gate*, New York: Onyx, 1990.

201. Walter, R., *Personal Communications*, Michigan Department of Corrections, Lansing, Michigan, September, 1998.

202. McDougal, D., *Angel of Darkness*, New York: Warner Books, 1993.

203. Jackson, T. and Cole, T., *Rites of Burial: The Horrific Account of A Sadistic Serial Killer*, London: Virgin Books, 1992.

204. Jarvis, C. and Swindell, S., *News and Observer* (Raleigh, NC), January 11, 1997.

205. _____ *News and Observer* (Raleigh, NC), January, 10, 1997.

206. _____ *News and Observer* (Raleigh, NC), March 20, 1997.

Index

A

W